"A wonderful life adventure ... one that most of us will only fantasize about!

"*Breaking Free* is a compelling read about a man who trades his successful business and family life for a backpack and a ticket around the world. Denis not only takes us to a multitude of countries, but he connects with the 'traveler' within each of us that yearns to break free of everyday responsibilities and submit to the adventure of redefining life—one with no self imposed limits or boundaries. This is a story of courage and love, of happiness and failure, of confusion and clarity, and of regret and completion.... This is a story of us!

"Denis's escape from his reality into new-found relationships and events that he encounters as he travels changes his perspective and his life.

"I invite you to read *Breaking Free* to experience the opportunity of the freedom that awaits each of us!"

—Frank John Zolfo (a fellow traveler)

DENIS HICKEY ran his first business at twenty-six and retired at forty-eight. He raised his family in Silicon Valley where he was a successful manager and entrepreneur with companies on the leading edge of four technologies. Later he co-founded the crisis management firm, Hickey & Hill. A man happy in his own skin, Denis traveled the world for ten years after retirement, and employed his talent for drawing people out to uncover amazing personal stories and insights.

He writes and lives in Warsaw, Poland with his wife, Malgorzata, and son, Sean.

BOOK 2

BREAKING FREE SERIES

THE
TRAVELER

A vision is that portion of a dream that is recurrent, focused, and deals strictly with the future.

DENIS HICKEY

Published in 2013 by Vingdinger Publishing LLC
Copyright © Denis Hickey 2013

The moral right of the author has been asserted.

All rights reserved. No part of this publication may be reproduced or transmitted in any form or by any means, electronic or mechanical, including photocopy, recording, or any information storage and retrieval system, without permission in writing from the publisher.

ISBN: 978-0-9888588-3-1 (paperback)
ISBN: 978-0-9888588-2-4 (ebook)
Libray of Congress Control Number: 2013944340

Front cover design by Paweł Jońca
Interior and back cover design by Jill Ronsley
Maps by Kazimierz Pelczar
Ebook formatting by Sun Editing & Book Design

Websites:
    breakingfree-thebooks.com
    vingdingerpublishing.com

Printed and bound in the USA

While this book is a memoir, the names of some people have been changed to protect their civil rights.

To Malgosia,

Sean Hickey and Audriel Hinds

Contents

World Map	x
Acknowledgements	xi
Prologue	1

Greece – The Trip — 5
1. Joe Reilly's Smile — 7
2. Speaking of Women — 13
3. Mykonos: Thunderclouds on the Road Less Traveled — 17
4. Santorini — 23
5. Crete: A Challenge for the Traveler Personality — 31

Turkey—Habits — 39
6. Rhodes — 41
7. Selçuk: The Clash of Islam and Christianity — 44
8. Women and Monotheism: A Story of Disempowerment — 47
9. Çanakkale and the Way to Istanbul — 52
10. Malgosia Comes to Istanbul — 60
11. Saying Goodbye to Love — 69

India And Nepal—Visions — 73
12. New Delhi: One Wild and Crazy Place — 75
13. Coincidence and the Taj Mahal — 84
14. Capturing the Baggage Car in a Bloodless Coup on the Train to Varanasi — 91
15. Death on the Way to Katmandu — 99
16. Second Challenge: Traveling with Janet and Auri — 105
17. Laughing with a Dead Guru in Pune — 113
18. Barney in Goa: Piecing Together How Visions Work — 122
19. Oh! Calcutta! Prostitutes, Lunch with a Beggar, Kibitzing with Mother Teresa — 131

Thailand—The Traveler — 139
20. Travelers: Who Are They? — 141
21. Laurie's Porno Movie — 147

22. Brush with Death on a Dream Island	154
23. Big Z Travels Light	163
24. Jungle Johnny, Z, and Understanding Women	167
25. Third Challenge: Z in Chang Mei	180
26. Women's Four Phases of Needs	187
27. Love Me Two Times, I'm Going Away	191
28. God, I Love Traveling!	199

Vietnam—Two Sides Of A Coin — 203

29. The Man, the Hole, and the Rat	205
30. Journey to Dalot and Nha Trang	213
31. Nha Trang: the Cost of War	221

Indonesia—Balance — 229

32. Indecent Proposal in Bali	231
33. Roosters in Action	239
34. Gili Meno: Bronte's Dilemma	245
35. Seeing Auras and Finding Joy	251

Australia—Re-Entry — 261

36. Like Plugging into an Electrical Socket	263
37. Sara from the Serengeti	265
38. Melbourne, Anne-Louise, and the Australian Open	271
39. Fishing with Little Mick	276
40. Confessing Thoughts of Home to an Ex-Priest	282
41. What a Time We've Had, Rosie!	288

New Zealand—Reunion — 291

42. Wwoofing with Shannon: Free Spirit Meets Responsibility	293
43. *The Vision* Pulled My Strings	299
44. Father and Daughter Swim with Dolphins	302
45. Reunion with Chimene	307
46. *Two Roads Diverged in a Wood*	313

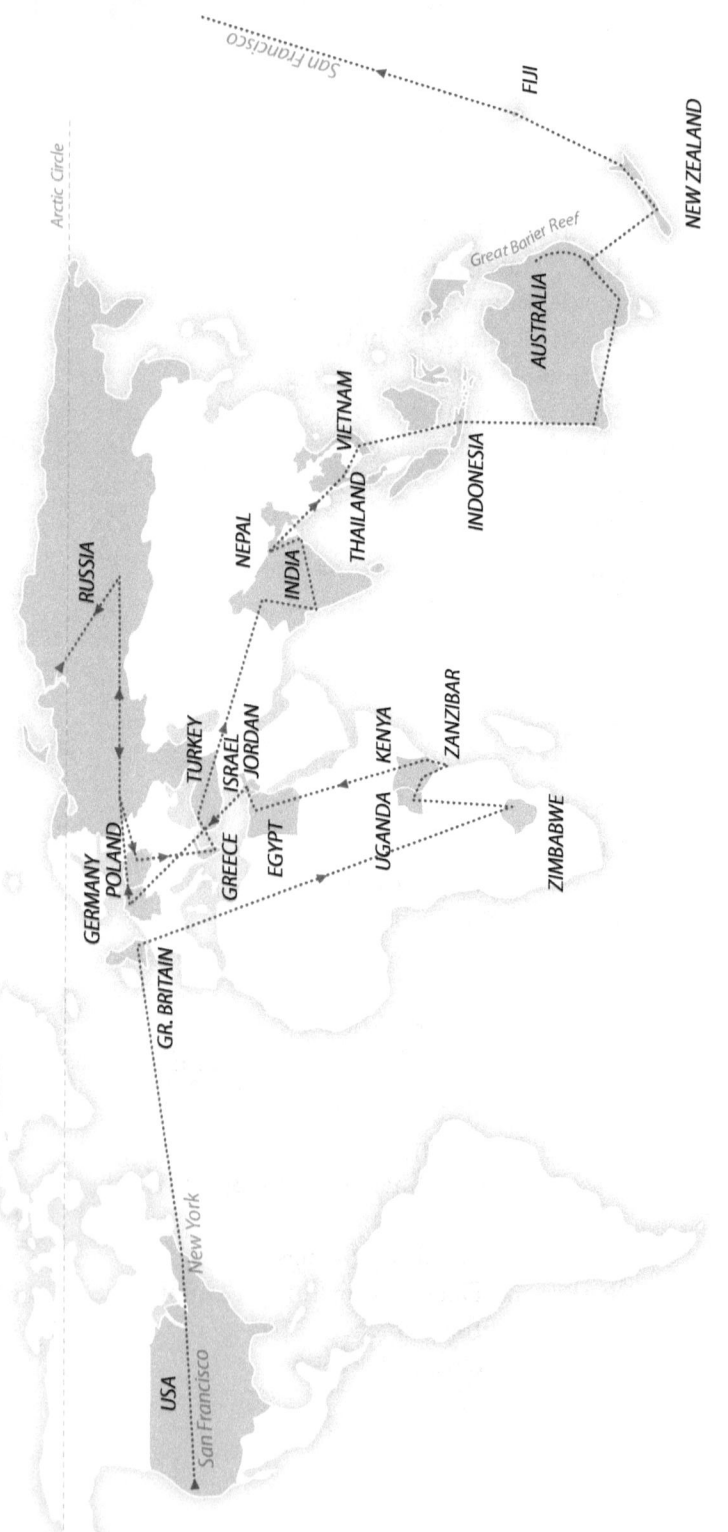

Acknowledgements

I WOULD LIKE TO GIVE my thanks to Joe Reilly for giving me the gift of a smile, and to the "Z" for being the "Z": a trusting friend, who lifts the middle of this book with his sense of fun and his wisdom.

Thanks to Barney for his expert help and advice on a variety of tasks, and to Kazimierz Pelczar for his maps, designs and sense of humor. Finally, thanks to Jill Ronsley for providing the final edit of *The Traveler*, its interior design and back cover, publishing advice, and of course for being the sweetest person.

My special appreciation to my wife, Malgosia, for helping with all the tasks she performed to make publishing manageable.

Introduction

A FRIEND'S HIGHLY UNUSUAL BUSINESS card has this quotation on the back:

*Life is not a journey to the grave with the intention
of arriving safely in a pretty and well-preserved body;
but rather to skid in broadside, thoroughly used up, totally worn out,
and loudly proclaiming: "Wow! What a ride!"*

When I first read it I felt as if I was truly dying—my life slipping into quiet desperation. I was barely nourished by a business environment that lacked passion and a great family that didn't need me anymore. My adrenaline-addicted pace of life left no time to waste on non-productive endeavors such as sending a thank-you note, expressing a small amount of fondness, or caring. Aging and living off stale love, I craved the kind of intimacy I could crawl into and savor. So I quit.

Six months later, I lay in my cabin on a sleek, forties-vintage, triple-deck Russian pleasure boat that was returning from the Arctic Circle. Malgosia had just left my bed for the first time. As she returned to her cabin, I listened to the rhythm of the Yenisei River as it caressed the contours of the boat. My body was limp and my mind mulled over the question she had asked me more than once: "Who are you?"

"A traveler," I had replied each time. Was this true? Or was I still the businessman and family man who tried so hard to be in control of his life? Nah! Not anymore. There was someone in me now who wasn't conscious before—a personality that had been hidden and waiting to come out.

The freedom of being in a completely different environment, one that encouraged new habits to flourish while old ones were put aside, was transforming me. I felt as if I had been resurrected or reincarnated. I was not now father, but had been a good father. No longer a husband, but a man who knew how to be a good husband. I had been familiar with wielding authority, but now desired humility. There was a sense of adventure, comfort with intimacy, and a feeling of unlimited time.

Six months earlier, I'd traded my Mercedes for a backpack and headed out to see the world, shuck my busy life, and wipe the slate clean of responsibility. For one year, I could be anyone I wanted. And I had become a traveler. I'd crossed seven time zones to catch this elegant boat to a Siberian city at the top of the world. On the voyage, I'd learned how the Russians see history, become entangled with a striking Siberian woman who spoke no English, then fallen in love with the only person on this boat who did speak English well—Malgosia, a smart, beautiful twenty-three-year-old from Poland.

Propped up on my pillow, I peered through the porthole at the expansive green tundra of the far north of Siberia. The Arctic Circle was the key to the direction and timing of my journey. To catch a boat heading north and avoid nasty weather, I had needed to be in Siberia in July. That dictated the route through Africa, the Middle East, Western and Eastern Europe, and finally here in Russia.

The strong control I exercised in my prior life had been drastically reduced—limited to where to sleep, what to eat and drink, and where to relieve myself. I was responsible for just my backpack and its contents. The freedom of having so little control was intoxicating. I was a kid again, plunged into a world of newness from the very second I stepped off the plane in Africa—marveling at the vastness of the sky and the masses of people.

Since then I had tasted adventure and fear: a wild car ride to reach the primitive jungle islands of Ssese by nightfall; confronting a savage African lion; getting lost as night fell in Jordan's abandoned desert city of Petra; and facing near-death on the Nile in a felucca.

And I had seen some of the greatest sights in the world: the incomparably majestic Victoria Falls; the ancient city of Lamu in Kenya, where Muslim chants floated out to sea like wishes on the wind; the grand antiquities of Egypt such as the Valley of the Kings and Ramses's 3,300-year-old temples; and the magnificence of St. Basil's in Moscow's Red Square, whose emerald and gold, pear-shaped cupolas unexpectedly reminded me of the palace in *The Wizard of Oz*.

Above all there were powerful insights gained from conversing with ordinary people: how the Masai men regarded multiple wives and what they termed "female circumcision"; how Muslim mores are being influenced by the West; and what it meant to have lived under Communism in Russia. Many of my initial judgments and biases were revealed to be wrong—or were at best only one side of the coin, one slice of the pie. There was always another piece to understand.

As my hair grew long and body toned, fellow travelers helped bring out the mellow hippie buried inside. With travelers I didn't experience conflict. There was instead the closeness of people going someplace for many of the same reasons. We knew nothing about each other except what we communicated, yet what we communicated was often deeply intimate. We had all the time in the world to explore intricate issues with a common level of understanding that comes from being physically and mentally present.

When you have a year to travel there is time to absorb life and understand how it developed and why, to consider change, and learn how change is accomplished. And now I had six months left to travel the rest of the world. I had broken the old Humpty Dumpty and put myself back together again. Yet here I was somewhere near the Arctic Circle wondering if those changes would stick. Did I have what it took to strike a balance between three conflicting desires: family, money, and no strings? And how would Malgosia fit in when I returned? How *could* someone a world away fit in?

GREECE
THE TRIP

1

Joe Reilly's Smile

I first saw Joe Reilly's smile on a balmy mid-September afternoon in 1966. Jaywalking on a mildly busy Denver street, I had my head filled with the second week of graduate studies when a voice shouted: "Hey, this isn't New York! Out here in the sticks we wait for lights to turn green." I recognized the face from class—handsome, faded freckles and bushy brows on a clear Irish complexion. He dressed neat-casual and had a pleasant bearing that fit his fine brown hair, which was cut—as it still was nearly thirty years later—business-close. An inch taller than me at five ten, Joe was lean with long legs that had an easy sway to them, like corn stalks in an evening breeze. But what I noticed most were his deep blue eyes and that disarming smile.

"Let's say I'm in the checkout line of a grocery store," he said later when I remarked on his expression, "and I notice the clerk having a bad day. I smile! Ask how she's doing. She forgets her problems for the moment and smiles back. Both our days are a little brighter." I took Joe's smile with me as I traveled.

After graduate school, we accepted jobs in New York City. Joe barely furnished a studio apartment with a TV, love seat, mattress, and a coffee table made from the cardboard box the television arrived in. Possessions never meant a whole lot to him. On Thursday nights, he and my brother Dave took a bus from Port Authority to New Jersey to dine with us newly-weds at our apartment and tease Kathi until she blushed. At the time, I thought if anything happened to me, Joe and Kathi would make a nice couple. But he was a meteor among planets in the Big Apple—he just passed through and returned to his home out west.

We lost touch till the trauma of his divorce brought us back together. Then we met once or twice a year in some out-of-the-way place. We discussed typical and atypical male topics from the esoteric, such as out-of-body experiences, to, of course, women.

We were simpatico, relating in the supportive way women do rather than giving in to the temptation to disavow the other's opinion just to prove a point. At one of those getaways, when the weight of unrelenting responsibility was crushing our sense of romance in life, we decided to abandon our worries and take off on a long trip. Although we knew it would have to be sometime in the undefined future, we did begin to plan it. Joe opened a special bank account, in which we both deposited a quarterly check.

Sometimes just the presence of an idea—such as this trip—can push us to achieve our passion. Those quarterly deposits probably drove me to blow a fuse in the Transamerica Pyramid in front of all those high-priced lawyers, bankers, and senior executives. When I lost the link between the onscreen presentation and my brain I was left standing speechless like a fool. It shocked me into changing the busyness of my life and severing the strings I mistakenly thought I was pulling.

Now here I was, waiting for Joe to join me in Athens. Except for an occasional skirmish, my friendship with him had the type of trust that didn't need a blowup to air it out. We were going to need that trust because Joe was coming from a regulated life to join me on a trip with few rules and many choices. He was also realizing his dream—three months without responsibility, beginning in the sunshine and splendor of Athens.

"Welcome to Shangri-La, mate!" I said to Joe as he hunched towards me balancing a navy blue backpack. His eyes shone with that fresh look of discovery, and except for a few crevices that time had inscribed in his forehead, he hadn't changed since graduate school. Meanwhile, I felt like Zorba, my body odor overwhelming his deodorant as we hugged.

"We have tons to tell each other!" I exclaimed. "I can't believe you're finally here!"

"I can't either! It was impossible to keep my attention focused on work. All I could think of was no appointments, no getting up early, no ties, no shaving.

"Jesus, Hickey!" he said as he scanned my features. "You look like Tarzan with those colorful clothes and long blond hair. Do you have *any* body fat?"

I laughed, squeezing the solid muscle on his upper torso. "Speaking of Tarzan, looks like you've added bulk?"

"Guy's got to keep fit." He smiled. "How the hell are you? I missed kicking things around with you."

Jabbering like crickets, we hopped a local bus that threaded and fumed through dusty streets, finally dropping us in the heart of the city. At the pension, Joe filled a chest of drawers with the contents of his backpack, while I briefly recounted my trip so far. I confided about meeting Malgosia in Russia, how I'd traveled a quarter of the way around the world, from Siberia to Warsaw, just to tell her the truth about my family life, and that we'd planned a rendezvous in Istanbul four weeks hence. I suggested that maybe a day or two after we arrive in Istanbul, Malgosia and I could slip off on our own for a few days, and that it might be a good time for him and me to take a break. Joe didn't ask questions about my trip and took in the suggested plan with a shrug.

He flipped me a package wrapped in a plastic bag with rubber bands around it. "Kathi gave me this at the airport when I stopped over in San Francisco. She said to give you a kiss and a hug from her. I told her I'd beg off on the kiss."

The bag contained letters, a headband with water-absorbing pellets to cool the skin in hot weather, a small package of homemade chocolate-chip cookies, and a leather necklace from which dangled a circular turquoise stone the size of a bottle cap. Suspended from a hole cut from the middle of the stone was a hematite ball. A sweet note from Chimene, my youngest daughter, read: "Hematite is my favorite, Dad. Rub the ball and I will be with you." Sitting on the bed rubbing the ball, I heard her voice and the advice she gave at my going-away party: "Think of this trip as a mid-life opportunity."

"I don't know what's up with Kathi," I said, reading one of her letters. "She tells me she misses my body next to her, and then alludes to a book about women taking on a lover to supplement a deficient relationship. What do you make of that?"

"It could be worse. She could have skipped the part about missing your body next to her. Come on, I'm dying to see the sights."

Under blue skies in late August, Athens smelled of roasting lamb. It also sounded hollow, empty, since its residents had fled city life for late summer holidays on island beaches. We walked leisurely along charming, restaurant-studded streets towards the Acropolis. Food was on my mind, but Joe pointed to historical sites like a boy discovering buried treasure. He was equally fascinated with the sexuality that drenched Athens. Postcards of satyrs with stiff penises as long as javelins, posters of sumptuous naked women, and a plethora of men's magazines featuring breasts reminiscent of Busty Russell and her Twin Fifties. Real women on the streets wore long black hair, four-inch stiletto heels, and short skirts.

"Do you think males or females buy penis postcards?" I asked.

"I think it's a woman's thing," Joe said thoughtfully. "The last time I heard a guy talking about penises was in high school. What I can't figure out is the appeal of those gargantuan breasts."

"Maybe there's a need for extremes in society because it's changing. You know, like the huge muscles of wrestlers. Because brains are replacing brawn and we need nature's extravagant side to show us being macho is still possible."

"The less realism, the greater the fantasy?"

We trudged up a high bluff to the Parthenon and looked down at the sprawling city. Joe read a passage from a travel book that said the great Athenian statesman Pericles commissioned the white marble building as a temple to the goddess Athena Parthenos, erecting it with help from massive numbers of slaves.

"Did you know," he read, "the Parthenon served as a Christian church, palace, citadel, mosque, and even a seventeenth-century storehouse for gunpowder?"

"I like that it's big."

Joe leaned against a marble pillar and wistfully looked around. Then he tossed me one of those "We did it!" grins, full of pride that we'd converted years of discussion into a dream come true. I grinned right back.

Over the next couple of days, as we began to get used to one another again, Joe's outward self-assurance was punctured by occasional bursts of irritation. I chalked it up to him transitioning between two lives, not thinking that my new traveler personality might have also changed the synergy between us. But there was something else.

The night before leaving Athens for the islands, as we were searching for a movie theater, Joe opened up to me about a mysterious illness he was experiencing.

"It's symptomatic of multiple sclerosis. My nervous system can get disoriented, and I have occasional uncontrollable twitches."

A fogginess clouded my brain—the sensation you get when you're suddenly slammed with the realization that something life-changing is happening.

"What do the doctors say?"

"They can't pin down what's causing it. So I've been dabbling in alternative healing techniques—that's why I meditate in the morning now."

"How long have you had the symptoms?"

"Six months maybe. The sensations started about the time you left. I didn't think much of it at first, just an annoying twitch."

"Do you think it's serious?"

"Enough to get me to consider the meaning of life."

"Jesus, Joe!"

The revelation was shocking. Part of me was worried and anxious, but I was also glad he was with me and out of the anxious hustle of American life.

"That's serious. Are you scared?"

"Yeah!"

We had become so absorbed in our talk that when we eventually looked around we found we were lost in a web of busy neighborhood streets. Joe tried using his map but it was like trying to find Venus on a cloudy night. He got annoyed when I asked directions from the locals, saying he was in control of the situation. Feeling slightly abused, I distanced myself from him and began to walk a few feet ahead. Then I figured it was the illness and got back in step, feeling guilty for not immediately understanding. Eventually we found the "theater"—a screen wedged between the hanging balconies of apartment buildings. It sat fifty people in the open air, not counting non-paying customers in the balconies.

Munching popcorn, we watched Al Pacino pursue Michelle Pfeiffer. The smell of home cooking drifted down from the apartments as did the sounds of corks popping and the *tink tink* of silverware on plates. On screen, Frankie and Johnny were also cooking and serving food, while trying to solve the problem of loving without hurting.

2

SPEAKING OF WOMEN

Early the next morning, we boarded a ferry the size of a three-story building at the port of Piraeus. During the voyage to the island of Mykonos, I looked over the railing—mesmerized by the Aegean's blue, crystalline waters smashing against the hull. While Joe was stretched on a deckchair immersed in a juicy novel, my thoughts went, as they often did, to Malgosia.

"You know," I said turning towards him, "serial monogamy keeps romance alive in our society, but how do you keep it alive with the *same* person in a long-term relationship like mine? When I talk to Kathi, it's like I'm talking to a stranger. The first ten years we would be salivating to hear from each other."

"You can answer that better than me," he said from behind his sunglasses. "How about a mistress?"

"There's historical merit to that point of view. Maybe long term needs *risk* for romance to survive. Couples are so close these days. There's no space to spread your wings to avoid loving and hurting at the same time. Malgosia adds risk. We had the type of intimacy I thought I'd never feel again. If we live a good life, don't we deserve another dose of romance?"

"Romance means different things to different people. It could be serial monogamy, or spontaneity. To me it's living life the way I want, without being stifled by superficial societal standards."

"Like what?"

"Those that don't reflect real-life situations. For instance, the idea that men are womanizers. But you need both a man *and* a woman. Yet we get the rap. That's what I mean by superficial.

"The reality is that strong chemicals affect men's minds and bodies. Everyone in our society is bombarded with images of sexy, slim girls. We're expected to remain pure of mind and women are expected to be thin. We wind up kidding ourselves. We are trying to live up to relationship expectations we can't achieve."

"I read somewhere," I said after considering Joe's point, "that when a young man gets a hard-on a half billion sperm gather in one spot hooked up and ready to leap. Wouldn't you say we're walking-talking nuclear reactions waiting to happen?"

"It explains our temporary insanity sometimes."

I chuckled. "What about women's chemistry? Have you ever wondered why after a steamy night of sex, when neither of you can get enough of each other, women aren't chomping at the fucking bit to have a go the next night?"

"They seem to be able to take it or leave it."

I pulled a deckchair up close to Joe and sat down under the balmy sky.

"I felt proud that someone found me attractive in Russia. I craved the intimacy. The most intimate times Kathi and I ever had were when we were totally honest. We were vulnerable. Too much of the time I didn't expose what I really thought about some things, and she held her inner thoughts sacred."

"Exactly!" said Joe, putting the book aside. "We get hurt or mad at someone for telling the truth, and all that does is create a liar. I lost the woman I wanted to be with forever because I was truthful about an affair. I abhor the dishonesty in hiding what I really feel, but hate the conflict that results from exposing my inner feelings. I'm not very good at conflict."

"That's the dilemma! If Kathi and I talked openly about my experience in Russia, we could air out a lot of our dissatisfaction with each other and reach a higher level of intimacy."

"It didn't work for me. Honesty is a lot about the other person's ego and taking a risk, don't you think?"

Before I could answer, Joe looked at me with a hint of admiration. "What I like about you is that you take risks and it rubs off. I'm on this boat to make my life bigger. You helped get me here."

"Thanks. We helped each other." I felt honored.

He had that lost look of a person thinking deep into the murky past. "We didn't fight much in my family—pretty much kept things to ourselves. It created harmony. Of course, lack of conflict is a double-edged sword. Holding emotions in didn't prepare me for marriage."

To change the subject, Joe—finally!—asked how I felt about being with such a young woman.

"Before my travels, I fantasized about falling in love just one more time. At airports I'd study the faces of young lovers as they stroked each other's fingers like they were intricate works of art. With Malgosia I fell in love after one kiss—though we'd talked the whole night before, till seven in the morning. She enchanted me. And I have to admit that I had great ego satisfaction that someone so young found me attractive."

"How about the sex? You know, was she … ?"

"Yeah! She was. I was practically shaking in anticipation before touching her. Her breasts and body were firm and vibrant, coiled almost. She was hungry. I was hungry.

"It's like Jack Nicholson said—and he's the only man I can think of that can get away with this comment—that there's a reason why men of all ages find women of child-bearing age attractive."

"Nicholson has a way of stripping away the superficial. Why do you think she liked an older man?"

"She said it was the clothes I wore that made me look interesting, that a woman notices how a man dresses. I wore color in Siberia, African clothes like these," I indicated my bright blue, flowered African shirt and dark blue, striped string pants. "Plus, she liked that I was talking to geese congregating in a mud puddle."

"Geese?"

"Yeah! Seems strange, huh?" I laughed. "Unbeknownst to me, she and her older cousin followed me around this muddy Siberian village where our boat stopped. I was trying to relearn how to sing from a sheet of my favorite songs. Suddenly, I was passing this mud hole when a gander—I guess trying to protect his group of females—made threatening gestures my way. We had words. It was then the cousin whispered to her, 'Why don't you talk to the American hippie?'

"She came up to me in the boat's elegant piano room where I was writing. She was the only one on the boat who spoke English fluently. Later she said women are curious, and older guys are more willing to share their knowledge and feelings. Her best male friend is this cousin. He's fifteen years older than her and brilliant, with a good sense of humor. Maybe he paved the way."

"What are you going to do about her when you get back?"

"I don't have a fucking clue. She's halfway around the world and beautiful. What are the odds?"

I wanted to talk more about this subject, about how the age difference disappeared when we were together, about perceptions, destiny, and options. But Joe picked up his book, found his page, and the conversation was over.

3

MYKONOS: THUNDERCLOUDS ON THE ROAD LESS TRAVELED

Mykonos Town, the island's capital, showed few signs of the quaint fishing village atmosphere where Shirley Valentine traded her housewife blues for romance with a Greek tavern owner. Its maze of streets buzzed with bars, restaurants, and boutiques displaying glittering gold and silver to tourists in skimpy clothes. The locals had deliberately laid these streets out in a confusing, disordered way to stall pirates as they came ashore and give themselves time to gather their valuables and skip town.

We settled in a characteristically whitewashed stucco guesthouse with a sky-blue roof and trim. The smell of fried food drifted in from the beach and soon lured us to a nearby waterside restaurant to devour fish and chips. Afterwards, we spread our towels and relaxed as fighter jets thundered across the skies flexing Greek military muscle. A carpet of glistening Caucasian bodies broiled in the sun like so many franks on the grill. Tanning lotion so filled the air that you felt the sea-breezes barely made it to where you were lying, much less their smell. Aside from the planes, the *whap-whap* of paddleballs, and timid splash of the waves, the beach maintained a bright beauty and European quiet.

Looking through sunglasses, Joe pointed across twenty yards of bodies to a prone figure with snow-white breasts exposed to a scorching sun: "Women love to expose themselves," he observed, "and I love to watch." He shifted his attention to a particular strolling Aphrodite. "Do you think butt-thongs are attractive?"

"Butt-thongs? Aha, I see what you're referring to." This needed pondering. "Personally, I like mystery in my objects of desire."

"Speaking of objects of desire, I remember handing Kathi a pack of matches with a picture of a naked woman on back. I asked her what she saw. She said, 'Tits and ass!' and took off on the theme of 'women as objects.'

"I saw tits and ass too! But also soft, shiny hair, thick lips, an interesting smile, and nice legs. The pity is that these days only a few men I know are able to converse about the beauty or intricacies of women. It's like guys are physically uncomfortable with the topic."

"I know what you mean. I get uncomfortable too. Maybe it's natural, or maybe all the focus on male abuse in movies and TV is making us gun-shy. You know, like we actually *are* bad guys. I don't think our fixation with women's beauty is any different than women seeing power or material possessions or security in us. Do you suppose we'll ever get tired of watching women?"

"It's a tribute to nature that men *your* age still have desire."

"Fuck you, Hickey! If I ever outgrow that tingle when a beautiful woman walks by, shoot me will ya?"

"They have such power over us, don't they?"

We shrugged—that was a given.

"Speaking of beautiful objects," I said, "how come you don't have more beauty in your life? You got to admit, except for your piano, your house is plain."

"Plain?" He sniggered. "I guess you're right. I don't have to own beauty to enjoy it. My mom and dad were living next to their parents in Kansas when grasshoppers ate my grandparents' crop. Mom and dad figured they were next, so they moved to Spokane because the grass was greener. It's always greener somewhere. They had ten dollars in their pockets when they drove west in a '35 Chevy coupe, with my older brother's crib in a wood crate built on to the trunk. We all slept on mattresses in the first house. Didn't need a lot of stuff. Mom used to say that people buy stuff they don't need with money they don't have to impress people they don't like."

"I like your mom."

Late that evening, I got out of bed, dressed, grabbed my money belt, and slipped out of the room leaving Joe snoozing. Nightlife in Mykonos started *late*, and I needed a taste. It wasn't the loudness I craved; it was the lateness and the conversation. I had gotten used to staying up all hours talking to people about all sorts of things.

I found a quiet bar, sipped a tall glass of beer, and chatted sporadically to an Australian who worked summers to pay for her travels. Mostly I thought about what it was traveling in a pair and the different habits you notice. Joe and I were alike in that we were quick to laugh, were generally friendly, liked talking about relationships between men and women, and were fiercely independent with strong opinions. We were also opposites. He was a private man—proper, polite, and mild-mannered. He showered every day, was careful of the bright sun on his skin, and, although a good conversationalist, was quite comfortable with silence. I didn't care what I wore most of the time, showered every second or third day, and talked a lot, especially after the necessarily limited conversation I'd had traveling through Russia.

In the morning, Joe's smile was gone. He was sitting on the edge of his bed bristling mad. "How could you be so inconsiderate, slamming things around in the middle of the night?" He worked up to fever pitch as I tried to blow away the night's cobwebs. "You woke me up!"

He was right. I should have just apologized. Instead I defended myself. "*Slamming?* Why are you exploding at me? And, by the way, it's not the first time."

"You're so self-absorbed," he said, "and while I'm at it, you're insecure about your writing, and you talk too much." He added a few other choice morsels about our traveling together such as not treating people like I should—whatever that meant.

I pouted, noticing an unusual reluctance in myself to pursue this conflict to a conclusion.

"You were inconsiderate the times I visited you in California too!" he added, as if as an afterthought. "Too *busy* to pick me up at the airport. Kathi and I were always waiting for you to get home from work." He looked tired.

A fatigued, sinking sensation took hold of me too. I felt defeated and submissive, as I imagine Kathi felt when I was in a bad mood and something she did caused me to get upset with her. I believed I was at fault and that his anger was justified.

"I'm sorry, Joe. I guess I was inconsiderate."

After a while of silence, Joe visibly softened. "I didn't mean to hurt or embarrass you," he said. "Nor the part about you talking too much. Maybe I'm reacting to old, pent-up issues."

We got up from our beds and embraced. I felt needy inside, but I did not feel any resolution. It was like leaving a hotel room wondering if you left something under the bed.

However, our strained emotions dissipated after a quiet day of being careful and considerate of each other. And before long we were on the ferry to Naxos, slicing through frothy waters and past misty silhouettes of other islands. I rested my chin on the bow railing, and absentmindedly rubbed Chimene's hematite ball.

Unlike Joe, I had quit my regulated life months ago, and been trying ways of living I would never have imagined. After Russia I felt invigorated, walking confidently on the periphery of society. I didn't have to fit anyone's mold, and enjoyed the new feeling of being without conflict. And if conflict came, I could always step off the bus at the next stop. Maybe the bigger issue wasn't waking Joe up, pent-up issues, or his health, but that I was a wild card in the making. Would friends and family of my previous life, like Joe, accept my new personality? Or would I have to step off their bus?

Like other Greek islands, Naxos recalled California cattle country—hilly and dry, the air filled with the scent from scattered clumps of thyme. Markets, bakeries, and restaurants with awnings lined the wharf for a kilometer. Resting on a small cliff poking out from one side of the wharf were the columns of an unfinished temple to Apollo, begun in 530 BC, which looked like off-white football uprights with a marble crossbar. On the opposite side of the wharf, atop a jetty of boulders, a pier jutted into the Aegean. The pier shielded a half-empty beach from view—none of Mykonos's claustrophobia of basting bodies.

At sunset, we walked along the beach to the pier and a lone porcelain-clean cafe and bar. Serenaded by Chopin from the speakers, we sipped rosé from delicate crystal glasses. Out the window, fishing boats inched across the dark crimson sea toward the hazy islands.

"You know, this has got to be one of the most romantic places in the world," Joe said. "Wouldn't it be great to have our women with us? Then again, I like just the two of us.

"Remember when you visited Spokane before leaving, and Kirsten and I asked you to write down qualities you wanted to bring along on the trip and those you wanted to let go?"

"Which we ceremoniously burned and buried?"

"What did we burn?" Joe snapped his fingers to aid my memory.

"A dominant persona. I held on to a friendly smile, sense of adventure, and few possessions—one of them is that diary you gave me with the Robert Frost's poem inscribed." I gazed at the distant boats and recited:

> *Somewhere ages and ages hence:*
> *Two roads diverged in a wood, and I*
> *Took the one less traveled by,*
> *And that has made all the difference.*

Several minutes passed before Joe broke the silence. "I've dreamed of exotic places like this since we deposited that first installment in the bank. Let's drink to *the trip!*"

Our glasses clinked to the life-affirming sound of Vivaldi's *Four Seasons*, but the music provoked another wave of nostalgia. "When Kathi and I were younger, marriage carried such desire, such playfulness. I couldn't keep my hands off her. But then the years passed and I woke up wondering where the love songs went."

"Is it possible to keep love songs going forever?" Joe wondered. "What if love travels along like notes on different scales? One scale is young love—all whipped cream and wild sex to Ravel's *Bolero*. Another is children and all sorts of memories. Does that make sense at all?"

"Yeah, it does. Maybe that's why love is so confusing at times."

"Perhaps the confusion comes when we lose harmony, when the enjoyment of sex, health, or money is not as important for

21

one as the other. Kirsten and I both love classical music, the outdoors, same foods. Then again, she works all sorts of hours, and I like to start work late, leave early, and take three-day weekends. If we're fortunate, we might slide along together long enough to harmonize on a different scale."

The stars twinkled, the wine sparkled, and the candle barely flickered in the enveloping night. Would Kathi and I ever find that harmony again? I asked myself and then said aloud: "Be nice to hit the high notes on a regular basis, Reills."

4

Santorini

Santorini (also called by its Ancient Greek name of Thera) is one side of a volcanic crater whose middle section violently exploded into the atmosphere a few millennia ago. The explosion obliterated all land above water except the eastern crater wall (Santorini) and some surrounding small islands with Nea Kameni, the newest islet, in the volcano's center. A cobblestone road led up the crater wall to Santorini's capital, Fira, which was no more than a large village. The sunlight glistened off white churches with royal-blue domes and blue and snow-white apartments built into the cliffs. Restaurants, perched on the crest of the crater wall, gazed down twenty-five hundred feet to where fishing boats left scratches in the blue sea and seagulls serenely flittered in and out of white-capped swells.

We stayed on the outskirts of Fira, renting a moped for travel. While Joe and I listened intently as the attendant explained the ins and outs of our bike, a young couple renting another moped blasted impetuously out into the traffic. Actually, the guy blasted off, leaving his girlfriend briefly suspended in midair. Her crash-landing left her sprawled inches from oncoming cars.

After running to her aid, Joe apprehensively climbed in back of our moped, grabbing hold of my stomach. "Hey, Hickey," he said nervously, as we set off into the town. "How much do you know about driving one of these things?"

"Experienced, but rusty! Just lean into the flow." Personally, I hated being in back—it was like saddling up on a barely controllable horse.

The lower streets of Fira were flooded with curio shops, overpriced eateries, and tourists. We had a breakfast of paper-thin ham and cheese on toast that looked like it had been retrieved from under an old mattress.

After stopping briefly at the crater's brink to admire the scenery, we motored south on a winding two-lane road, along semi-arid hills terraced with vineyards. By now, Joe was more comfortable riding double. He clutched less and leaned into the flow. However, at the same time, he did look quite exhilarated and grateful each time we stopped. His mysterious disease appeared to have melted away.

Our destination was Kamari, a beach with black sand (small pellets of dark lava). We laid sarongs down under a multicolored umbrella—one among three parallel rows of identical multicolored umbrellas. Unlike the youthful bodies lying on other islands, the shaded bodies filling beach chairs around us were older, with affluent, lumpy flesh, more vulnerable to death.

"Did you notice that guy walking to your left?" I asked, trying to get comfortable on the oversized sand. "That's the third time he passed us."

"You mean the hunched-over guy with a blasé appearance, nose like a dagger, blue safari hat and pink bathing suit? I'd say unemployed KGB assassin."

We looked suspiciously at each other. As words have a way of doing, the mention of "assassin" triggered a conversation about death. Joe opined that we placed too much importance on life. "When we're buried what remains of us is a snapshot on someone's wall for a generation or two, then it's up into the attic. If we're interesting or good-looking enough, we might be sold in a rummage sale. I can't remember my great-grandmother's name, so why take death seriously if we're just a snapshot on the wall of life when we leave it?"

"Yeah, lucky thing we don't take death seriously," I replied, but the word was already triggering memories. "When my brother Steve died, I felt grateful. Steve never really had a chance. He wasn't going to grow old. I figured I'd grow old with Dave though. As a kid, I was always so glad to see my oldest brother walking down the driveway, just home from college. He was bigger than life."

"Must have been tough to lose two brothers and your father so close together."

"It was like nature thinning out the weak." It had been so long since I gave voice to their deaths, although the trip had given me time to look back to when we were kids.

"I remember the times Dave and I came to your apartment in New Jersey," Joe said. "We had different views on life. He was more a product of the fifties, more religious. He had that fast, nervous way of speaking his mind. I loved his humor—quick and natural."

"My whole family had a great sense of humor. The thing is Steve and Dad had been mentally ill for so long they couldn't cope. I took their deaths too well, the pragmatic, humanitarian approach. Steve was better off dead than living in a mental institution, and if Dad had died after Mom, who would have taken him in? At Steve's funeral, Shannon said I was keeping the pain inside to be strong."

"I guess with so much illness in the family, someone had to take control. The stiff upper lip."

"So to speak!"

"I was at an alumni get-together in San Francisco to watch my old college team play basketball in the NCAA tournament. I literally bumped into a high-school and college classmate of Dave's in the crowded bar. Dave, Steve, and I went to the same high school and college and this guy knew the family. He asked me how my dad was. I said he was killed in a car accident four years ago.

"'Oh no!' the guy says. 'I'm sorry to hear that. What happened?'

"'Drunken driver.'

"'Ah, that's too bad! Say, how's your brother Dave? Haven't seen him in ages?'

"'He died too!' I said, starting to feel sorry for the guy, but thinking I'd be glad when this line of questioning was over. What could I say?

"The guy says, 'What happened?'

"'Suicide.'

"I figured Dave needed more of an explanation than Dad. 'Life had gotten too complicated,' I said, 'too much responsibility.'

"There was a pregnant pause. 'How about Steve?' he says, treading gingerly. 'What's he up to?'

"'Steve's dead too.' I told him how Steve had been mentally ill for years and he'd died before Dave in a New York City mental institution. I didn't confess how. Obviously, the first chance he got, this guy slinked away through the crowd of alumni. He'd heard enough.

"They said Steve fell off a couch. An accident! No fucking way! Dave and I identified his body at the morgue. It was badly scarred around his face. We figured Steve had gotten into one of his "tough guy" moods with the wrong fellow. Otherwise everyone loved Steve. Those big blue eyes and innocent sense of humor. We would do John Wayne together—Steve did the walk while I did the talk. And whatever he was thinking came right out his mouth.

"I hated visiting Steve in those grungy places," I continued, opening up to Joe. "Even the brown clumps of grass outside the brick buildings were depressed. Steve used to say that he didn't see how they could cure anybody, because most of the doctors had a hard time speaking English. He seemed normal to me most of the time, and he was really good at analyzing his various doctors' analyses of him.

"Steve's first job out of college was a social worker in a hard-core mental hospital. Six months later, he was on the other side of the bars. In the end, he was a schizophrenic with too many years in too many institutions."

Joe shook his head.

Sifting the black sand through my fingers, I stared at the water beyond the small waves cresting to shore, fixated on the sea's vastness. Why couldn't I cry during each of these tragedies? Was it Dad's drinking or my fighting with him that hardened me? Or had I become just another unfeeling businessman handling one more crisis?

That evening, we parked the moped in Fira and followed the whiffs of fried food down flights of narrow stone steps to the Ippos restaurant, which was built gracefully into the crater walls. The evening clouds were like smoke signals on the fading blue sky. Dressed in jeans and long shirts to ward off a slight chill in the air, we munched on calamari and casually speculated on the depth of the crater below the water. Trams carried tourists down to ferries, which delivered them to "Love Boats" moored offshore. The illuminated cruise liners looked so bulky and out of place they could have been tethered white elephants strung with Christmas lights.

"What happened to Dave?" Joe asked, picking up the conversation about my brothers from that afternoon.

"After you left New York, Dave went to California with his roommate for a change of scenery. A year later, his roommate put him on a plane home. When I picked him up I'd never seen anyone so defeated. His hair stood three inches straight up, as if it was the only part of him that wanted to live. My beautiful brother!"

"Life trips us up sometimes."

My eyes watered as I recalled Dave's despondent look, his struggle with living. It took me years to regain his confidence after I became the "successful" sibling, the one who always gave him advice. It happened eventually when, one day at a bar, I confided a weakness or two. Dave added some more weaknesses he'd observed in me and told the bartender to set us up. That was it—the key to having his confidence was my humility and a few beers.

"Anyway," I said to Joe, "he slowly recovered and after a couple of years got hitched. His wife and kids gave him something to shoot for."

"What put him over the edge?"

"Money. The last time we sat at the bar, he was neurotic about the cash going into building another bedroom in his house. He had built a security blanket and was consumed by the thought it was slipping away. That's the last time I saw him. I wanted to grow old with Dave."

"The drive for money carries such pressure, and men don't have much of a support group to unload on, do they?"

The waiter came down the wooden steps from the kitchen with our main course: spinach pie, meatballs covered with eggs and lemon, and stuffed eggplant. Sunset faded as Joe changed the discussion to his daughter moving out on her own.

"I was proud of her. Also relieved. I felt liberated that I was now only responsible for myself—even if I'd still be on the phone asking what she had for dinner, and cringing as she described something mixed with peanut butter! There are times as a single parent when you want to say, 'Fuck it, let me out of here!' Guys are expected to be responsible for others, but what prepares us growing up for that subtle prison?"

"You think responsibility is a prison?"

"Sometimes."

"Huh. I thought I was prepared for the long haul. But I realized during this trip that I've been dealing with emotional responsibility since I was a little kid. My dad, confidant to Mom, protecting Danny because he was smaller, raising my own family."

Danny, my twin brother. He started with a lot less than most folks and lived without what are usually considered necessities such as self-esteem and romantic love. Dyslexia preceded psychosis and a nervous condition that left his neck frozen. But he was intelligent—in a slow way—and had a wonderful sense of humor, the family trait. The slowness allowed him to be totally honest at times, such as: "How did you like dinner, Dan?" "I didn't like it." I envied him the honesty that didn't have to abide polite fibs. And the older I got the more I appreciated him. He managed without help, yet I felt responsible. He was my twin.

"I thought I could help Steve until I realized it was a lifelong effort," I continued. I welcomed this opportunity to unburden about my family. "Then Dad suffered a nervous breakdown and doctors were sticking electrodes in him saying how shock treatment would inhibit the anxiety. Steve and Dad must have had fifty shock treatments between them. Neither was good at handling responsibility, and then it was stripped from them."

"It's like your family was cursed. How did you escape?"

"People used to ask me that all the time. My mom's side was very strong. She is the most courageous person I ever met.

"Once she went to court when Steve got everyone in his halfway house drunk and started a fight. She convinced the judge, through the intensity of her motherly feeling, not to throw Steve in jail. Once in a rare moon, she'd cry in my arms.

"She'd say: 'Maybe this wouldn't have happened if I had stayed home like the other mothers instead of working.' Can you imagine five kids and working full time as a nurse? I'd tell her how valuable her work was and that it would be positive in the long run. I said she'd have to let Steve go or she'd nurse him forever without a life of her own. How do you let one of your kids go?

"It wasn't as bad as it sounds," I said, though I felt close to tears. "Most of this happened in my early twenties. Before that, except for Dad, we were a normal dysfunctional family. But I was always the advice-giver, the rock-solid personality. I don't want the job anymore."

"I know the feeling," Joe commiserated. "We're much alike that way. When Jane and I got divorced, I felt so isolated. It was as if she'd died. No more warm glances or touches. I was a single parent just starting my tax practice. There wasn't much money coming in, and, like Dave, I didn't have a support group. It was like I was roped to a heavy plow. When you divorce you get to seriously thinking your life is worthless. The weight of the world makes you think how much simpler it would be to end it all.

"But I've always been the strong one too, ever since I was a little kid playing football. They put me in the line when I wanted to score touchdowns. One year, I just said I was a halfback. No one challenged me, so I scored touchdowns. I control my little world. But here with you I'm out of my nest. It's scary and exciting at the same time."

"I keep forgetting that you've only been traveling for two weeks. I've been flying free—nobody's dad or husband or brother. You think we're selfish?"

"Freedom's a selfish concept. But we only have one life, why waste it? What's that saying? Most people tiptoe through life just trying to make it safely to the other side."

"Pass me the wine, O Assuring One," I said, only half-joking. "I wouldn't like a steady diet of freedom. I like my other life too. But Dave's death made me realize that the control I thought I had was a ruse. Business and family had more control over me than I had over them.

"When I was on the brink of disaster—during the first video game shakeout—my friend Frank Zolfo asked me to think of myself as eighty, and visualize what I'd accomplished. I said I saw myself out of business by fifty. Shortly after that, you and I set up our travel account."

"The account worked for me too. Each time I made a deposit I thought of beginning a more exciting life."

"Fifty can be the beginning of a new life, rather than the beginning of decline."

"What's that?"

"Something I learned from my grandmother. She died recently—aged ninety-nine."

That night, I mulled over my childhood. I found no regrets. I'd inherited many of my father's talents, for which I was eternally grateful. And, admittedly, a few habits that this trip was changing. Dad, with all his faults, sang like Caruso, played the violin, was a four-letter man in college, had interesting hobbies such as carpentry and boating, and told uproariously funny jokes in every brogue you'd ever heard. My siblings and I would inch our way down the stairs to hear him entertain friends, who were busting a gut. Dad's laugh boomed. When he was happy, life was a charm.

The flip side was he had no sense of what people were thinking and so we'd always end up arguing. I couldn't recall ever having a *real* conversation with Dad. This "dialogue," driving back after picking my parents up at the airport when I was already in my thirties, was typical.

"What do you think about the Flood?" Dad asked. He had a book closed on his lap in the front passenger seat.

"What flood?" I said.

"*The Flood!* Sons of bitches! I send you kids to Catholic school and you become atheists."

"You mean Noah's Flood?"

"What other flood could it be?"

"It could be the one in Iowa."

5

CRETE: A CHALLENGE FOR THE TRAVELER PERSONALITY

Our sleek hovercraft departed at 9 p.m. and raced for three and a half hours to Iraklion, the Cretan capital. The city was close to the ancient town and palace complex of Knossos—the capital of the goddess-worshipping Minoan civilization. Some historians speculate that the explosion of the Santorini volcano around 1600 BC may have helped destroy the Minoans and was the origin of the Atlantis legend.

Iraklion was now a bustling Mediterranean city filled with jewelry shops and, for some reason we never figured out, telephone booths devoid of phones. Older men twirled worry beads as they walked and talked. Their voices sounded like gravel being dumped. But the song and sizzle of Zorba was missing—maybe because of the time of year. The local late-season sentiment was summed up by an inscription on the back of a shirt: "Send more tourists, the last ones tasted great."

Joe and I came to Crete to follow a map my daughter Shannon had prepared. It showed me some of her haunts during the six months she traveled after we'd given her a $2,000 college graduation present. It had these instructions: "Take the bus to Chora Sfakion. It's a sweet little fishing village you dream about. Then take a twenty-minute ferry to the smaller fishing village of Loutro. Hike up a rocky trail into the copper mountains behind the town. It leads past abandoned ruins and down into the even smaller hamlet of Nikos, where a cute hotel sits on the edge of a rocky beach. Try the yogurt with honey and tell them I sent you. Then, hike west a quarter of a mile and take a look at the cave I lived in for a month when my money was low. Climb the slopes above the cave (be careful it's steep) and walk along the mountain ridge to Marble Beach."

A picturesque bus ride later, Joe and I were relaxing on the balcony of the pleasant Hotel Alkyon overlooking the turquoise waters of the Mediterranean. As we nibbled sardines and fresh baguettes, we toasted Shannon and proclaimed to each other, "*This* is heaven."

After two days devouring fresh fish and Greek delicacies, we boarded the morning ferry to Loutro. It was a perfect day, the early sun casting its lazy spell over the tranquil sea. On the ferry, we were told that everyone was related to everyone else in the isolated village. Approaching the shore, we could see the settlement was carved out of the rock-shale hills looming in the background. At either end of a stony beach the length of a football field, there was a three-story white hotel with the standard blue shutters and awnings extending lazily over its waterfront restaurant. Inevitably, one cousin owned the left-side hotel and another the right side. No cars or bikes disturbed the village's calm.

We checked into a sparsely furnished room in the right-side hotel, and, without much ado, began to follow Shannon's map down the beach on to a path into the hills. A half-kilometer up, we found decaying remains of a Venetian castle whose walls had one-foot arrow slits at ten-foot intervals. A twenty-foot turret with a hole blasted through it—I imagined it had come from a direct hit by a pirate galleon—loomed on the seaward side. A statue of Poseidon searched the Mediterranean below.

We trudged up craggy ridges accompanied by an eerie wind and piercing silence and then down into a green-speckled valley. Occasionally we passed horned goats, bells dangling and clanging as they nonchalantly munched thyme or begged shamelessly for handouts. After a few kilometers, we reached Nikos and the "cute hotel" Shannon had written about.

Under the restaurant's blue awning, Joe lunched on Greek salad and red snapper while I tried the yogurt and honey Shannon suggested. Twenty yards from us a bearded man standing ten feet into shallow water pounded octopi against a large rock, tenderizing the meat for dinner, I guessed. Joe had a glazed look on his face. We talked to a shepherd in his early thirties who remembered Shannon, while two gray-haired women in heavy black dresses and shawls shot suspicious glances our way as they cleaned fish. We were the lone customers.

After lunch, we walked about a quarter of a mile down the beach to Shannon's marble cave. It was carved wide and deep (maybe a hundred and fifty square feet inside) into the mountainside and high enough up so that the tide wouldn't flood it. All but sandy patches of the floor were marble. Yet there was enough sand to sleep comfortably and elevated nooks to store clothes.

The cave felt inviting. Shannon said a couple of travelers handed the cave over to her after their extended stay. Inside, I could feel Shannon's presence and imagined where she put her sleeping bag and laid out its contents. They would, of course, have been strewn around. Was she scared and lonely here? Her determination must have been put to the test.

Thinking of her brought on a powerful sense of nostalgia. The same nostalgia that Chimene's necklace gave me. It had been five months since I had seen my family, and I missed them.

"I'm glad I found out about this place after the fact," I told Joe. "I would have been concerned about Shannon. I admire her for braving these conditions and being able to make her money last. She was so enthusiastic about her cave."

Joe just nodded and appeared anxious to move on—as if there was something in Shannon's cave that bugged him.

When we left the cave I began to head eagerly toward the next landmark on Shannon's map—Marble Beach. It was as if I was compelled by her spirit to meet her there. Joe began to walk in the opposite direction. After a few steps, he looked my way and we locked eyes. "I'm heading back to Loutro," he said.

There was toughness in his gaze and tightness in his walk that I could not comprehend—and never did. I felt a strong, unreasonable determination to go on without him, without discussion. I sensed combativeness in Joe for something I did and, like a cat whose tail was being pulled, I had to go the opposite way.

We had reached a crossroads. Our eyes lingered on each other, and then we turned and went our separate ways. The unspoken words consumed my thoughts—so much so that I hardly noticed I was walking along a steep cliff that dropped menacingly down to the undulating aqua sea below.

I was surprised at my behavior. Normally I would have gone back with Joe and returned to the beach the next day. That was the way I was—the path of least resistance unless it was vital. In this case, I had a manic desire to follow Shannon's instructions, as if they were the call of home. Was it this "manic" that bothered Joe? Or simply three weeks of differences had piled up and needed a pressure release?

Joe might have been worried about pushing himself given his strange illness. There had been little sign of it and perhaps the absence of the Western speed of life had made it go away—like all my aches and pains—or maybe it was there under the surface. I felt guilty thinking the walk may have been too risky for him. But the strong sense for someone's energy, which traveling had given me, told me that if Joe's demeanor was like the last time we quarreled, it was not anything I wanted to be around again.

When I returned to Loutro in early evening, time had smoothed over whatever problems had surfaced. We enjoyed dinner in the usual mellow fashion. And there was no sign of tension the next day as Joe and I rented plastic kayaks and paddled the scary swells the mile or two to Marble Beach. Like two Robinson Crusoes, we nervously explored forbidding caves along the way before spending a relaxing day at the beach. It was only that night as we sipped ouzo at a small seaside bar that the strain in our relationship resurfaced. We were innocently bragging about our grandmothers living to their late nineties.

"What in their lives do you think made them live so long?" I asked.

Suddenly, Joe's eyes turned cold.

"You don't care what made them live so long," he spit out. "You're just patronizing me, like a father with his young son, because you've figured out the answer like you usually do. You always know the answers."

The words were like a karate chop. I ask questions, lots of them, but I would never ask Joe questions in a hurtful manner. Fuck it!

Crete: A Challenge for the Traveler Personality

"Instead of alluding to the past, why not unmask it?" I snapped back in an icy tone that had lain unused for a long time. "I'll start. For instance, what about your jealously?"

"About *what*?"

"My travels, my family, my business life! All the things you never ask me questions about. The areas where I'm successful." My response was a delayed reaction to his outburst in Mykonos—and all those stings from his Scorpio personality over the years.

"Yes, your time was always so important," he repeated sarcastically—the only evidence of the famous Joe Reilly smile was the crow's-feet around his angry eyes. "Your family was always the greatest! When I visited you in California, it was Kathi who picked me up at the airport because you were too busy making money to put our friendship first. I waited for you to come home for dinner, sometimes until nine o'clock. You disrespected me. I always met you personally when you flew to Spokane."

"Our friendship! What about all those years I was the only one keeping in touch because you were apathetic? It wasn't until you got divorced and needed someone to talk to that you contacted me on your own volition!"

There was silence.

"Why are you so angry?"

"I'm not the angry one, you are."

We argued about who was angry. It was silly. We should have laughed. A few caring words would have thawed the atmosphere. But my "traveler" personality had disappeared and someone else had stepped in. His rage was unstoppable. He was the one who had to have the final words when I was a kid fighting my father. And he had shown up occasionally during the darkest days of my marriage.

"You pay the fucking bill, Joe!" I rose from my chair and stormed off.

Back in the room, I packed my bag, walked on to the balcony, and waited for Joe. The packing was more a consequence of hurt than an actual desire to leave. I expected Joe to apologize because he'd vented first. Then I would unpack. That was what happened at home when I got angry: I'd react extremely and, voilà, there'd be a resolution. Or was I reacting a new way: the traveler getting off the bus at the next stop? It was confusing.

When Joe did show up he eyed the backpack quickly, then shrugged. "Maybe it's best if we split," he said.

"Yeah" was all I could muster. I wanted him to suffer before we talked. But we never did.

That night, I twisted and turned in my bed with stifling unease. I heard Joe doing the same. My mood alternated between waves of anger and frustration, and a consuming fear of losing a friend I loved. Friendships are fragile, not flexible like marriages where there are time and chances to redeem a multitude of sins. Joe and I never had much practice disagreeing and hadn't set up rules when we started out traveling together. A growing sense of loss fought against a shaky traveler's conviction that whatever happened, happened for the best. Outside, the wind picked up in the dark of early morning. That eerie whistling in the hills must have been the sound Odysseus heard abandoned on his remote island. Finally, I dozed.

As daylight returned so did my fear. My hands and legs were swollen. Joe was gone. I wrote a letter and left it on the night table, hoping it would be a bridge to the future. The essence was that I didn't feel our confrontation represented the essence of our trip and that maybe my questions were aggressive.

For six months, I'd been the easygoing traveler I wanted to be, but couldn't yet change my feelings in real time if another person vented. I couldn't yet think from the other person's perspective.

I did find Joe, in the restaurant, and willed him to stop me from leaving. There was so much I wanted to say to him. Instead we hugged goodbye—a little too stiffly—and parted—a little too amicably. Such fucking egos we had! Such jerks!

From the deck on the ferry to Chora Sfakion, I looked back at Joe sitting in the hotel restaurant. He was staring at the ferry as if lost in a fog. He had dreamed of exotic places since we deposited that first installment in the bank. Now he was alone for one month before meeting his girlfriend in Portugal. And I was heartbroken.

The loss triggered the tears I couldn't even muster at my brothers' funerals. The last time I cried I was ten and Steve had broken my tooth.

Maybe Joe had been upset that I suggested we take a break in Istanbul so that I could be alone with Malgosia. We never discussed this break. I'd failed to communicate with someone from home who helped me make my life bigger. How many other relationships would need retuning to harmonize with the man I'd become?

I kept imagining Joe and me meeting up in the next town on our itinerary to patch things up. Yet maybe we needed to take our own paths home. Frost's words came back to me: *Two roads diverged in a wood* ....

I reached for Chimene's hematite necklace to rub it for comfort. I forced myself to conclude that good and bad happen along the road, but whatever happens, happens for the best—if you're positive.

The necklace was missing.

TURKEY
HABITS

6

Rhodes

I waited anxiously at the boat terminal in Iraklion to see if Joe would show up to take the ferry to Rhodes as we'd planned. He didn't, and the boat was cancelled. I decided to go by plane. I drank lots of water, as if somehow it would wash away my loss.

At the Iraklion airport, I listened to babies cry and watched people sit and stare, laugh, and drink beer. I kept reminding myself to find the positive. But I was tired, needed a shave, and my hair was shedding like a wolfhound in winter. My left armpit gave off a stronger body odor than the right. An old pain flared in my heel. And a tension knot, similar to the one I carried during insecure times in business, squeezed my innards. I needed support, so I wrote Kathi a letter about what had happened, and said I needed her right about now.

Then I met Dirck, a rather callow, thin-faced, young Dutchman. He wore thick glasses and droopy jeans, and spoke with an intelligence that gracefully mixed book learning and personal experience.

By the time we arrived in Rhodes, a Greek island in the eastern Aegean Sea, we'd become good buddies and decided to room together at Steve Kefala's for the two days I stayed in Rhodes. Kefala, a delightful sixty-five-year-old repatriated Greek, had handled logistics for famous Montreal nightclub acts before returning to entertain tourists in his jasmine-scented pension off Omiros, a tidy cobblestone street in the "old town."

Rhodes was an honest-to-goodness, walled-in castle city, girdled by a dried-up moat. Cobbled streets melded into a honeycomb of cream-colored stone houses and shops that made you feel you were wandering through catacombs. The city mixed a fourteenth-century battleground with the tranquility of an earthly paradise.

Traveling with someone I didn't know and having all the time in the world to speak honestly was therapeutic. My experience with travelers was that they liked to talk and were, in general, positive and curious about everything around them. And as we explored the high walls overlooking the sea and traipsed the city's maze of alleys, Dirck and I talked as much about the history of Rhodes as our own lives.

Dirck told me that though there were Neolithic settlers on the island from about six thousand years ago, things really got going with the arrival of the Minoans in the sixteenth century BC, followed quickly by other Ancient Greeks.

"It became illustrious," he said in his academic way, "for its scholarship and the various diplomatic allegiances to the dominating culture of the time. Perhaps the island is most famous for the Colossus of Rhodes, one of the ancient Seven Wonders of the World. As the story goes, Antigonus, one of Alexander the Great's generals, sent his son to lay siege to the city in 305 BC. His equipment included a 180-foot, 360,000-pound battering ram and siege tower—the Helepolis. After a year of siege, Antigonus relented and signed a peace treaty. When his forces left Rhodes they abandoned a huge store of siege equipment, which the inhabitants of Rhodes sold. With the profits they erected a giant bronze statue in the harbor to honor the sun god, Helios. The Colossus was destroyed in an earthquake in 226 BC."

Dirck summed up his history of the island by saying that the capital also was destroyed many times over the years, but the current Rhodes dated back to the fourteenth century. Then, as travelers do, he moved seamlessly into his personal history.

After studying in France—in one of the four languages he was fluent in!—Dirck had journeyed six weeks overland through southern Africa and then voyaged down the Nile. Now he was exploring the Mediterranean region. He traveled to acquire knowledge and was hoping for an insight into what to do for a career. Even though we only spent a few days together, his curious mind and sense of humor was exactly what I needed to bring back the spirit of the traveler.

Dirck and I parted company when I boarded the Rhodes ferry to the Turkish coast. I realized that in my time with him I'd come to grips with my trauma with Joe. It was clear that working twelve-hour days in the upper echelon of business had made me impervious to heartache and left little time for friends. The pain of loss was strangely refreshing. In business, there are times when a company has to prove it has the right to exist and somehow friendships and marriages share that need.

While I thoroughly enjoyed being with Joe for the most part, I was now back to no rules. I talked to people more frequently. I didn't have to watch what I ate, how I smelled, or worry about waking someone up at night. I was free again. Traveling is about having one foot in the past, while the other is always stepping into the future.

My future was to rendezvous with Malgosia in Istanbul in less than two weeks. As the sparkles from a bright sun bounced off the ferry's wake, I had flashes of her slim features, classic Ingrid Bergman looks, silky blond hair, and her satisfied sense of self. Flashes that made me hunger to be in her arms.

7

SELÇUK: THE CLASH OF ISLAM AND CHRISTIANITY

THERE WAS NOT EVEN A wisp of a cloud when the ferry discharged me on the docks of Marmaris in southwestern Turkey. Surrounded by low mountains, this fishing port had the feeling of an easygoing grandparent—attractively simple and exceedingly slow. I walked to the bus station asking directions from people who, except for their sandals, looked like they'd been transported from the forties in America—baggy slacks and close haircuts on guys, mid-calf dresses and kerchiefs on women. Jeans had yet to be invented.

The bus took me north along the Aegean coastline to the town of Selçuk. The road was surprisingly smooth. I'd expected the kind of rutted, broken, dangerous roads that crisscross Africa. Perhaps this was because my entire knowledge of Turkey came from *Midnight Express*. In the movie, a drug-smuggling American is tossed into jail and brutalized. The message: Turkey is barbaric. But what was this culture was really like?

Selçuk was named after the Seljuk Turks who arrived in the eleventh century. They'd left their Central Asian home and battled across the Middle East and into Anatolia, the ancient name for what is now Turkey. Along the way, they converted to Islam. At the time Islam was a fledgling religion compared with Christianity. Seven centuries earlier, Roman emperor Constantine had converted to Christianity. He also built a new, more strategic capital for his empire on the old Greek city of Byzantium—Constantinople, which is now Istanbul. After the fall of Rome, the Eastern Roman (or Byzantine) Empire continued. So when the Islamic Turks arrived, the two religions were on a collision course.

The air-conditioned bus swayed through hilly terrain entertaining its occupants with the shrill beat of Turkish music. The rhythms were nothing I grew up with, but expressed the mystery of an ancient culture. Out the window, the sight of people in work clothes and shawls laboring in the countryside took me back to Siberia. Inevitably my thoughts drifted to Malgosia.

To the cloudy-cool day in Krasnoyarsk when we'd parted beside the Yenisei River. The scene on the dock was wrought with emotion. Malgosia stood hands on hips, eyes boring into mine, as she waited angrily for Vitali, the *Chkalov*'s navigator. While Vitali, amid drunken tears, wrote my address across the palm of his hand under the captain's fierce glare from the bridge. Behind Malgosia, a tour bus loaded with her fellow Poles, staring and ready to encourage her, revved its engine. I was leaving to catch the train back across Siberia. She wanted me to take the plane with her to Moscow—otherwise we might never see each other again.

"Miss the train!"

"Malgosia," I implored, "I'd love nothing more, believe me! But if that train comes on time, I know I'll get on it. I'm a traveler."

She kissed me deeply. Her fellow countrymen on the bus cheered.

"Miss the train!"

My desire to leave her was, I knew deep down, also a way of avoiding a painful future back home. But what were the odds of maintaining a relationship with a beautiful young woman halfway across the world?

The train was on time and I boarded. I had three and a half days to Moscow to think about the ramifications of my decision.

At the beginning of the second millennium, somewhere in the vicinity of Selçuk in southeastern Anatolia, two of the great monotheistic religions battled for land—and souls. The result was the Islamic Seljuks crushed the Byzantine Christian army. The victory opened the country to Turkish migration and conquest. It also sparked the Crusades.

In modern-day Selçuk, the few backpackers coming off the bus were efficiently whisked off by a "tout" (in the backpackers' vernacular, a tout is a person selling something on the streets) to his uncle's Spanish-style pension for check-in. Then we were off to his cousin's rug shop for a thirst-quenching spot of tea and a low-pressure carpet show. I bought two double-knit rugs and mailed them home.

That night, after a tasty chicken barbecue at the pension, I called Kathi. She said my romantic letter from Greece had brightened her birthday, which hadn't begun well after a thief broke into her car and ripped off speakers and three weeks of computer analysis on her doctoral thesis. For the first time on the phone during my trip, her voice lost its formal, distant tone. She told me she'd read the letter four times and was lonely for me. I also felt pangs of loneliness. I felt them in the pit of my stomach. And slowly after the conversation ended they made their way into my mind.

However, I felt no guilt mixing thoughts of Malgosia and Kathi. I was two different people living two different lives, each comfortable in his own environment. One life was ten thousand miles and six months away. The other was currently in a ten-dollar-a-night room in an old city with colonial-style streetlamps, outdoor restaurants serving people in the warm night air, and pregnant animals roaming the streets.

The truth was I missed the passion of falling in love, the intimacy of knowing a person's body and soul for the first time—the taste of it. I had needed that loving feeling back. And it arrived with Malgosia. I remembered again the passage in Chekhov I'd read on the long train ride from Siberia to Moscow. "Needless, petty, and deceptive were the things that keep people from loving each other. They ask themselves, where this affair will lead me. In judgments about love, start with something higher than happiness or unhappiness, virtue and sin, or make no judgments at all."

8

WOMEN AND MONOTHEISM: A STORY OF DISEMPOWERMENT

THE FOLLOWING MORNING, I TOOK a day trip north to Ephesus, a spectacularly preserved city of antiquity. Surrounded by sun-scorched hills, Ephesus had been around since the tenth century BC. Its natural harbor on the Kaystros River near the Aegean Sea supported a city of a quarter of a million inhabitants. The city was the center of trade and commerce, linking the Greco-Roman world to rich hinterlands of Anatolia and the East. It boasted one of the original Seven Wonders of the World—the lavish Temple of Artemis, the many-breasted goddess of fertility. The road from the sea to the Temple of Artemis glowed with torches at night, making Ephesus one of the first cities to have streetlamps.

Colonnades lined its stone boulevards, and cobblestone streets connected the upper and lower districts of the city. Walking with other tourists along the "Marble Way," I could almost hear the sounds and movement of bygone Ephesus. We passed under the huge arches of a stone aqueduct whose water was distributed to the city through a system of baked clay pipes. Herons had now built straw nests along the tops of those arches. Following the aqueduct to the lower city, we came to the remains of a major market and the spectacular double-tiered, marble Library of Celsus with its bold columns. At one time, this library housed 12,000 scrolls and had an underground passage leading to a brothel on the other side of the street. Thus, in ancient times, an educated man could read up on his fantasies and then take a walk over to the wild side and partake of them.

The Marble Way took us to a handsomely preserved amphitheater, with grass growing through cracks in the stone. It served as a testament to the remarkable understanding of sound that the Greeks and Romans possessed. The concept of the amphitheater evolved from performances in Greek grain-threshing circles, which were then developed into semicircles with tiered seating. More recently, in the twentieth century, this twenty-four-thousand-capacity theater hosted performances by rock bands such as Jethro Tull. What would the ancient Greeks and Romans have thought of Jethro Tull?

I sauntered farther along one of the stone roads to upper-level homes whose mosaic floors depicted brilliant starburst designs and frescoes of polytheistic life. They reminded me of similar frescoes in Egypt and Greece, graphically showing earthy passion between males and females. What chain of events caused the shift to male-dominated, monotheistic religions, with their austere codes and suppression of the sensual and feminine?

The chain of events that caused the demise of Ephesus began with excessive lumbering, charcoal burning, and overgrazing of the land. These led to the topsoil slipping into the streams and silting up the harbor. This soon created malaria-infested marshes, which in turn caused a migration from the city. By the time the Crusaders arrived it was little more than a village and by the fifteenth century it was abandoned. It remained largely unknown for five hundred years until excavations began in 1863. By which time it was miles from the sea.

Riding a van back to Selçuk, I met an older couple from Scotland—a chubby, amiable woman who rehabilitated young criminals and a stoutly built mid-lifer with cynical eyes and salt-and-pepper beard who was studying fine art after thirty years of diffusing bombs for the British air force. They invited me to join them for dinner at one of the several adjoining outdoor restaurants. Over shish kebab, rice, eggplant in tomato sauce, and string beans—all washed down with a clear ouzo-like alcohol—we discussed homelessness. They were struck by the relative lack of it in Turkey compared with the UK. But the evening was made most memorable by the arrival of three scruffy dogs, thin as greyhounds, walking among the tables of the restaurants. Two males were pursuing a female who scurried along with her ears drooping and eyes defeated.

"Oh no, not here!" cried one of the diners, as the squeals of the female rang out.

Minutes later, the female and a black mongrel were standing ass to ass within inches of a very staid-looking middle-aged couple. Fully illuminated by a streetlamp and unable to separate themselves, the dogs looked embarrassed. Meanwhile, the third mutt jumped back and forth over them, looking for an opportunity.

Last time I saw anything like that was as a kid in the countryside. We diners continued to fork food into our mouths with gentility, but there were too many Australians in the crowd to keep the happening decent. They cheered the third dog, howling: "Try the other side!" The restaurant owners at first joined the jeering Australians, but as the pair unhitched and more dogs arrived they quickly drove the pack into the night. The female nervously scampered away followed by the determined gang of sniffing mongrels, with a trailing Scottie trying to keep up on his little legs. All the while, the proper couple chewed their food as if the turmoil next to their table existed in another dimension.

While traveling, I often became embroiled in thinking jags. Then invariably I bumped into someone knowledgeable about the very subject I'd been contemplating. So it was with the history of religion. The day after my visit to Ephesus, the 'someone knowledgeable' sat down next to me during a two-hundred-kilometer bus junket to the springs of Pamukkale. A distinguished looking gentleman in his late fifties with softly graying hair, he told me about his two-month dream trip through Turkey, Syria, and Israel, adding that he was a lecturer in ancient religion at a university in the Netherlands. Fluent in multiple ancient languages, he had, among other things, read the Dead Sea Scrolls.

"Just yesterday," I said, shaking my head in amazement. "I looked at paintings of gods and goddesses, wondering about women's role in monotheistic religions. And you appear out of the blue!"

I told him of my recent fascination with the religions of the area and their origins. Then I asked him point blank, "Who do you think should get credit for being the founder of Christianity?"

"What precisely do you mean?" The twist on the topic caught him by surprise. And he pushed his glasses farther up his patrician nose to study this long-haired hippie.

"I mean there are a billion people who believe in Christ. Who possessed the passion and talent to develop and market this religion to begin with? Christ had died!"

"That is an interesting way to look at beginnings—from a business perspective!" He closed his eyes for a minute in deep thought. "Hmm, I would say without a doubt that *Paul* was the guiding force, the entrepreneur. As a matter of fact, Paul was a marvelous orator and writer. Now that you mention it, he must have been extremely extroverted. He lived a portion of his life around Ephesus. And you may not know that Paul never met Christ. He wrote his famous letters nearly thirty years after Christ died."

Outside the window flower and vegetable gardens bloomed amid the mostly barren country. Heavily burdened donkeys, gangly chickens, and barely nourished dogs wandered along lonely dirt streets. Men in loose-fitting dark trousers and woolen caps sipped coffee at endless cafes, while women wore scarves and full-length black or mid-calf green dresses. Kids walked to school in uniforms—blue jackets and gray flannel pants for boys and dresses and white blouses for girls.

"So then where did the concept of *virgin birth* come from?" I continued.

"In mythology, gods and goddesses often copulate with mortals," he answered. "Why do you ask?"

I told him my thoughts about the passion and beauty between males and females in the frescoes I'd encountered in Ephesus and Egypt, and how that contrasted with the shift to male-dominated religions and consequent suppression of the sensual and feminine. "When a single god became dominant in the religion the women's role seemed to diminish. I don't understand what happened."

"Well, let us think this out together. Hmm, monotheistic religions, especially Christian, seem to have a particular dislike of material possessions. At least in theory! Their spiritual worlds, on the contrary, offered heavenly rewards to a constituency whose lives were disenfranchised and often brutal. Paul recruited among these people. If one were to look at religion as you do, from a marketing perspective, one would conclude that redemption and a happy life-after-death were pillars of his market positioning and recruitment speech.

"One could suggest that, since time immemorial, people conceived religions reflecting their surroundings and circumstances. Those unhappy with their lot in life changed the emphasis from the here-and-now to the kinds of after-death rewards previously reserved for pharaohs and kings.

"If the present life was to be endured, then those who brought us into this misery—namely women—might be subconsciously unworthy."

"And scrapped from the theological design."

"Precisely! And without goddesses and their sexual nature to balance out the theological design, why would you need more than one god? Thus monotheism! Caesar! The chairman of the board!" the professor concluded with gusto, quite proud of himself. "It's as good as any other hypothesis."

I laughed. We were approaching Pamukkale. It looked like a ski resort with the hills above it covered with snow and glistening in the hot sun. Up close, the hills were a mass of layered terraces and trenches formed by overflowing rivulets of water. The water carried calcium from mineral springs, and its white deposits, a rock known as travertine, created the look of a wintry hillside with hundreds of waterfalls.

Once off the bus, the professor and I joined a multitude of kids and extended families playing in the aqua pools and trenches that contrasted brilliantly with the whiteness of the travertine. Despite searing heat, the rock surfaces felt cool and adhesive to bare feet. Afterwards, we swam in the fabled calcium-rich waters at a pool in one of the Pamukkale hotels. An old Turkish woman and I smiled at each other. Her fragile eyelids looked like the remains of burned waxed paper.

9

ÇANAKKALE AND THE WAY TO ISTANBUL

THE PROFESSOR STAYED THE NIGHT in Pamukkale, but I returned to Selçuk. The next morning, in search of a Turkish bath suggested by a couple of travelers, I walked along a quiet red-bricked promenade lined with black lampposts, and asked a policewoman for directions. She wore a blue uniform with trousers and a holstered gun. In a country ninety-eight percent Muslim, I didn't expect to find female police. But then the prime minister at the time was also a woman. I suppose that this was what Mustafa Kemal Atatürk, war hero and prime minister after World War I, had in mind when he replaced Islamic law in Turkey with a secular, Swiss-based civil code *and* gave women the right to vote well before the Swiss. "Humankind is made up of two sexes, women and men," he is reported as saying. "Is it possible for humankind to grow by the improvement of only one part while the other part is ignored? Is it possible that if half of a mass is tied to earth with chains that the other half can soar into skies?"

Inside the baths, I passed through a pair of airtight metal doors into a foggy oval room with smooth white walls and a ceiling dotted with recessed holes that welcomed a modicum of light from outside. Towels wrapped around their hips and standing barefoot on the marble floor, two powerful and mustachioed men diligently worked soapy lather into the pores of a half-naked blond European woman who lay on an octagonal marble slab the size of two queen beds. The guys seemed to concentrate on her generous naked breasts. One of the men motioned for me to lie face down on the marble adjacent to her. When they finished, they led her to a cold shower where her toweled boyfriend waited. She appeared pleased with the results. Despite his liberal leanings, I doubted Atatürk had envisioned mixed baths.

Just one of the masseurs returned and began scraping the travel dirt off my body with abrasive rubberized gloves. He lathered me from a small bag of suds for ten minutes before pulling and pounding my front and backside into relaxed oblivion. Big-breasted European women must be much more difficult to massage, I concluded, since they required the attention of *two* strong men.

That night, a cat, which looked like skin and fur glued to a bunch of bones, crept into my second-floor room at the pension. It closed its eyes—one blue, the other bleary-white—as I stroked it, burrowing its tiny head into the cleft between my thumb and forefinger. Clothes and writing materials lay scattered around the room. Holding the cat, I flipped through family pictures. In one, Chimene was tucked into Shannon's lap when the girls were two and three years old. Other pictures captured memories of high-school graduations. The girls were tall and slim and had terrific smiles. Shannon looked like a model, her strawberry-blond hair flowing down her shoulders on to a jean jacket. In keeping with her character, Chimene wore a black tux and bow tie, her gleaming brown hair cut short. In other pictures, Kathi beamed with her arms around the girls, or she was dressed in black, her dark hair skirting bare shoulders.

A single word rattled around my mind after the discussion with the professor about monotheism and women. So I grabbed my pocket dictionary and looked under d's for *domination*. It read: "The rule or control by a superior power or influence that represses or suppresses natural impulses." That was the most insidious thing about domination, it was natural. Sports announcers, the military, and business executives extol its virtue. And what would sex be without it?

My grandmother's self-esteem had given me the strength and body language to avoid being dominated. And as a parent I encouraged the girls to be strong within themselves. But Kathi and I were born of a period when male domination was the norm. Although I was controlling, it was not my intention to be so. And relationships are always full of control processes, which I wasn't aware of as a young man. Thus, while the girls were liberated, their parents played an old tune.

I placed the sleepy cat softly on the floor as my mind walked backwards a few years to one of those never-ending arguments that solve absolutely nothing. Kathi and I had just walked into the house after a therapy session with our marriage counselor. We argued. I could see us: me, jaw thrust out, righteously demanding logic, and Kathi, tears hanging in the corner of her eyes as I cut her words short. At that time in our marriage, my heart was stony from feeling underappreciated and used, and I was oblivious to the power of her tears. Hopelessly frustrated, she ran up to the bedroom. A few seconds later, sounds of shower water penetrated the stillness, followed by her screaming.

I hurried to the plush, carpeted stairway to our bedroom, then halted and listened for her condition. A vice of guilt crushed my heart. I had never heard Kathi scream before. Standing on that stairway, I envisioned her slumped and sobbing against the marble wall. *Marriage forever?* It had become an exercise in torment. How could I be the source of such unhappiness?

I left Kathi a note and checked into a hotel for the night. Lying on my back in the dark, I combined meditative trance with Gestalt role-play, slipping into Kathi's mind and facing an angry Denis. The depth of that dominating personality left me claustrophobic. Drenched in sweat, I curled up like a pill bug exposed to sudden light. I was witness and all-knowing prosecutor. To snap out of it I reminded myself that Kathi *was* used to me. And that she married me because of who I was: the intense young man with a vision and sense of humor, who loved swinging kids in the air and making her laugh.

After that night, we separated for a year. I couldn't be anyone's bad guy anymore.

Kathi had hated the thought of separating, but the girls confidently encouraged us to expand our individualities during the cooling-off period. That was five years ago.

The separation changed me. It's hard to express in writing my feelings back then. Maybe it's a male thing? I guess there's something about relating deep feelings that sounds like bitching or blaming someone else, or a violation of "the strong silent type" that men are meant to be. I could go deeper into what was wrong between us, but instead offer a friend's comment when he was getting divorced after twelve years of trying to solve the issues. "It's not about communication—we've been to more marriage counseling and couples communication retreats than any two people that ever lived—it's that we just can't live with each other anymore."

During that period of the separation, I often felt like an outsider in my family. As time went on, the women seemed unable to empathize with my issues. It was as if my feelings didn't complete the journey to their consciousness. I bitched about it in our family meetings. We all had the right to discuss issues without judgment, why was I now the exception? But my issues must have reached them, because they all gave me their blessings and were genuinely happy for me when I took off to travel for a year. Or maybe they were just thinking: "Whoo, what a relief, we don't have to hear about male-female issues anymore."

And the gamble of separating worked. We bought time to stitch wounds and get our hearts pumping again. In the end, I was able to accept Kathi's habits, because she wasn't going to change. While her willingness to rekindle our romance during the separation successfully diffused anger that had been building in me. It's hard to stay angry with a sensual woman.

Spacing out on the bed in Selçuk, I realized that—except for the occasional person from back home who traveled with me, which basically meant Joe—I had no conflicts here. On my own, I was a good guy.

Leaving Selçuk, I bussed to the seaside town of Çanakkale on the way to Istanbul, dropped my stuff at the Yetimoglu Pension with its rose-studded garden and went to explore. Along the brief walk to the center, I stood to watch uniformed children running wildly, wrestling like kittens, or congregating in cliques in a local schoolyard. It felt good for me, a man, to be in an environment where I could look at youngsters in a playground without feeling like a derelict, which was how I'd feel in America.

Seeing the kids reminded me of the times when Kathi would pack a picnic lunch and we would take our giggling girls from school on the pretext of a dental appointment. After picnicking, we'd see the latest blockbuster movie matinee. "Once a year for the rest of your lives," I warned them, "expect us to suddenly appear at your school or work to take you to the dentist."

On a roped-off thoroughfare in the center of Çanakkale, a wedding reception was in full swing—literally. Hands held high, only the men danced, hips swaying to the local music. I turned down an offer to join the party. I was in a pensive, not festive, mood. But I watched for a while before the intoxicating smell of sea air led me to the harbor where boats bounced and Turkish flags flapped wildly from masts. I wandered into a park that lay at the water's edge.

Leaves scurried along a sidewalk in the stirring wind. Islamic chants carried over the ten-story buildings and small shops that surrounded the park. The breeze brought whiffs of men's cologne, cooked peanuts, chestnuts, and the shish kebab hawked by husky voices at kiosks. The vendors called out to the couples, old and young, with and without kids, who strolled hand-in-hand along the waterfront. Children ran ahead and then back to snuggle in their father's arms.

The way of life here reminded me of my childhood before all the social changes of the sixties—the conservative clothes and haircuts, lots of kids, and a romanticized patriarchal society. Witnessing the role of the family here, I reflected on my changing perception of Muslim culture.

The individual's right to chart his or her own course was a principle enshrined in the Declaration of Independence—and one which I totally subscribed to—yet Western media and much of my society had, I felt, done an injustice to people who did choose to live differently. We mourned the breakup of the family and preached against a decline of morals and values, while at the same time denigrating other societies who did have strong traditional families.

I had a dilemma. I'd always supported the idea of equal partners in a relationship. But I had become aware while traveling that the thought process necessary to achieve equality had put my family life at risk. The idea of equality focused on life, liberty, and the pursuit of happiness, not on the family. Divorce rates in the United States had skyrocketed over the twentieth century.

We criticized Muslims, but we certainly hadn't yet offered them a societal example of equality *and* a healthy family. Roles and values were clearly defined under the old system, but had become ambiguous and evolving under the new. After visiting several Islamic countries, it was apparent to me that Americans who thought "Muslim" was just another way to say "terrorist" or "wife molester" should experience that culture's family life.

On a rare rainy day, I took a bus from Çanakkale to Istanbul, five hundred kilometers to the northeast. I sat next to a young Turkish woman, dressed in a bulky skirt and a bright yellow scarf, who completely ignored me for the first hour of the five-hour trip along the Sea of Marmara. But when a bus attendant squirted lemon-water into our hands to freshen up I took the opportunity to initiate conversation. Speaking with a heavy nasal inflection, she said that she was an accountant in her uncle's store in Istanbul, and asked if I was Australian.

"No, I'm American."

"I thought you were Australian. Many Australians visit this area because of the battle of Gallipoli." Gallipoli was where, after the Ottoman Empire was defeated in World War I, Kemal Atatürk won a great victory over a combined Allied force, with a heavy involvement of Australians and New Zealanders, she explained.

"They wanted to possess our country because of its location, but General Atatürk organized an army and pushed the enemy from the center of our country into the sea at Gallipoli." She described his army as tattered professionals and farmers, and Atatürk as a great hero.

"He was raised in a small village and formed our country into a nation. He organized many reforms, because he said we were falling behind the West."

"What kind of reforms?"

"He encouraged women to work and wear Western fashions," she said, staring straight-ahead, and only occasionally glancing in my direction. "Also he improved education, especially for girls."

"Your English is very good." I was pleased to speak to a Muslim woman and had found that complimenting someone's English never failed to endear.

"Thank you very much. I learned in school."

"Do you mind if I ask why you wear a scarf around your head? I notice that most women wear scarves on their heads."

"Your question is quite a good one," she replied with a giggle, while unconsciously tightening the scarf. "I believe in the words of Prophet Muhammad. He teaches women must be modest."

"Are women with scarves treated differently than those without scarves?"

"Men don't bother women wearing scarves."

"What do you think about women who don't wear scarves?"

"I respect the right of other girls to wear what they want. Many of the girls want to dress in modern clothes, like they see on television."

"Does the Koran require women to wear scarves?"

"The Koran instructs us how to live each day. It is not specific about scarves." She giggled again, this time into her hands.

That was why Muhammad focused on protecting women! It became clear to me. He was a family man and father of several girls. Christ, on the other hand, was a bachelor and traveler. So he focused on the individual's right to future reward. Atatürk must have realized that if you link individual rights and the future, you unlock vast creative resources. And that leads to rapid development. Strong family systems rely on male chauvinism to survive. And in my experience male chauvinism squelches creativity.

Approaching the ancient walls of the dusty northern entrance to Istanbul, formerly Constantinople, we paused in our conversation to absorb the bustle of city life. My neighbor told me that the Muslim Ottomans progressively captured all the lands surrounding the well-fortified city. They were content to receive tribute from the Byzantine emperors in Constantinople until the money ran out. Then, in the fifteenth century, young Mehmed the Conqueror dramatically breached these walls, thus ending the Byzantine Empire and beginning the Ottoman one. The emperor at the time of the changeover was, appropriately, the last of the Constantines—number XI. Gradually the name "Istanbul" took over, too, but it only finally became official under, of course, Atatürk.

"Do you like working?" I asked, bringing the history up to date. "I understand most Muslim women stay at home."

"Yes, I like to work. Many women work because their families need money. My sisters and my friends will leave their jobs when they have children. They say, 'Let the men go to work. It is their responsibility.'"

10

MALGOSIA COMES TO ISTANBUL

Loose on the streets of Istanbul, I searched the area around Sultanahmet Street to find a place suitable for Malgosia, yet not too much above a backpacker's budget. Someplace nice. I was lucky enough to get a room on the fourth floor of the And Hotel, a six-story wooden building with an elevator and large rooms. The room overlooked the sprawling lush grounds and buildings of the Topkapi Palace built by Mehmed, and to the right was the otherworldly Blue Mosque. Perfect!

Looking out over this ancient city, I recalled something Joe said to me before I left home: "Somewhere on your trip you will be one of a kind, and people will treat you special." Russia had been that place.

Once I left Moscow, I didn't meet another Westerner until I returned a month later. At first, I was afraid, but I let destiny guide me. And the Russians didn't disappoint. They treated me like a star. Picnics, vodka parties, and tearful goodbyes on the train. While on the boat to the Arctic, the crew took care of their *friend* and the passengers all wanted to meet and do something nice for the American. It was a blast!

True, on board the *Chaklov*, I helped destiny a bit by becoming a divorced man ten years younger with two suitably aged kids. A decision influenced by a group of very good-looking young Russian women. When they corralled me on the second night and tried to force me, in broken English, to reveal my background, I opted for a fictitious one that wiped clean the slate of history. A clean slate sets you free. Thus, when Malgosia and I eventually met I was a "single man."

On the way back to Moscow from Siberia, the *cha-chunk, cha-chunk* of train on track mixed like music in my mind with Malgosia's repeated command, "Miss the train." This refrain reinforced the guilt of telling her a life story that was only partially true.

She must have benefited from the love affair too, and known it was unlikely we would meet again. Nevertheless, the lying, combined with countless mental repetitions of what would have happened if I missed the train, changed my plans. Instead of going to Greece via the Ukraine and Black Sea, I found myself in Warsaw to set the record straight.

I called a severely shocked Malgosia at work and arranged to meet her at the Marriott Hotel across from the railroad station. We resumed where we'd left off. It was only a day later, at a very nice traditional Polish restaurant; I worked up sufficient courage to tell her what had been left out the first time. I was *still* married and my children were older than I'd said because I was older. My excuse that my "divorced" persona had already been established on the boat before she and I met cut no ice. The truth may have set me free, but I was now the *bad boy*. She used silence to torture me as I followed her around Warsaw while she shopped for necessities.

Finally, as we entered a tram that belonged to the mysterious Eastern Europe of the Cold War, I told her I loved my wife and expected to be married forever, but that I loved her too. Tears flowed from under her sunglasses.

Our relationship deepened immensely during the four days I stayed. Based at her place near the university, we never left each other's side. We had quiet moments, introspective moments, wild moments, and moments of pure fun. We set a date to rendezvous four weeks hence in Istanbul. I wondered what in the world I was getting into, but followed Chekhov's advice about love and made no judgments at all.

The next morning, I was awoken, almost serenaded, by dueling chants from muezzins. As the one at the Blue Mosque ended his chant, another across the city began. The emotion was overpowering. I felt small and far from home.

Yet I slid out of bed in a very good mood. I was going to meet Malgosia. After two weeks of counting the days, we were just minutes apart. Dressed in shorts and my fancy African shirt with its white lace V-neck, I admired the magic the sun had worked over the past seven months on my hair—the frazzled brown of a sedentary, high-stress life was now long, soft, golden curls embellished by graying temples. It looked so healthy. I headed to the airport. Anticipation warmed me more than the bright Turkish sun. Who was this woman?

I waited with about fifty people at the gate. We peered through a large glass wall trying to spot the arrivals. There she was! Wearing meticulously fitted white pants and a red summer jacket that contrasted with her blond hair and light skin, she looked stunning. Her beauty was humble yet unbowed. Her petite body and fresh face made Malgosia the epitome of *wholesome*. If she were in the movies, she'd be a heroine my mother would like.

She looked round nervously at the waiting Turks, then walked gracefully into my welcoming arms. Her smile was meant for me alone. And her warm touch and sweet smell made my heart race. We held each other tight—not talking, just feeling. It was as if, having been severely deprived, our bodies were trying to fill the empty space. We kissed—exploring, communicating, tasting, and promising. I was hopelessly captivated.

I swung her in my arms, hooting and smiling at everyone. She laughed with me, but immediately after I set her down, she looked around again with that same nervous look.

"I have been told by several people," she whispered, "that it is dangerous for a blond woman in Turkey."

I laughed, still holding on, not wanting to let go.

"*They* always say something like that. The truth is that it's dangerous for other men to see such a beautiful sight. They could die on the spot with envy."

"Of you!"

"You better believe it."

She laughed shyly as I disengaged.

"Come, I have a nice place that I picked out. I think you'll like it. I want to lure you to my lair as soon as possible."

"You picked it? Did you visit many places?"

"A few. This is the nicest."

"A woman feels good to know her man takes care of her."

On the way to our hotel, we traversed a street lined with restaurants. Long shallow pans displayed tasty food across the width of the front windows. Shepherd's salad, rice pilaf, koftas (meatballs), lamb strips with yogurt, eggplant stew, kebabs ... on and on! Istanbul was where East and West converged, I told Malgosia. Good recipes flowed here, to the center of the Ottoman Empire. While I liked Greece, it was no match for the friendliness of people, variety of terrain, or the food of Turkey.

We crossed the trolley tracks near the Blue Mosque and stopped to stare at its magnificence. Six gold and white minarets surrounded the pewter-blue mosque, which grew into the sky in four layers of progressively larger domes—each one having the look of a colossal turtle shell. The top three domes were guarded by round turrets with javelin-shaped spires, while the highest was crowned with a golden spire.

The And was upscale compared with the places I had been staying. It had an elevator, charming little bar, friendly staff, and plain-but-nice rooms with white, see-through lace curtains. Malgosia surveyed the room, its two sturdy double beds and simple, stained-wood bureau. She unpacked her clothes from the new backpack she had purchased in Warsaw and placed them carefully in two of the four bureau drawers. Then she lined up both our shoes neatly under the bed by the windows. She peered out, marveling again at the mosque and palace grounds. I lay on the bed closest the window and watched her.

"Very nice choice," she said, her eyes turning to catch mine.

I guided her back towards the bed, kissed her shoulder and hair, and began unbuttoning her blouse. There is nothing quite like the thrill of undressing a woman.

Before long, we broke out of the prison of restraint and ripped at each other's clothes, pulling them off with delight. I felt like swallowing her.

Soon she was on top, her back arched and her fine, bright hair surrounding our heads. I felt as if we were together in a small cave. Pleasure consumed her face—a squeezing, pulsating pleasure that made her bite her lips. She slid her hands down along my stomach and thighs feeling the muscles that had become particularly strong and hard with travel. Enveloped in ecstasy myself, I said softly that I loved her and that in some other time we had been great lovers. How else to explain our synchronized movement? Eyes closed, she smiled.

We lunched at a restaurant on one of the streets converging at the Blue Mosque, contently devouring spinach pie with goat cheese and lamb strips in yogurt. Sounds of buses and trolleys and the voices of food sellers filled the air.

"How do you like the people here?" she asked.

"So far they have been friendly. I've been invited home to dinner twice, and to a wedding with lots of kids. I feel like I've been transported back in time to when uncles and aunts and cousins and grandparents lived close by. People were friendlier and more polite. It's such a contrast to my country where families are small and spread out."

I told her my thoughts on religions with a single god versus those with a pantheon of gods and goddesses, speculating that nature used monotheism to speed up evolution. A single god could focus the energy of masses of people on a few simple concepts, such as life after death. Away from my old life, I had been struck by energy—its all-encompassing nature, so alive and godlike.

"I like that idea," she said. "But what about Islam, they focused on one god too and they have not—how do you say—speeded up evolution?"

"Maybe strong family systems inhibit creativity."

"You do not believe that Christianity has a strong family system?"

"I think Christian dogma is focused on saving individual souls. And I am beginning to believe that the natural extension of that theology is that individuals in the new society, in general, don't have the time, marital tenacity, or traditions that strong family systems require. Nature is moving away from strong families and the West is leading the way."

"It is sobering to think that individual expression might be at the expense of the family. In Poland, under socialism life was slower. Now under capitalism, people work hard and have less time for family."

After a strange interlude during which the restaurant's cook invited Malgosia to wear his tall, white chef's hat and survey various pans of food he had laid out for customers, our discussion meandered into travel.

"My uncle was a traveler," she said. "I like traveling also, but I was afraid to come here. And excited too! Are you afraid when you travel to new places?"

"Men aren't supposed to be afraid," I joked.

"Not on the surface."

"Three things scare me the most: an unsafe vehicle, bad roads, and fearless drivers. Traveling in the Third World, they all come together at the same time. Being driven across Africa by a series of fearless young men in overcrowded cars on dangerous roads, I learned one thing: Look for a driver that has lots of gray hair! Gray says: *I have survived and don't need macho.*

"Mostly, though I'm excited to go to the next place. I have found that a positive attitude and good smile leads to positive experiences. Like finding you."

She placed her hand across the table on mine.

We removed our shoes before entering the Blue Mosque, while an attendant found a white cotton shawl to cover Malgosia's hair. The interior was uncomplicated yet expansive. Stone columns rose to the domes. No benches, no jewels, no statues, no human icons of any kind. Only floor mats on gray stone, and lots of bulbs hanging down. I liked the simplicity of the place. Christ would probably have been more comfortable here than in the cathedrals loaded with the trappings of wealth erected in his name.

Outside again, we crossed the street and walked to the gates of the Topkapi Palace. To the right stood the Ayasofya, the former Byzantine cathedral Hagia Sophia which dated from the fourth century, with dark green marble columns and a fifteen-story dome.

"The Ayasofya was so beautiful," Malgosia read from her Polish guidebook, "that the Islamic sultans didn't have the heart to tear it down, although they plastered over its mosaics. The same could not be said of the crusaders. It says the Christian knights burned Constantinople almost to the ground."

Manicured lawns, bushes and gardens surrounded the Topkapi Palace complex's pavilions, state offices, dormitories, barracks, mosque, and library. The palace itself boasted bright tiled walls with veins of gold for grouting and an interior that glowed with mosaics and color. As grand as the palace was, the main attraction—and the only one with a line of people that day—was the sultan's harem. With over a hundred rooms, slave quarters, outdoor baths, inner courts, and a hospital, it once serviced five hundred wives and concubines. His favorites occupied the largest quarters. Although an African eunuch was responsible for the running of the harem in the old days, the real power inside lay with the dean of women—the sultan's mother. Malgosia and I speculated on when the first feature film would be released retelling all the spicy events that must have taken place.

After breakfast the following day, we strolled under the bright sun to the Grand Bazaar. Tens of thousands of square meters in size (estimates vary), it consists of sixty-one streets, two mosques, fountains, and over four thousand back-to-back shops. Any woman coming here would think she'd died and gone to heaven. The bazaar sold everything from carpets, leather goods, and dazzling jewelry to fruits and vegetables, spices, and barrels of rice. Vaulted stone ceilings sheltered the sellers, creating the largest covered market in the world. Mehmed originally constructed it to provide traders with a safe and orderly place to do business.

To the wailing of Turkish music, we ate popcorn and drank fresh orange juice. Scents from pyramid-shaped mounds of green, orange, brown, and astonishing red spices floated through the air. Malgosia shopped for a necklace and I for a leather coat for Kathi.

The salesmen aggressively mixed sexual innuendo into their spiels—bragging of their conquests or even suggesting they could hire a young virgin for ten dollars in Thailand. "Buy a rug," pleaded one, while licentiously eying Malgosia, "and wrap your girlfriend in it." I chalked the banter up to sexual repression, but it got on my nerves.

At a necklace shop, a clerk with bulging jowls and a jelly belly that stretched his belt to capacity ogled Malgosia. She nonetheless dickered with him over the price of a gold chain. Dangling it in front of her eyes, he made tedious sexual remarks. His crude body language amplified the impact of his words. He began to seriously piss me off. Finally he pressed his fat lips to

Malgosia's neck, just below her ear, and whispered loudly: "For you. You get free if you treat me nice." She stretched her neck away to avoid his lips, her eyes fixed pleadingly on me. He repeated the proposition.

That was it! "She gave you a price." Steely-eyed, icy-voiced, I enunciated each word slowly and clearly. "take it! or leave it! What the hell is the matter with you? You think you're desirable?"

We exchanged hard looks. Then I squeezed the beefy part of the fellow's arm, pushed him to one side, and grabbed Malgosia's hand and took her away.

"Thank you," she said, after a few steps. "I froze. I cannot explain why. I felt so powerless. It happened so quickly, and I just stood there."

"A good kick in the nuts would have done the trick."

"Nuts, what 'nuts'?"

"It's a term we use." I demonstrated the kick. She laughed.

We found a leather jacket for Kathi in a shop thick with carpets on the floor. I was barely courteous to the merchant. I just couldn't purge the fighting instinct to go back and smash the other guy's jowly jaw. The *controller* had re-emerged from the deep. Malgosia, however, wasn't bothered anymore—her attention consumed by the joys of shopping.

In the hot sunshine outside the cover of the bazaar, a tout in leather sandals accosted us. He yanked a pair of socks from a wooden pushcart. Normally, I figured a tout's job was to get whatever money he could out of my pocket, and mine was to keep as much of it as possible. I had always been in a good mood traveling, but recent events had left me ornery.

"Listen to me very carefully," I said through clenched teeth. "I do-not-want-to-buy ... ANYTHING!"

"Good approach," Malgosia whispered.

He put the socks back into the flimsy cart, and grabbed underpants packaged in plastic: "No like socks? You buy pants!"

Weighing the bottle of water in my left hand, I thought, "Enough already! I'll get this little bastard!" I shoved the bottle into his chest, and tried another tout response—one I'd used with some success in Israel.

"You buy wa-ter! You buy! You buy!" I shouted. "It is good wa-ter. Best wa-ter in Istanbul. You buy! You buy!"

"Not much water!" he countered, looking at the two inches of jouncing water.

"You my last customer. Good for you, good for me! You buy. Good deal."

This tactic didn't faze the skinny little man at all. He smiled at me and then at Malgosia. "No!" he said, pushing the pants softly into my gut. "You buy from me."

On it went. A crowd grew around us. Haggling over underpants and water, I could feel the anger drain from my body like sand falling in an hourglass. The controller was leaving, the traveler returning. The energy of this man's smile absorbed and converted my anger to admiration and humor. Finally, to my surprise, the stubborn merchant agreed to buy the water! I immediately stuck out my hand for payment.

He, of course, reneged.

Eyes wide, head thrust back, arms out, palms up, I appealed to the crowd like the victim of a petty heist. They burst out laughing along with Malgosia. Some shouted to the tout: "Pay him!"

"Okay! Okay!" I said, also laughing. "No charge if you leave me alone."

"No charge, no sell," he agreed with a broad grin.

Something very powerful occurred in that exchange: I recognized how easy it was to change the energy. For so much of my life, I had been engaged in conflict of one sort or another—often lacking a good means of extricating myself. Now I had a tool, but I wanted to understand more about how to wield it.

11

SAYING GOODBYE TO LOVE

MALGOSIA AND I HEADED OUT farther east on the Black Sea coast. We lounged on its dense sand and swam and teased on its barren, rocky shores. While we enjoyed the local food and people, we enjoyed each other more. We touched. We gazed at one another. We went to sleep spooning each night and woke up cuddling in the morning.

I enjoyed sharing in the novelty of her first experiences. I thrilled even more to be the instigator of her hearty laugh. We shared our past. I found myself falling deeper in love with this person who I hardly knew and yet knew completely. I told her so.

"Falling in love with you was my pleasure," she replied.

Back in Istanbul, our deepening attachment created a dramatic mood for our last night together. We took a tram to an expensive restaurant overlooking the lights of the old city. Malgosia wore a sleeveless, black blouse and loose, flowered skirt with a slit up the side. Her hair was up, emphasizing her high cheekbones, and silver earrings dangled above her delicate, now slightly tanned, neck. My dress was more modest, hair in a ponytail, dressy short-sleeved shirt, blue slacks worn by travel, and Tevas. Tevas gave me the opportunity to show off my symmetrical feet. Although seldom exposed, my feet were the real deal, my claim to fame. They were beauty incarnate.

In the candlelight, we gazed into each other's eyes—hers clear, more green than gray-blue. We talked about our ages, a common discussion that I mostly initiated.

"What does a proper woman like you think of being in love with an older man? When you're forty-five, I'll be over seventy. And when you're sixty, I'll be in my eighties."

"What do you think?"

"I think we would have to have a flexible—that means that it can bend—relationship. Most times it doesn't occur to me that there's an age difference between us. We have lots of interests in common, I guess. I think my comfort with younger people is why I travel so well with them. My grandmother always used to say: 'You're as old as you feel.'"

"I think I would like your grandmother. Is she alive?"

"She died when I was in Kenya."

"Are you sad?"

"She was ninety-nine."

"Holy smokey!"

"Actually, it's holy smokes!" I said with a laugh, in which I heard an echo of my grandmother's laugh. "When we were in Poland, sometimes I paid attention to people's looks, you know, the 'You depraved older guy with a young girl' look. It made me consider our ages."

"I do not think age matters to the couple," she said, after listening intently, "but it matters to others. My cousin Anjay is my best male friend, and he's fifteen years older. I enjoy his company because he has knowledge and is interesting. You are not old to me. I like how you look—your face, your ears—and your personality, the way your mind pursues everything interesting. And you know very much that I like your muscular calves.

"I love when you hold me strongly that I am almost breathless, when you kiss me a lot, when you touch me, when you look into my eyes and at my body. What does it matter that you were born earlier?

"This is it!"

"Okay, I'll be honest with you," I said. "I think of your young body all the time. It's magnificent."

She sat back and smiled coquettishly.

"You make me feel young and cocky," I continued, grinning. "There's a lack of cynicism in you that appeals to me. I keep pinching myself, thinking, 'This is not real.'"

"You did not have trouble finding *real* young Russian women on the boat," she teased.

"I was one of a kind in Siberia. I could have been missing a nose and both ears and still been attractive."

"You are different, and this is what I love about you," she declared, as tears rapidly filled her eyes. "What will happen to us?"

"I don't know. I'm just going hour by hour these days." I studied her eyes. Then I uttered something that surprised me and made me feel bold.

"I will love you forever."

"I don't know what can possibly come of that statement," I continued, "except that I needed to say it. I loved you from the moment I saw you."

"I have this sense of destiny with you," she said, her tears coming faster, "and know that I will also love you forever. I don't want to lose you. You chose a good time to come into my life."

"What if," I said haltingly, "you go back and fall in love with some young guy and have kids, will you love me then?"

"Yes! I will love you then."

"Would you have sex with me?" I kidded.

"No," she said thoughtfully, "I'd be married. A woman must be proper. I would be your friend."

"That doesn't seem right. Suppose you were married with kids, and ten years from now I show up? You'd be horny."

"And you would be too old."

I laughed so hard I dropped my fork, the orange sauce splotching the white linen tablecloth. Malgosia started to laugh too, stopped, and began to cry again.

"Will we see each other?" she pleaded.

"Yes!"

"But you are married, and you love your wife."

"There's plenty of love in this world. I'll be loving you forever, and then you will meet another guy," I said, wanting to settle our future, to settle something that couldn't be settled. "You're young and beautiful and live eight thousand miles from me."

"I do not want to talk about that," she said determinedly. "I love you, and do not want to talk about a future that we cannot know. I will be your mistress. Then one day someone will come along, and we will be friends."

INDIA AND NEPAL

VISIONS

12

NEW DELHI: ONE WILD AND CRAZY PLACE

STILLNESS PERVADED THE NEW DELHI airport. The only activity was the buzz of a lazy fly reconnoitering a mango peel. This stillness was an illusion—or, at the very least, deceptive. For, outside the airport's calm, under a blazing October sun, the real India lay in ambush.

Soon I was in a black, bumperless cab right in the whirl of Delhi's dusty, crowded streets. Cutting through heavy air, the cabbie zigzagged around trucks and buses spewing black fumes, beeping scooters, honking old cars, bikes, rickshaws pulled by skinny men in tattered clothes, donkey carts piled with hay, wild cows, dogs, chickens, and even an elephant. Everywhere people in baggy shirts and pants or saris milled about. In my memory, only Africa competed in numbers of children and pregnant mothers. Swaying along with the cab, I felt a mellow calm that comes with traveling for an extended time. Sure, it was thrilling stepping into what for me was a completely bizarre culture—with nearly a billion people living in a space a third of the size of the United States—but I was going with the flow.

The New Delhi Tourist Camp existed peacefully beside a busy two-lane road on the seedy side of town. I wasn't particularly anxious to walk on the wild side, but after staying in subdued London for the previous two weeks I was looking forward to being with travelers again. The camp compound consisted of a two-acre, grassy plot with sixty or so rectangular, rust-colored cells separated by reddish paths. Everything was tinted with a fine layer of whatever had been thrown up from the neighboring thoroughfare. At the far end of the compound was a snack shack surrounded by a six-foot, weathered picket fence. In front of the fence, two travelers in bulky shorts and smudged T-shirts played hacky sack in the dirt.

I paid six dollars in rupees for two nights; in return I was given a key attached to a chunk of wood with "89" daubed in thick white paint. Number 89 had delux room painted in white across its sky-blue door, which was secured by an iron bolt across the middle. The "room" had the size and look of a jail cell—sandy cement floor, tiny window eight feet up, clear light bulb fixed to the ceiling, and a very single bed with a hard pillow. The fan hung two feet above the pillow, its blade unprotected by screening. The "delux" part must have referred to a dirty curtain and the threadbare sheet on the bed. I had stayed in a cell like this in the jungle in Uganda's Ssese Islands, so I wasn't shocked by its Spartan nature. It was how I imagined a monk in an *extremely* poor monastery might feel. What had become of my businessman self who slept in $250-a-day rooms? I slung the daypack over my shoulder, grabbed my water bottle, and left to find camaraderie in this new land.

The hacky sack was being bashed about by four heavily traveled hiking boots. Judging by their height and looseness of body, the hacky sackers looked to be Americans in their late twenties—one with short, blond hair, the other dark and long—both sporting beards. Was it the steroids in meat that made young Westerners so big?

"Wanna play?" asked the dark-haired one in, as I'd expected, an American accent. He juggled the sack a few times as he spoke, then flicked it to his partner with the heel of his boot.

"Sure," I said, never having touched a hacky sack.

"I'm Derrick," he said, momentarily stopping play to shake hands. The other fellow, Tom, welcomed me with shy eyes. I was struck by the number of gold rings he wore—nine pierced his left ear, with one in his right, and another hanging from his nose.

After about ten minutes of my feet connecting with the sack only by complete chance—who thinks up these games?—we decided not to suffer my apprenticeship any longer and went to drain a few Kingfisher beers at the snack shack.

Derrick began by immediately saying he was Jewish, as if it was his main characteristic. After that, I discovered both were twenty-five, hailed from Port Washington, New York, and were Deadheads. They'd traveled through China and Pakistan before entering India. Despite his young age, Derrick dreamed of retiring at thirty after building a string of restaurants. Tom's ambition was to be part owner of a flower shop.

"What's China like?" I asked.

"It's big!" Derrick said. "The food's fair, railroad's comfortable, and the people are suspicious of strangers. Not like India. The fuckin' Chinese are notoriously apathetic when it comes to service. One time, Tom and I asked for a room at this guesthouse. The dude at reception made a *no rooms* gesture with his hands. They don't give a shit! Figure they get paid whether the house is empty or full, so why clean another room?"

"So we unzipped our backpacks," Tom continued, "took out the sleeping bags and laid them on the floor near check-in. We motioned that we'd sleep right there for the night, thank you very much. The guy freaked—"

"Guess what, dude?" Derrick picked up the story. "An empty room miraculously appears."

Derrick invited me to join them for a tour of the city. At our first stop, a park with almost no greenery, touts immediately descended offering massages. At just two dollars each, we thought, why not? So the next hour consisted of two master masseurs expertly pounding our flesh. Another loitering specialist swabbed wax from my ears using chopstick-like utensils dipped into a special oil, purportedly to avoid infection.

Pounded and cleaned, we entered the heart of the city through India Gate—a ceremonial stone arch not unlike the Arc de Triomphe in Paris. Grinning children in faded clothes played with balls of rolled twine and pushed wheels with sticks. Unusually for a traveler, Derrick paid attention to the kids, pulling funny faces and making them laugh.

On the way to visit a museum, we saw some women wearing sprigs of white jasmine plaited into their long, black hair like clinging vines. I asked the guys if they noticed how few women, compared with men, were in this city.

"Yeah, it's freaky," Tom agreed.

Derrick explained that women stay on the farms and men journey to the city to get work. "They also abort females. An article I read quoted that out of a thousand abortions in Bombay last year, nine hundred ninety-nine were females. A Jewish woman aborted the male."

"Just as well," Tom opined, "the child doesn't have to live in a society that places so little value on her just because of her gender."

Later in the afternoon, we joined affluent Western tourists for a sound and light show at the Red Fort—the former residence of Delhi's Mughal emperors. After the spectacle, the tour groups streamed back into their colossal air-conditioned buses, which would whisk them away to four-star hotels. It was no wonder visitors perceived poor countries such as India as starving when they looked down through tinted windows and never saw into people's eyes. Sometimes you need to be on ground level among locals to make distinctions between starving and poor people.

The dark of night crept in ever so methodically as we drifted from the city's main arteries into the confines of its narrow veins, which thrummed everywhere to the country's unique musical cadences. Bereft of streetlights, the crowded alleys were gorged with three-wheeled tuk-tuks and crawling with vendors and beggars. The workers in the endless fix-it shops chit-chatted next to their worn wooden tables and barrels of grease covered with soot. The pavement was littered with rubbish, which was nosed through by scavenging dogs and wandering cows. Clouds of steam floating above cauldrons of boiling water in the makeshift food shacks added a hazy eeriness to the darkening atmosphere.

A woman with a suckling baby cried: "Please give me fifty rupees. Touch my baby's body. Please give me."

"Jesus!" Derrick bellowed, mopping his brow. "There's no air. Not even enough of a breeze to blow the dust off windows."

"I hope you guys learned to be tough in New York," I replied, "because this place gives me the willies."

"Yeah, it makes the Bronx look like Park Avenue," Derrick said, shaking his head.

It wasn't that any individual was scary. It was the prevailing atmosphere. Sweaty crowds in dirty, narrow spaces stared at us constantly. Their, often broken, teeth were stained from chewing the addictive *paan* (betel leaf usually mixed with the areca nut and tobacco), which was to the street Indian what coffee was to Americans—a drug to make the day pass with flavor.

"I hope you guys can find your way out of this maze," I said. "I have no sense of direction."

"Tom can find his way out of a coffin buried deep in a pyramid using a glowworm, can't you, Tom?"

By way of an answer, Tom pointed to a light on the upper floor of a two-story building: "Dinner!"

As we took the only empty places in the dully lit, grungy five-table restaurant the other patrons stared at us shamelessly, forgetting all about their food. The menu was in Hindi, so we ordered by guesswork and pointing. Miraculously, within minutes, the waiter delivered bowls of rice and a circular tray with separate plates of spinach, potatoes, yogurt, and hot chili and mint sauces. We supped and exchanged the details of our lives under constant eyeballing from our fellow diners, including a middle-aged, toothless man who inquired every few minutes: "You like food? Eat. You like?"

"Ever since we were kids we dreamed of this trip," Tom said. "Derrick and I grew up in the same neighborhood before his dad moved up to the big time. The thought of traveling in the wilderness of the world kept us in touch."

"What does your dad do, Derrick?"

"He's a venture capitalist. He makes dreams come true," he said with a hint of sarcasm. Before leaving for China, Derrick had been a very junior member of a group that started a hamburger restaurant chain. The selling point was that the food was upscale and the service had flair. He was responsible for the flair. "The only thing better than a restaurant," he said, "is the restaurant bar."

True to Derrick's word, Tom led us home through the maze of streets brightened by the crescent moon. We all had our New York antennas up, scanning for danger. Mainly, though, slumbering silence prevailed as dust and smells settled for the night. In alleyways behind restaurants, men lined up in neat rows, legs folded as if sitting patiently for a yoga class to begin.

"They're waiting for leftovers," Derrick remarked nonchalantly, "the direct approach to serving the poor."

We passed sleeping figures slumped in rickshaws and curled up on anything elevated: wooden sidewalks, tables, chairs. Bodies were scattered everyplace, except where cows decided to park, even on the concrete median of the road that bordered our camp compound. My heart went out to them—the hopelessness of it all, the loss of life and limb if a car went out of control.

The New Yorkers' suite, delux room 121, looked as if a tidal wave had swept through it, leaving clothes and photographic equipment strewn about. As we swapped travelers' tales, Derrick grabbed a cube of brown, compressed resin, heated it and chipped pieces into a cigar-shaped pipe. He held the pipe in an awkward position to get the smoke flowing.

"What the hell is this thing?" I squealed when it was my turn, unable to make it work.

"It's a chillum. No, no! Not that way," Derrick replied, grabbing and adjusting the pipe in my hands. "The sadhus, who are Hindu holy men, use them to smoke hash."

"What is hash exactly?"

"It's pollen that sticks to the leather aprons of people working in a mature marijuana field—kind of how pollen sticks to the behind of a bee going from flower to flower."

I was all thumbs trying to use the chillum and began to laugh at myself. It was a hearty laugh, with the unrestrained energy of youth. Laughing like this was a new sensation for me. Most of my life I made people laugh, but had so controlled my own laugh that it must have been barely evident.

Tom grabbed his guitar and began singing Hotel California.

"That has to be the most widely sung song in the world," I said, swaying to the beat. My friends and clients would have been shocked to see me now—hanging out with one guy who looks like a mountain man and another with ten rings in his ears and one in his nose. Not to mention the chillum.

I had already experienced some adverse reactions to the changing direction of my life. Just prior to my travels, I worked in the kitchen at Esalen, the center of philosophy and psychology in Big Sur, California. Esalen was geared towards people who wanted to change their lives. I was there on a work scholarship for a month, trying to trade my affluent habits for simpler ones. I worked in a kitchen that fed eighty to a hundred people three times a day. In exchange, I got to attend a month-long seminar. I chose acting.

Somehow a former client tracked me to the kitchen phone to ask a question. In the course of the conversation, he learned my purpose there and laughed as if I'd run into a tree while skiing and lost my sense of direction. I knew it had taken me on to a higher, slower path—one that gave me time to ponder other pursuits than business.

The familiar music attracted other travelers and locals into the New York suite. As the small throngs drifted in and out, Derrick and I escaped to cool off in the miserly night breeze. He began talking about the expectations his Jewish parents had for their only son.

"Dad believes that since he can cut it, so can I. He talks about vision. I tried a vision, but the hamburger chain failed. Traveling has given me time to lick my wounds and figure out if I'm ambitious enough to risk failure again."

"There's a lot of risk traveling, don't you think? It's been my experience that learning to risk something is key to achieving a vision."

Sparse traffic and the croak of a gecko punctuated a few moments of silence. It was only then that I realized the little lizard must have been named after its cry—ge-cko. Derrick inhaled the cool night air and restarted the conversation, asking what I did for a living.

I filled him in on my years in Silicon Valley—semiconductors, then computers, then video games, finally biotechnology. Talking about high-tech felt so good. I couldn't help enthusing about the late seventies computer startup where I was chief financial officer.

"It was one of the first new age computer companies. The founder literally started in a garage making electronic boards about the same time as the Apple guys did. He inserted the boards into a metal box and called it a 'microcomputer.'

"Early on, we didn't know much about who our customers were selling computers to, or exactly what the end users were doing with our machines. What we did know was we'd be very rich if the company survived the eighties. Unfortunately, it didn't. But by that time I had already moved on to help start a video game company.

"I ended my career reorganizing troubled companies, so I guess you can say I started out helping to build companies with visions, and ended trying to fix those with busted ones."

"What motivated you originally?" Derrick asked.

"A vision, I guess."

"Do you think there's a difference between a person's dream and a vision?"

"That's an interesting question. I've given a lot of thought to dreams and visions over the last several months. I like to think a vision is that portion of a dream that is uncluttered, recurrent, and deals strictly with the future."

"A vision is kind of a focused dream?"

"That's a good way to put it. The harder the dream to accomplish, the more focused you need to be."

"I don't know if the dream to build a restaurant chain is mine or my dad's. Don't know where his dream leaves off and mine begins. Silicon Valley is loaded with entrepreneurs with visions. How do they work?"

"The thinking process is this, Derrick. You start with what you want the future to be, and then plan backwards to the present. Then you take a risk. That's how we got to the moon when Kennedy had a vision."

"That's the uniqueness of Americans—taking risks. Can you imagine the risks our ancestors took leaving their families and way of life forever? To go where no dream was impossible. In a sense, every country is part of us since they all contributed ancestors. The US means *us*."

"What an interesting thought," I said. Once again I was fascinated with the character and wisdom of young people I met. The nice thing about traveling with them was that their minds weren't yet made up. I wanted to explore more about Derrick's sense of vision and how it related to my own experience.

"The computer company where I worked was originally funded by a VC group known as the Page Mill Club," I continued. "It was comprised of early Valley entrepreneurs who liked investing in young guys full of juice like us. Building companies was in their blood and they liked the vicarious thrill of it all. Bob Noyce represented the group on our board.

"You may have heard of him, he co-invented the integrated circuit and founded Intel. Noyce once told me, 'The trick with a vision is to make it so simple that employees can carry the concept around in their heads. Then it will drive you.' So we spent a month working on the first two sentences of our business plan. It was our vision."

"My dad says business plans are blueprints for the future. They bring the future into the present, so that we can do something about it now."

"Nice phrasing. I like it."

"It sounds like the recipe for a vision is a simple passion that you want to achieve in the future and a strong dose of risk taking."

"Tenacity! Add tenacity. It's the same as focus. There is real power in a vision, Derrick, but it's also a burden. I risked my money and marriage on this trip to complete mine."

Derrick's recipe for a vision rang true, but it took me the rest of my time in India and Nepal to grasp *why* the recipe worked.

13

COINCIDENCE AND THE TAJ MAHAL

THE BUS TO AGRA BOUNCED for six hours on roads deeply rutted from overuse and inattention. Water buffaloes and cows strolled indifferent to the traffic—as if they were members of an exalted class. And, in a way, they were. Our driver treated cows with utmost deference. The humans, inside and outside the bus, were expendable, but the cows were sacred. In India, these beasts could truly watch the grass grow. Life went on around the cows, I remarked to a thin older man sitting next to me. They already knew, as a friend once said during one of my dark days, "Crises come ... and then they go."

Responding to my earlier observation, the thin older man said cows were not the only sacred animals in India. Rather, Hindus believed that all life shared a universal soul and therefore the resources of the earth. Animals were respected as potential havens for departed spirits whose karma needed fulfillment.

"Do you believe in reincarnation?" I asked.

"Yes, of course!"

"I have problems accepting reincarnation as a possibility. I believe the genes in our bodies store the attributes and experiences of *our ancestors*. So if our genes come from our family, how can we be a reincarnated spirit from somewhere else entirely?"

"Why is it not possible for the body to have many spirits?" he replied without hesitating.

His answer was so simple! Why couldn't the body be host to many spirits? One spirit developed from one's ancestors and another spirit—or spirits—also deciding to inhabit the host, for whatever reason. Multiple spirits could explain multiple personalities.

"I like that thought," I said. "A few years ago, I read about this multiple personality case. The woman's primary personality was a severe diabetic. But when her second personality was out, she ate as she pleased *and* her eating habits didn't harm her body, which was meant to have diabetes."

He dropped his head on his shoulders as if he were about to sleep. Then he looked up at me. "The body adjusted to the spirit?" was all he said.

"Hello, sir," a little girl in rags called out at the Agra bus station. Her dark eyes sparkled as she grinned. She held out a dirty hand. I placed five rupees in it and patted her head. She dutifully brought the money to her mother sitting on the dusty floor of the depot. The mother hugged her daughter. Easily worth five rupees, I thought.

I negotiated a daily rate with a dignified tuk-tuk driver, Halim, who was younger than me in age but older in looks. He assisted me checking in at a nice hotel, then we set off down a street crowded with stands of fresh vegetables, fruit, and symmetrical piles of vibrantly colored spices to see the Agra Fort and the Taj Mahal at sunset.

The sixteenth-century fort was a barrel-chested, magnificent edifice in perfect condition. Constructed of dazzling red brick, it easily encompassed five city blocks. Turreted walls protected numerous rooms where olden-day Muslim warlords entertained and conducted affairs of state. Sitting inside the citadel on a teal-green marble bench on a marble balcony, I gazed down over a grassy park to a coconut-colored sandbar on the Jumna River. From the sandbar, I tilted my eyes upward and got my first glimpse of the distant white dome and minarets of the Taj Mahal.

On the way to the Taj, Halim recounted how Shah Jahan (and twenty thousand workers) built the mausoleum in the middle of the seventeenth century in memory of his favorite wife, Mumtaz Mahal. He also repeated the myth that Jahan killed his chief architect so that the Taj would never be duplicated.

Once inside the mausoleum complex—after fighting my way through all the touts outside—I could see why it attracted so many myths. I passed under a grand brownstone arch and strode down a long white stone promenade surrounded by fresh, rich grass and billowing bushes and trees. At the halfway point, I joined a young German couple on a white marble bench. We were all transfixed by the sight at the end of the promenade. You could never describe or even take a picture that would do justice to the Taj Mahal. It was much more than its image.

I headed eagerly to the end of the promenade to explore the stunning structure—and the magnificent red sandstone mosque and its companion building, which guarded either side—more closely. The three edifices stood on a cliff that dropped hundreds of rugged feet down to the Jumna River—so far that the silhouette of a camel pulling a cart below was barely visible.

Touring the river side of the Taj's outside balcony, I impulsively slid in my socks across the sparkling marble tiles, mildly startling the other visitors. There wasn't so much as a hint of resistance. The inner chamber, above the crypt, was devoid of gold and silver, but none was necessary. Again, words could never capture the beauty and craftsmanship of the carved stonework.

Outside, the evening sun cast a scarlet glow that climbed up and reflected off the marble, which changed color depending on time of day. But before long the descending darkness carefully covered the world and one of its most beautiful buildings with a somber blanket. *Don't wake me up, this must be a dream,* my mind whispered.

After bathing in comparative comfort back at the hotel, I dealt with some pressing communications needs. First, I phoned Frank Zolfo and made arrangements for meeting him in Bangkok in November. Along with Joe Reilly, he was one of the old friends I had planned to meet up with along the way.

Then I sat and wrote Kathi. I wanted to simply state the things I adored about her: her talents as a mother and lover; her sweetness and elegance; her thoughtful gifts and surprises; the way her mind worked and its eclectic interest in so many subjects; her cooking; and lastly, the patience to support an ambitious man. I drifted off thinking that if only we could parlay the qualities we liked about each other to make up for the qualities that drove us apart.

Early the next morning, I revisited the Taj to enjoy its colors changing as the day unfolded. Away from the beeps and honks of the traffic, I lay on the lush grass under the shade of a tree with heart-shaped leaves and listened to the chatter of birds and murmuring wind. The faint whiff of burning leaves tickled the air. In front of me stood the most beautiful work of art I had ever seen.

I realized I'd come full circle on monuments to God and wealth—those glorious, sometimes gaudy, cathedrals, mosques, temples, and jeweled palaces built with the sweat of the poor. The Taj Mahal convinced me that lasting beauty *was* worth the sacrifice, and that both poor and rich should be able to take pride in their achievement.

Three good-looking, mustached, talkative Indian students joined me on the grass. They wore Western clothes—white shirts, jeans, and sneaks—and studied engineering and political science at the local university. They didn't hold back on their questions—quickly ascertaining my nationality, family statistics, occupation, date of birth, and favorite chewing gum.

"And what kind of music do you like, Denis? What are your favorite groups?"

"I like blues, rock and roll, sevenities soul," I said. "I have no memory for names of musicians, books, authors, or movie stars. But I like Paul Simon and The Eagles."

"Ah, 'Hotel California'!" said the smallest of the three. He preferred The Smiths, whoever they were.

We moved on to the philosophical and spiritual. They said Hinduism had already existed at the beginning of the Egyptian empire and that it was better to describe it as a philosophy of life rather than a religion. Its polytheistic pantheon of gods and goddesses, as well as demons and spirits, were really symbols of the natural world. The central belief was the energy of destiny, karma, that transcended the body and lived within individual souls. These would keep taking birth until they had learned to shed ego and find the real self, which was God. They theorized that the caste system derived its politics from this evolution of souls, each successive incarnation representing a moving up (or down) in whatever form was needed to teach a lesson.

They then described the Indian education system. It shut out the poor, the students said, because they didn't have money or the primary learning required by the universities. Women were not considered equals, but that they were regarded with kindness and respect. They said the old ways were changing.

I offered water from my bottle. They drank, holding the mouth of the bottle two inches from their lips. Whether this was because of manners or sanitation I wasn't sure. Perhaps both.

"Do you go out with women?" I asked, since the topic had been broached.

"In India, we are having two systems," said the most relaxed of the three, "one for the upper and lower classes, and one for the middle class. The former have access to drugs and females. The middle class is more conservative, only having access to drugs."

As non-threateningly as possible, I asked if they were virgins. They looked at each other and me, then we all laughed.

"Yes, we are virgins," said the second student unabashed. "Ninety-five percent of middle-class males are virgins before having married."

"Virginity is the greatest burden of adolescence," the third announced humorously.

Before catching the 23:15 train to Varanasi, Halim putt-putted me to a cozy five-table restaurant in the center of town. I spotted the German couple I'd run into at the Taj and again earlier in the afternoon. They asked me to join them and over a dinner of curry and chicken baked in a *tandoor* (clay oven) I tried to find out more about our coincidental meetings.

"Okay, this is the third time we've run into each other in the last twenty-four hours. What's the link?"

The link was that we'd already met. Cristoff studied architecture in Munich with a German girl who'd spent her junior year abroad in high school with *us* in California, Nicola Disko. *And* Nicola had introduced him to me, her "American dad," at a party by the riverbank in Munich's Central Park the previous June when I was passing through Germany.

Nicola, tall and intelligent, graced our lives as an exchange student from Germany when Shannon spent a year in France before starting college. Both our girls eventually lived in small towns in France, relearning how to "waste time" when our lives had gotten so busy. It was an important lesson and when Nicola returned to Germany she sent me a small novel by Michael Ende, *Momo*. I told the Germans the story of Momo, a little homeless girl who lived in the ruins of an old Roman amphitheater in a nondescript town in Italy.

The people of the town visited Momo because she brightened their day and was a great listener. Then the *time savers* moved in. Wearing gray top hats and gray suits with round watches dangling, they convinced the townsfolk that if they saved their time in a bank, they could retire early with all the time in the world. The people began to deposit *time* previously "wasted" on family and leisure and worked harder and harder. Their visits to Momo became fewer and fewer, until even her best friend, a little boy, was far too busy to chat.

Then the time savers went after the only remaining time waster—Momo. Eventually the spirit world intervened to help Momo avoid the clutches of the humorless villains, and the townsfolk learned what they knew originally: that time "wasted" was often as valuable as time spent productively.

"A relevant story in today's world," Cristoff agreed, with a shake of his head. "And what an amazing coincidence meeting you in Agra. I cannot wait to tell Nicola."

"Maybe coincidence is a poor word," his girlfriend, Berit, offered. "In my travels I have felt an energy that connects people. It seems like coincidence, but many travelers I have met feel the energy is cosmic. Perhaps the cosmic karma that Hinduism speaks of. Perhaps coincidence is merely attraction."

"*Ja*," Cristoff picked up the thread briskly, "Berit and I just this minute, before you arrived, talked about reincarnation and coincidence. Perhaps *coincidence* is really a familiar energy that connects a spirit in one body to a spirit in another body, bodies that came in contact with each other during a past life. Both spirits drawn to familiar energy like iron to a magnet.

"Perhaps in a previous life, a spirit residing in us *now* lived in the same body as a spirit in the person that attracts us. And subconsciously they recognize each other. Thus, déjà-vu!"

Whoo! I thought, the analytical capacity of Germans was outstanding.

It was like the energy surrounding startup companies. Back in Silicon Valley, just when we needed a person with a particular talent, someone miraculously appeared. It was like the company's energy reached out and grabbed them. Like Berit, I also felt an energy when traveling. I knew that in each place I visited, I would see something and meet someone I'd never seen before. It was as if an energy field surrounded me attracting compatible energy. As if out here in the world, people were waiting to meet me.

14

CAPTURING THE BAGGAGE CAR IN A BLOODLESS COUP ON THE TRAIN TO VARANASI

THE CROWD THAT MILLED AROUND the dimly lit railroad station in Agra was sleepy. Well, it was 11:35 p.m. Children rubbed at the fatigue in their eyes and whole families cozied up on the wooden floor, trying to catch a little shut-eye under light blankets. A scruffy beggar with stumps for legs sat on a grimy skateboard, paddling along the ground with his hands. I gave him a few rupees.

I was the perfect paranoid traveler. Would I take the wrong train? Or worse watch the right one leave while standing on the wrong platform? After four people confirmed to me in sign language that the Varanasi train would depart platform seven, I relaxed. The wheeled beggar returned grinning and pointing to a cup of chai in his hand.

I'd heard that every day Indian trains carried the equivalent of Australia's population. Most of them seemed to be on this train. I squirmed through the multitudes searching for my assigned bunk. Compartments designed to sleep six were instead crammed with scores of people. And, like the others, when I reached mine it contained a legion of Indians merrily singing in the dim lighting. My bunk was history. If it hadn't been so late, I might have joined the festivities, but instead I struggled to turn around and maneuvered back through the car door and down iron steps on to the dreary concrete platform. Breathing air and sighing with relief, I began to search for an official who could assist. It was fruitless.

Dispossessed and weary, several other backpackers retreated from exactly the same situation. Without introductions, we formed a survival group—steeped in confusion but united in purpose. Led by an outraged Canadian, we headed for one of the two baggage cars. Once we'd violated its perimeter, we claimed squatter's rights from a surprised and indignant assistant guard.

Before long, a squad of armed soldiers surrounded this car. The situation could have seethed with intensity, had it not been for the smiles on the faces of the soldiers and their encouragement to hold our ground against the assistant guard. The situation was intense but also baffling. I searched my daypack for pen and paper, asked our leader his name, and began to compose a news bulletin for my comrades without arms.

AGRA INDIA APPROX 12:15 A.M. MULTINATIONAL FORCE OF BEDRAGGLED INSURGENTS CAPTURED BAGGAGE CAR ON VARANASI TRAIN IN BLOODLESS COUP STOP AFTER BRUTAL STRUGGLE TO OUST INVADERS ASSISTANT GUARD SURRENDERED TERRITORY VOWING REVENGE STOP INSURGENTS PREVAILED AGAINST ATTACKS BY HIGHLY TRAINED ADMINISTRATIVE REGULARS STOP UNIDENTIFIED SOURCES CONFIRM INSURGENTS GALLANTLY LED BY CANADIAN DANIEL MCCARTY STOP MCCARTY RELAYED THIS MESSAGE VIA SOLDIERS SYMPATHETIC TO INSURGENTS' CAUSE SURROUNDING BAGGAGE CAR STOP WE WILL NEVER SURRENDER! STOP WE WILL FIGHT TO BITTER END OR VARANASI WHICHEVER COMES FIRST STOP

Eventually, the heretofore invisible chief guard arrived outside our car and politely agreed to a truce. We were appeased by the offer of berths in car S-3. Unfortunately, waves of locals at successive stations had different ideas and soon car S-3 resembled a rugby scrum. Shouting matches broke out as newcomers flashed tickets with "our" seat numbers.

After a while, the travelers and locals, garbed in turbans and white kurtas or colorful saris, reached a compromise—some sharing bunks while many of the Indians slept barefoot on the grungy floor. Only our fearless leader, Dan, held out.

He stubbornly negotiated for an hour with an Indian gentleman over occupation of a disputed bunk. The man, wearing a baggy, brown suit and a very concerned expression, kept pointing to his ticket, then to the number on the bunk, all the time weathering the seething look on Dan's angry face.

"You are having the wrong seat. Look here, number twenty-two!" the man insisted. "I should say straight away, there is a problem. Answers must be found. In addition, ticket numbers and costings should be considered."

The first "answer" they found was to split the bed in half. However, Dan couldn't get comfortable with his length of body and the solution fizzled out in a tangle of legs. Finally, they took turns sleeping while the other scrunched up at the bottom of the bunk.

For the next twenty-two hours, we lumbered the six hundred kilometers to Varanasi, with only a brief stop for an hour and a half at Lucknow. The break, we discovered, was because the locomotive was no longer attached. It had disappeared. A substitute eventually came. Still we waited. We clunked forward a teasing twenty yards, then sat for another forty minutes.

It is in such unusual circumstances that traveling groups get formed. Our guards drop as we are in constant contact and we begin to bond. My group consisted of Dan, his traveling buddy, Dave, who'd recently graduated from medical school in London, and Maria, a Spanish schoolteacher traveling alone. Four was a good number. It meant two double rooms and therefore reduced costs.

Once in Varanasi, we hired a pair of tuk-tuks and went to check out budget guesthouses. The dusty and dimly lit roads were lined with earthen homes no bigger than typical US kitchens, yet they usually housed ten or more people. We parked on an anciently narrow street filled with dilapidated brick buildings. The far end of the road pulsated with music and sparkling lights that might have come from a Christmas tree. A wedding party, a local man told us.

While my companions went to inspect potential accommodation, I remained in the tattered rickshaw nursing the pain in my lower back. An old disk problem had flared up. In the past, regular exercise warded off discomfort, but then I wasn't scrunched up in a crowded train or carrying a forty-pound pack.

Dusty humidity permeated the quiet night air. A group of children in a brick alcove the size of a small pantry caught my attention. Two little girls, neither older than three, slept spread-eagled with their bare bottoms sticking out. One, lying face down, bent her knees inwards and feet outwards like a frog to avoid falling into the street. Beside them a handsome boy of seven slumped forward, one arm dangling on to the floor, despondency heavy on his face. The other arm stroked a third little girl nestled in his lap. She was no more than two. His amber body was bare except for flimsy tan short pants.

For me, he symbolized the sadness of a society that overburdened the land from which it drew sustenance. He gently lifted the tiny girl aside, inched over to the edge of the alcove, and puked sallow, stringy gunk into the street. The little girl's face wrinkled with cries of abandonment. She crawled after him, lifting herself on to his back for comfort. The boy's patient haunted look never changed as he waited for the slow intermittent waves of nausea to pass.

We checked out two guesthouses and settled on the second. Maria and I walked into the guesthouse room we were set to share. We tossed our daypacks on the beds, opened the window slightly to let in a little air, and then joined the others for a late night supper. When Maria and I returned to the room and shut the door behind us, we slowly looked at each other with mouths agape. Something was drastically wrong. Exactly what took a few seconds to register. But when it hit, it hit with a vengeance. Walls, ceiling, bed, everywhere was black and moving. Bugs!

There were thousands of them—black, green, and red—dropping on the twin beds like rain, clicking away. "Oh shit!" we cried in unison, running too late to close the open window. My sore back was forgotten as we grabbed pillows and started blasting. Dan and Dave heard the ruckus and joined the fray, along with the landlady and two other travelers who happened to be passing by. But we knew we were fighting a losing battle and soon the landlady ushered us to another room.

Breathing a sigh of relief, we lay on the firm clean beds. Maria prepared a joint. She had a dark, pleasing complexion, short, curly, brown hair, plain features, and a slightly pudgy build. She was a woman battling within herself. She'd left her teaching job and beachfront home in the Canary Islands after a difficult divorce, and was following her dream of backpacking around the Indian sub-continent.

She felt low self-esteem was her enemy, and had already challenged her fears by taking an adventurous route to the roof of the world in Ladakh, northern Kashmir. Then she'd worked her way across northern India. Like the rest of our band, she planned to head north from Varanasi to Nepal. Her aim was the arduous Annapurna trail in the Himalayas. At forty, she was the oldest backpacker I'd met. She was also my third female roommate, which fostered an unspoken, but definite attraction.

It was the attraction that arose when two strangers of the opposite sex lay close and spoke intimately. Not an overwhelming desire, more of a "let's get together." Perhaps it was a genetic reminder of the fundamental necessity to preserve the species. With the openness I loved about travelers, we discussed this phenomenon—a mutual feeling—and decided to abstain.

The next morning, we rode off in a pair of rickshaws through the jungle of markets and narrow streets of one of the oldest cities in the world. Raw sewage trickled along gutters so ancient they were turning into dust. Dust was ubiquitous. It was incessantly swept or watered down by shop owners, and filled the air with gray clouds. Brown bodies roamed everywhere.

An old woman squatted on the ground amid a swarm of flies, slapping cow dung into circular pies. Her yellow feet were cracked and her forehead streaked with red signifying "married." She slammed the completed pies against the wall of her hut to dry, and to be used later as fuel for cooking.

We passed a man in a red gown with silver hair flowing down his neck drinking chai and caressing a cobra wrapped around his neck. He unleashed a wad of red betel juice into the street like a baseball player spitting tobacco. Our destination was a weaving factory employing four thousand people. We watched fascinated as silk garments and carpets were created by hand on the looms in front of us.

I was getting to know Dan and Dave. Dan, like Maria, was also a teacher, who'd taken a year off to travel. He liked to negotiate with locals—much too hard I thought. His smile appeared far too infrequently. Yet he reminded me of the cynical but curiously likable Englishmen I'd met in Jordan—negative but who said things close enough to the mark to demand respect.

Redheaded Dave from Wales had just finished a series of punishing eighty-hour weeks as a medical internist. He was out to see real individuals and disprove to himself the notion that people were only numbers. With his easygoing confidence and humor, he and Dan were opposites. Where Dave was quiet, Dan was brash. Where Dave was thoughtful, Dan barged ahead. Where Dave's pale, Celtic body seemed out of place in the sun, Dan's wiry muscles welcomed the rays. Opposites might not always attract, but certainly sometimes they complemented one another.

In the afternoon, we made our way through the back streets to the Ganges. At the sacred river, we climbed aboard a long wooden boat steered and propelled with a bamboo pole by the English-speaking Sahir. Wasting little time, he and his betel-spitting assistant pushed off into the Ganges as the yellow sun's glory penetrated a dusty mist to meet the shimmering dark flow of the water. The resulting sparkles on the holy river looked like the dawn of nature.

The Ganges flowed two and a half thousand kilometers from the Himalayas east through the plains of India to empty into the Bay of Bengal on the border with Bangladesh. It wasn't a crowded river, but several other boats with casually dressed tourists drifted nearby. We slowly passed large terraced mansions overlooking the river. Monkeys frolicked along their eves and gables and jumped on to branches of banyan trees. Further along, we came to the famous *ghats*—broad stone steps built along the edge of the river, which descended into the water.

Locals milled about on the ghats. Some, holding brass goblets, chanted and prayed. Thin men in drooping skivvies and jutting rib cages belly-flopped into the water. Others stood in the water scrubbing their tongues and teeth with a stick, a string, or their index fingers. Women in thin, colorful saris stepped gingerly, submerged themselves elegantly, and washed under their garments. An old matron, skin wrinkled like a raisin, bared her upper body. While an immersed water buffalo, its dripping black snout sucking air, enjoyed a break from the heat and waded among the bathers.

As he poled the boat, Sahir explained why the water was peppered with burned cinders. "When Hindus die the privileged rest in the holy river. People, all castes, travel long distances in trains and buses, often three days, to bring dead. Those of wealth burn corpse—like that."

He pointed to a smoky area on the shoreline not far from the bathers. The wood pyres belched orange flames. "They push body remains into river," he continued. "Those not wealthy use government crematorium."

I was awestruck by the goings-on, unable to question, and satisfied to observe. While in the bow, Dave bent towards Maria and spoke in a hushed tone: "I was told the families of blokes who can't afford cremation wrap the body like a mummy, tie it to a rope with a heavy stone attached, and give it a heave into the water."

"Why burn the body?" Dan demanded brusquely.

"Burning purifies the soul," Sahir replied.

Out of Sahir's earshot, but loud enough for the rest of us, Maria said, "I read that in the old days a man's spouse was thrown alive on the burning pyre to share the afterlife with her husband. And they abort female babies. But the locals I have met are so nice. I do not understand these people."

"Cuts the population growth, doesn't it?" Dan said sardonically. "Abort a man and you decrease the population by one. Abort a *woman*—God knows this land can't take any more people."

Maria shot Dan a sour look. Dan may have been crude, but I was beginning to think that many tribal traditions that appeared cruel or perplexing to today's Western society may have been introduced to solve practical problems, such as matching population to available food supply, or polygamy could save a woman (and her children) who might otherwise be destitute after the death of her husband. Dan's comment gave me pause to recall what Montaigne said of traveling: " … the mind is constantly stimulated by observing new and unknown things … No propositions astonish me, no belief offends me, however much opposed to my own."

Maneuvering closer to shore, Sahir said babies and holy men go directly into the water because they are already pure and don't need to be purified. Under the afternoon sun, we watched an affluent corpse burn on the ghats. The body was wrapped in gold, red, and white swaths of linen and silk. Eventually, it popped from the buildup of gases in its head and torso. The eldest son, I guessed, with a shaved scalp and wearing white, poked the burning body of his father while sprinkling a salve on the burned head. There were no women.

"Ladies do not attend these ceremonies," Sahir said, "because of the pain it would cause them."

That was when we spotted the head partially covered in burlap. It was bobbing up and down like a buoy, floating in the water between the crowded cremations on shore and the sparse boat traffic. With its black staring holes, it looked like the Grim Reaper directing his traffic.

15

DEATH ON THE WAY TO KATMANDU

My AILING BACK MIRACULOUSLY HEALED, leaving me exhilarated and ready to resume the rigors of travel. Our foursome boarded a crowded morning bus for the first leg of a two-day trip north to Katmandu in Nepal. We would sleep at the Nepalese border and change buses the next morning. Adding to my exhilaration was an anticipation of the familiar: Janet and Auri, friends from home, were waiting for me in Katmandu. But the elation would not last the journey.

While Dan complained about the tardiness of the bus, Maria grabbed seats for us in the driver's booth, which was enclosed in clear plastic. Under the rearview mirror, garlands and gold-colored tinsel adorned a statue of Shiva, the Hindu god of destruction. As we chugged along, the conductor squeezed nine people inside our booth, which was meant to seat three, because there was no space elsewhere. Overflow passengers sat on stools in the aisle or leaned against worn corduroy seats.

Like a swollen-bellied beast, the bus sagged and squeaked its way along unpaved roads towards Nepal. We stopped for accidents and swerved to avoid giant potholes. All the while, I sweated from the humidity, humanity, and near misses. Finally, at one of the many roadside stops to drink chai and munch on roasted chickpeas and bananas, Dan and I joined several of the backpackers on board and climbed the rear ladder to the roof.

Straddling backpacks and parcels, we exalted in the freedom to stretch out and breathe fresh air. The roof brought life to the countryside and stimulation to conversation. Dan told me that he started traveling with a mate from Canada, but they split in Africa. "I liked to go out, he didn't," he explained. "I was talkative, he wasn't. Didn't work!" Dan didn't care for Canada, said that it had become like *Brave New World*. He carried lots of pills and ate tomato sandwiches for breakfast and dinner, and his stomach was chronically upset. I hadn't had a problem eating what the locals ate, as long as it was cooked.

We crossed the India–Nepal border that evening, purchased visas, and found lodgings for the night. The second leg to Katmandu began innocently enough. Birds chirped, a flea-bitten dog nosed around our baggage, and a hotel attendant watered the dirt to keep the dust in check. Our new driver and conductor only spoke Nepali. Pointing out the nearness of the border, they politely motioned to us not to climb on the roof.

Stuck inside, I sat in the front near another tinsel-wrapped Shiva. My neighbor was a young French woman from Marseilles and we shared the booth with another Westerner and two Nepalese men with engaging smiles. Meanwhile Dave occupied a stool squeezed between the driver and the rest of us. Before long, three more Nepalese crammed into the booth. The flies buzzed and scavenged to the sound of Indian music and its high-pitched female voices, which I now associated with male-dominated cultures. Fully loaded, the bus wailed in an effort to conquer a steep slope in the foothills of the highest mountain range in the world. And promptly broke down.

Passengers poured out as the driver rummaged through a grimy, cloth-wrapped set of tools disgorged from an oily cubbyhole under his seat. He squirmed under the bus using wire and cloth to make repairs. Somehow drivers in the Third World always fixed the problem. There was no Triple-A. And they got plenty of practice. Our bus broke down six times before we forged into a large plateau town crawling with people and pregnant animals.

I had retreated to an aisle seat behind the driver and was wiping my brow from the rising temperature and cramped quarters when the French woman screamed. I simultaneously felt the thud. The memory of that sickening dull heavy sound bound us together throughout the remainder of our trip. I looked back out the window. A crowd was beginning to form.

"Oh my God! He must be dead," Dave's shaky voice cried. "He just walked in front. The old man jus—"

Dave shook his head and held up his hands helplessly. Another traveler behind me said he saw the body hurtling through the air and landing in a lump.

The diminutive curly-haired driver labored for three hundred yards before pulling to the side. Then he slid from his perch to the dirt road and conferred with the conductor. The French woman wept quietly. I envied her sensitivity. Part of me just felt relieved to be stopping. The rest of my mind leapt into crisis mode, calculating alternatives.

How long we would be detained? Who was the old man? Were hit-and-run accidents dealt with in Nepal like in Africa—instant justice? What would happen to us?

Whether it was a male reaction or the years dealing with crises, I didn't know. Slowly the driver climbed back behind the wheel, revved the engine, and pulled off, looking frequently into the side mirror.

What was this little man with a pleasant disposition thinking? Did he have children? Or an aged grandfather not unlike the man he'd hit? I watched his callused hands maneuver the wide black wheel, perspiration moistening his face as he nervously eyed the road behind. Everyone was stunned. There were sniffles from a few of the women, but not one of us said a word. We bumped along in silence. Should I tell the driver to pull over? He didn't speak English. So what! I was a pro at the language of gestures.

Kilometers ticked by—five, then ten. Suddenly, a pickup loaded with men passed the bus and stopped across the middle of the road ahead. Several of the occupants jumped out immediately to flag us down. As the driver coolly pulled over I tried to gauge their faces. Would they pound the driver to death? And us?

Seconds later, the police showed up and quickly herded our driver and conductor down from the protection of the bus, through the agitated crowd and into their car. Another driver climbed aboard, and, without a word of explanation, drove us five kilometers into a large grassy field behind a white, two-story police station. A policeman in khakis stepped into the bus, and, speaking politely in Nepali and English, asked the passengers to step out. He informed us that other buses bound for Katmandu would stop and we were free to go with them. No hit-and-run depositions. No reports.

Within an hour, two already crowded buses pulled into the dirt road beside the station. We boarded and jockeyed for space. I quickly decided it was too tight inside and joined Maria, the French woman, and five Israelis on the roof. The horror of the recent events faded in the pristine beauty of the Nepalese mountainside.

We climbed up and up, through a rich emerald wonderland of rice paddies that covered the mountainside like steps up a colossal stairway. An easy camaraderie developed among those on the roof. We laughed at four little boys shitting in unison off a deep cliff-face. We ate giant cucumber slices and guavas bought from grimy-faced boys and women with nose rings who tossed the food up to us.

The driver beeped his horn endlessly as he swerved his vehicle around the broken, boulder-filled, narrow roads. Sometimes the bus negotiated a hairpin curve or spit of land where the road had given way and couldn't accommodate the length of the chassis. The driver would lurch the bus back and forth until it shifted a hundred and eighty degrees, the wheels inching so close to the edge that we could see the remains of rusted shattered vehicles that had miscalculated far below.

As we climbed the mountains, I stopped trying to work out which way to jump off the bus in an emergency and instead gazed out at the exotic sights around me—cows and water buffalos scratching themselves on trees, the mountain people's primitive thatched huts, little girls in oversized frocks, and leathery old men. Rope and wire pulley systems ferried solitary passengers in canvas carriages across deep gorges and roaring rivers. As nature crowned the day with a sunset that made the river below sparkle like a bed of diamonds, we took off our bandanas and hats and let our hair blow in the breeze.

Dan, who'd been on the other bus, had already negotiated lodgings when we reached Katmandu. The four of us jammed into a van and took a winding road past small garbage fires in dirt alleyways and slant-eyed pigs drinking from roadside puddles.

This foul-smelling land, overpopulated and bubbling with human waste and humidity, had given me a nagging cough that wouldn't go away.

The Mitre Guesthouse was simple and clean. We devoured veggie chop suey, fried rice, and lumberjack bottles of Tuborg, while pouring out our feelings about the accident. In the middle of our emotional unburdening, Dan exclaimed: "If there weren't so many damn people, these things wouldn't happen!"

"You believe that life is cheap in densely populated countries?" Maria countered testily. "You think that old man won't be mourned?"

"So they place value on life," Dan bellowed sarcastically, "but what about pollution? Can you imagine what this place will look like in ten years and another half billion people? Everything goes on the ground."

"The people in Western countries pollute a hundred times more per capita than developing nations," she retorted.

"The only reason these people pollute less is that they don't have the tools to pollute more. Guess what? The tools are coming!"

"Do you want to shoot the excess population? These are human beings we're talking about."

"That's true, Maria," I joined in, "but what about animals and plants? A week ago, marauding elephants rampaged through the outskirts of Calcutta because their ancient trails had been built over. Animals are becoming extinct all over the world because six billion humans need more wood and space. Personally—and I know this sounds bad in light of the old man being killed—but I'd rather have another elephant than another human."

Maria's look said I'd been placed on her shit list, right beside Dan.

"He's right," said Dan. "We kill rats and cows and fish by the billions. We hunt to keep the animal population in control. What keeps us in control?"

"You cannot compare humans to animals!" Maria's face colored a fighting red. "We have a soul, and the ability to change nature to a higher order. Elephants cannot."

"Elephants," Dan hissed, half under his breath, "are not so arrogant and righteous."

"Hold on, mates," interjected Dave, who'd been content to listen until now. "We are evolving. Technology is changing the world—for the better. Tyrants can't mutilate without being spotted by TV cameras, and if it wasn't for modern birth control, Western families would still be popping out five babies on average.

"I reckon technology will find solutions. It's going fast enough. Remember that village we visited, Dan, the one that recently got electricity? People crowded around the place's only television to watch a drama featuring a modern family of three, with modern conveniences. Don't you think the villagers will dream of these things for their kids, and have fewer children to make the dream come true?"

"Dave makes sense," I agreed. "Maybe that's nature's bigger picture. The faster we develop technology, the quicker we save the environment."

"Seems to me countries like India should be forced to use birth control to speed the process," Dan opined.

"Who are we to judge the way countries solve their internal issues?" Maria said a little wearily. "But if you want to decrease the population of the world, empower women."

We relaxed on our beds, drinking beers. That was the appeal of long-term traveling for me—experiencing new places and lives and trying to get an understanding of things by lively conversation that didn't turn into an entrenched argument.

16

SECOND CHALLENGE: TRAVELING WITH JANET AND AURI

I HAD NEVER ENCOUNTERED SOMEONE so eager to meet me as Auri. Janet had walked up to me at a party at my California home with an even bigger grin than normal. "Do I have a surprise for you!" Behind her was another young woman, dark-haired with a full-faced smile of anticipation and penetrating brown eyes aimed directly at me. Auri was Janet's best friend from early childhood. And her look came from what Janet had told her about me. That made me proud and confirmed Janet's place in my heart.

Short and heavyset with lush, sandy-blond hair, Janet captured your attention because she so obviously enjoyed life. She started out as my daughter Shannon's friend, but quickly worked her way into the hearts of the whole family. Her giggly laugh and mischievous smile were infectious. Janet was instant fun.

We were her "honorary Jewish family." And while she was in high school I was her advisor on parents and money. Janet had a love-hate relationship with money—she loved to spend it but hated her dependency on it. At the tail end of phone conversations with Shannon she'd ask to speak to her advisor and gradually our relationship became a friendship. Being busy with business and family, I often cut short our discussions, but through her I began to refocus on how I related to young people.

Crossing the age barrier was a quality passed down from my grandmother. Having seen what it was like to live a long life, she advised me to make friends with the younger generation. Why put all those years into raising children and not see that they—and their friends—could also become your friends? Of course, being buddies with your kids wasn't always straightforward. We had a family democracy—but while the girls got one vote each, the parents had two votes each.

My relationship with Janet only matured when she was twenty-one and asked me out for dinner in San Francisco. During the meal, I lifted the heavy veil of age and gender and got to see Janet as an individual. Though I had an image among the parents as somewhat of an eccentric, having dinner alone with a young woman was risky.

"What do your parents think of you having dinner with Shannon's dad?"

"They think what all people your age would think."

"What do you think about that?"

"That's their business. What do you think?"

"Married men don't have younger female friends, Janet. Probably in most cases that's proper. But I like the freshness of the younger mind, so it's worth the gamble."

"There you are then. So what are you having for dinner?"

With the veil lifted, Janet matured in my perception and our voices changed to a pitch that befitted equality. She told me she lived for the moment and maneuvered around conflict because she didn't like messing up the moment.

With Auri, we became real friends during my first separation with Kathi. We hung out together, sometimes with her boyfriend, and discussed communication, psychology, philosophy, and subjects others conceal. Auri asked a lot of questions, and her analytical mind delved sensitively into my psyche and my marriage. It could have been dangerous ground, but our relationship remained platonic. If age and gender were severe barriers to close understanding, they were not fatal ones. I crossed those barriers back then, and now I fit in with younger travelers.

Taking a break between her master's and Ph.D. in psychology, Auri was at the midpoint of her six-month sojourn in India. She'd been studying with a community in Lucknow who followed the guru affectionately known as Papaji, a self-realized teacher born in the Punjab in 1910. Papaji's message was "Wake up! You are already free."

Second Challenge: Traveling with Janet and Auri

Janet had arrived two weeks earlier from California, fulfilling a lifelong dream. India had that spiritual connection that drew people. She'd spent her time in Pokhara, a village on Lake Pewa that served as a base camp for treks into the high mountains. The plan was that we would all travel together for two weeks, and then Janet and I would go off by ourselves for another two weeks before parting ways.

While we were all excited at the prospect of being together, I was concerned about Janet's newness to serious traveling. My experience with Joe Reilly in Greece was still fresh.

Auri and I met first. We had a low-key and sweet rendezvous in the tea garden of a three-star hotel in Katmandu. By an amazing coincidence, she'd been partying the night before with two New Yorkers who'd left early in the morning to go rafting—my buddies Derrick and Tom from Delhi!

Arriving at the hotel in the late afternoon, Janet screamed when she saw us: "oh my god! denis! auri! I'm *so* happy." We swayed in a circle, arms gripped around shoulders, kissing and hugging and shaking each other with delight.

"Ooh!" Janet cried in her jellybean bouncy way, "I missed you guys *so* much. We're going to have such a *great* time!" Then Auri and Janet did their own dance, jumping up and down with a playfulness stolen from childhood.

Janet jabbered all her news. First, the going-away party Shannon threw for her in California.

"Shannon got drunk," she said in her high-pitched nasal voice, "and went into a fit of laughter when I told a bunch of people, 'The thing about the Hickeys is that if you make a friend of one of them, you have to take them all. And you can *never* get rid of them!'"

Next was her arrival in Katmandu and trip to Pokhara. "I met this handsome Nepalese guy with beautiful brown eyes!" she said unable to suppress a wide, wicked grin. "His name's Ram. It's spelled R-A-M, but it rhymes with Tom. Anyway, he's really easy-going. We met at a restaurant on the lake, the Elegant View. He owns it!"

"You little weasel, Janet!" said Auri. "Tell us everything."

"He's here in Katmandu staying with a cousin," Janet replied starry-eyed. "He's Hindu. So we call ourselves the Hin-Jews. The cousin offered to take us to Pokhara in his van. It's maybe a hundred miles from here. What do you guys think? You'll love this place. The air is *so* clean."

I loved the sense of home Janet brought from so far away, and the thought of traveling with a modicum of control over the driver appealed to me.

The air on the shores of Lake Pewa was as good as Janet promised. A mist enveloped the lake's further reaches, and through patchy clouds we were presented with the majestic snow-covered peaks of the mighty Himalayas. The mountains nearer to us were carpeted with the bright green of early rice, right down to the edges of the water where water buffaloes and egrets peacefully ranged.

Janet seemed restless.

One evening, while Janet was furthering her romance with Ram, Auri and I hired a boat from a smiling gap-toothed man with stained teeth. Naked boys dove and swam by the dock, and an eight-year-old girl washed the hair of her wailing baby brother trying to keep soapsuds out of his eyes. We rowed, then drifted over the placid lake, content to absorb a quiet so loud you could hear a minnow splash.

"Feel the energy," Auri urged softly. "Papaji says freedom is living in the now."

She picked up a paddle as I slouched comfortably.

"Freedom is also watching someone else paddle," I responded.

"Papaji teaches that we are pure consciousness in the absolute here and now—already and always free! You don't need to attain it. You just need to realize it. He says that by quieting the mind we remove the world of thoughts and desires that the mind believes are real. Papaji says that when your identification with the unreal has vanished, then you will be what you have been, the spirit."

Or spirits, I thought. Nice philosophy. I was in the now.

"When I told my friends about your trip around the world, they asked your age, then said, 'A mid-life crisis trip.' They can't conceive of wanting freedom for its own sake, as opposed to rebellion.

"Knowing where I was going provided a sense of security," I said.

"Why put the pressure on? Happiness is now. People always plan for their happiness tomorrow, but often don't know what makes them happy today."

"I guess I was willing to sacrifice to buy this measure of freedom. I wouldn't want freedom all the time, but it's nice to know it's attainable."

"There's a lot of ego in that statement," she almost whispered. "But I find harmony in it."

The following day, Ram offered to take Janet and me hiking to the top of Sarangkot, a neighboring mountain, to watch the sun set and then rise. We would look down on creation from the top of the world. Auri demurred: "Why trudge up a mountain when you can bask in perfect near-tropical weather?"

We walked along the lake and then through rice paddies with manmade fishponds, past a thatched hut with walls of piled stones and a little girl holding a baby lamb in her arms. An old lady, bent under bundles of green hay, stopped me to pantomime an offer to take her daughter for my bride. The daughter, under her own bundles, flushed red when I acted honored at the prospect.

Ram led the way. He had the quintessential beautiful look of the Nepalese man: melancholy brown eyes with silky eyebrows, shiny black hair, and wiry build. His English was slow and rough. He occasionally described vegetation and local life, and responded to our curiosity about his Hindu faith. He left space for Janet and me to fill each other in on the year that had just passed. I asked her what was underneath the tension in her shoulders—she'd already wangled two massages by wiggling her shoulders and back and saying; "Please, please! I've been so tense lately."

"Things at home with my parents are not good," she said. "They have a hard time seeing me as an adult. I also hated my job and the thought of working ten hours a day and driving in traffic to earn just enough money to survive. I wanted to be out in nature, not staring at four walls and worrying about finding a man. I wasn't happy. So I started studying Hindu philosophy to find another option.

"It's such a transition getting used to the tranquility of traveling, such a contrast to the cynicism I feel sometimes. I needed a change, Denis. I was at a low point in my life."

After the challenging all-day trek, we reached the summit—a plateau with a village of scattered kiosks, huts, and wooden, two-story guesthouses. No electricity, no running water. While Ram talked to friends in the village, Janet and I continued our conversation in a candle-lit guesthouse dining room, which barely accommodated a six-person plank table.

"Don't you think I've changed since you left?" she asked out of nowhere. She didn't specify how, and I made the mistake of not asking. Rather I replied she seemed the same. To me, that wasn't a bad thing, but she was evidently hurt. I then compounded the error of not drawing her out by giving unsolicited advice—a habit I'd learned to avoid with young people during my travels.

My advice was that while traveling a positive attitude buys you everything.

"I don't want to talk about it if that's the way you feel!" was Janet's aggressive response.

Something snapped in me. I had been mellow, but now I had a relentless urge to understand and be understood, to have resolution. I didn't want the issues to follow me as they had in Greece. And I certainly was not yet adept at letting negative energy merely melt away.

"Why not talk about it, so we can get rid of whatever *it* is?"

"Leave me alone."

Whenever there was conflict traveling, you got off the bus. Who needed conflict?

"Janet, I can't travel with someone that gets upset and doesn't want to clear the air. Why would it upset you that I didn't think you had changed?"

"You don't want to travel with me?"

"Not if it's going to be like this!"

Of course, the male need to try to explain myself—as I used to do endlessly with Kathi—kicked in with a predictable results: frustration and Janet storming off to her bare wooden room for the night.

Ram, Janet, and I gathered to watch the rising sun in silence from the apex of the mountain. Janet uncharacteristically wasn't

Second Challenge: Traveling with Janet and Auri

talking to me, and Ram ignored the unspoken conflict. I now wanted to escape, so after initial hellos and comments as to the awesome morning, I wandered off to avoid Janet.

In the chilly mountain air, a girl in a baggy dress, rings in her ear, and snot in her nose cleared sleep from her eyes. Her mother, rings in her nose and baby in her belly, prepared chai for a wrinkled old man sitting on his haunches. As he waited he adjusted his turban and smoked. They must have slept outside. They were oblivious to the beauty of the crimson sunrise. The glow illuminated the fog-shrouded Himalayan peaks. Mist seeped down the mountain past where I stood, swirling around and between the huts to the green valley below. Almost as if the gray clouds were searching for the source of the Nepalese music echoing in the distance.

The silent conflict with Janet lingered even after we'd left Ram in Nepal and returned to India. Neither of us was willing to practice humility. Auri chose not to get involved. She instead brought us to Papaji's community in Lucknow. If our conflict was due to the power of ego, this was a good place to explore it.

The first morning, attending a circular group discussion, I sat on a pillow on a waxed floor next to Auri. Suddenly, a precocious ten-year-old girl asked me point blank: "Who are you, Denis?"

"I'm me!" I said. The simplicity of the response got a favorable reaction. But I couldn't leave well enough alone and elaborated with a loquacity that drew yawns. Afterwards, David, one of the longer-term disciples, handed me a book by Papaji, *Who Are You?*

At first, I figured I'd been had by the little girl, but I quickly came to admire the theme of the book. It postulated that by stripping yourself of desire you could come to the true self, the spirit.

"It is desire that fucks us up," David agreed. "When we get what we want it's never as good as we thought."

At the conclave, the group encouraged Janet and I to talk things out. Janet blamed me for what happened. I said I wanted to continue my journey alone. At that point, Janet cried. We eventually admitted to each other (and the ten or so people in the circle) that we were substituting the other for people in our lives that frustrated us. That was it. End of story. Except that I was now the bad guy once again—if not in Janet's mind, then my own!

To smooth things over, I treated Janet, Auri, and David to dinner at a restaurant where the guests were all foreigners—Western or Japanese. We ate French food and laughed like old times. But the estrangement needed time to heal. I was disappointed that I allowed our disagreement to dominate the time we spent together and for not heeding Papaji's advice: "Quiet the mind and remove the world of thoughts that the mind believes are real." As with Joe in Greece, instead of quieting the mind I wanted to run from discomfort.

The following day, the three of us explored the dusty city. Outside a vegetable store, I sat on my haunches next to a dark Indian begging on a rutted concrete sidewalk. His left leg was a foot shorter than the right, his legs pretzeled at right angles, and neither arms nor legs had flesh on them. I gave him money and asked how he got that way. Even though I didn't speak Hindi I felt he understood my question and answered. An answer I didn't understand. Then he flashed an infectious, wide, betel-juiced smile and grabbed my hand, pointing to the money and thanking me. The shop owner walked out, handed him a bowl of rice and lentils and told me the beggar had lived outside his store for twenty years. This horribly crippled man living a minuscule existence was happy. That was the power of positive energy. And yet so many fortunate people I knew found reasons to be unhappy.

Although Janet and I parted on good terms in Lucknow, the bloom was off the rose. I wrote Chimene that my new persona challenged old relationships and I hadn't acquired the skill to deal with it. How in hell would I cope with Frank Zolfo during our two weeks of travel together in Thailand? Frank was the most dynamic person I'd ever met.

The other side of the coin—and you could always find another side—was that I felt comfortable Janet and I were meant to travel together for the time we did and no longer. Something good or bad could happen along the road, and if you were positive, something good would happen as a result. Just ask the beggar.

Still, I knew I should have asked Janet what she wanted to change, or who she wanted to become.

17

LAUGHING WITH A
DEAD GURU IN PUNE

AFTER A FEW DAYS IN Bombay, I went to board a train southeast to Pune to visit the ashram of Bhagwan Shree Rajneesh, the man who never died, only visited earth between 1931 and 1990. In America, he was widely known as the sex guru who owned lots of luxury cars and got kicked out of Oregon. However, I was interested in learning more about meditation and whether it could assist me in changing a couple of bad habits.

Walking nonchalantly towards the station in Bombay, I failed to notice—and this will forever remain my worst visual oversight—human feces on the sidewalk. I promptly slid on the excrement like a surfboarder, my left sandal catching anything the right missed. It took all my balance to avoid a complete wipeout. The brown stuff oozed everywhere and started caking like mud between my toes. Wholesome it was not. But the thing I'd learned about India was that while these things were likely to happen, there was also usually a solution nearby.

In this case, the solution lay just inside the station: a twenty-foot-long trough with iron sinks and faucets normally used for more routine hygiene, such as brushing teeth. Nevertheless, I wound up sitting athletically on top of the sinks scrubbing off the feces as if it was the most normal thing in the world.

Things picked up once on the train. A middle-aged man with a slightly hooked nose immediately offered to buy me breakfast.

With a handshake, he introduced himself as Subhash Deo, and then placed his hand on his heart. In the course of asking me a few personal questions, he won my immediate adoration by expressing surprise at my age.

Subhash was an electrical engineer and eager to fill me in on his country. The finance minister was India's most important person, he said, TV was becoming widespread, and India would be a country to be reckoned with because of the growth of the middle class and its wealth of engineers. Why, I wondered, with the magnitude of its financial problems, didn't the US have a minister of finance? Treasury secretary was not the same thing. But not everything in India was perfect according to Subhash.

"Muslims pose a very grave problem. We Hindus believe in birth control, but not Muslims. They multiply like locusts. After the partition between India and Pakistan in the forties, there were thirty-five million Muslims in India. Now they are around a hundred million—over ten percent of the population! Also we are having serious issues with Pakistan over Kashmir. Pakistan is Muslim, you know."

He added that the government was drastically short of funds for education, and that inequities in the system also caused a major problem between Muslims and Hindu populations.

"Why?"

"Muslims do not have the same education level as Hindus, nor do they have a middle class. So, you see, the tax burden falls on the middle class. With mechanization putting millions out of work, who will support the unemployed and more babies? You do not have this problem."

The influence of the religious right in America had made it difficult for world organizations with US funding to encourage birth control. But would those same Christian fundamentalists support the growing multitudes in poor countries?

Over our breakfast of oily scrambled eggs on toast, rice pudding, and chai, I wanted to expand my knowledge of the Indian philosophy of meditation.

"My understanding is that to know who you are, you meditate to strip away desire. What's left is your spirit."

"I should say straightway you should see how people live here," he said, pointing to the shacks by the railroad line. "One gets to know one another in such neighborhoods. If one has a cold, or marries, or dies, or finds something valuable, the whole neighborhood is knowing. Privacy is internal, and desire is a very limited commodity."

I didn't quite follow the link to meditation, but his explanation was a start at understanding how India is the meditation capital of the world.

Subhash was going to the wedding of his brother and invited me to join him. I was very tempted but declined, opting instead to stick to my plan.

Halfway through my two-kilometer walk to Bhagwan's ashram, I began to feel a powerful pulsing energy. The tidy street leading to the ashram was lined with rickshaws, touts, and kiosks hawking fruit, T-shirts, trinkets portraying Hindu gods, and body-length maroon or white robes. Disciples, who were already wearing the robes, walked purposefully to and from the main gate, not looking at anything or anyone that wasn't a companion, a book, or blank space. You couldn't buy a smile.

New arrivals were welcomed with an HIV test before admission. If the test proved negative, inductees would receive passes with names and pictures. A maroon robe was worn at the ashram during daytime, with white reserved for the daily 6:40 p.m. meeting of the Osho White Robe Brotherhood—Osho was the name by which Bhagwan Shree Rajneesh was now known.

I returned the next day for the HIV test results. I'd passed. So, I haggled with an eight-year-old clubfoot boy over the price of the maroon and white robes, promptly donned the maroon one, and entered the extensive, manicured, lush green grounds. Two stylish-looking women with long, loose hair conducted the orientation session for newcomers. In soft voices, they informed us they'd been with Osho for seventeen and twenty-one years respectively. That Osho did not die—he'd left his body that was dead. The purpose of the robes was to join people's energy. And drugs were forbidden.

"The commune is for seekers who come to immerse themselves in the energy of the Buddha field through meditation, therapy, and Osho Multiversity," the older one explained. "The Multiversity teaches centering, healing, Zen martial arts, meditation, mysticism, Tibetan pulsing—which is directing pulse-beats towards areas damaged by negative sexual experiences—and transformation to intimacy by playfully accepting and expressing ourselves."

We were then taken along slate walkways across the immense complex, where three thousand people studied and worked. The air was clean and the landscape inviting. Modern buildings sat serenely amid lush gardens and ponds. The tour leader pointed out dorms, mediation rooms, cafeterias, classrooms, a library, exercise rooms, tennis, basketball and badminton courts, a massage room, sauna, and a swimming pool with a black bottom. Buddha Hall, where the Brotherhood convened, looked like a circus tent, only it had a white marble floor and you had to pass through a metal detector because Osho was paranoid about being shot—the result of constant hounding in Oregon by the CIA and FBI.

The overall atmosphere was one of people trying to rid themselves of the rush of Western society in order to find nothing less than the elusive *self*. However, while the greenery and fresh air invigorated me, people walked like zombies with few smiles, little eye contact, and no hellos. Then my elusive self whispered: "Give the Westerners a fucking break, be positive about them." All of a sudden, I noticed the hugging and laughing.

The following morning, new inductees were given individual counseling sessions. My counselor, Eric, was a young-looking forty-nine-year-old Jewish bachelor. (I didn't know why I'd bumped into so many Jewish people in India, but it did seem to be a trend.) He led me to a small, sterile room with a desk, two simple chairs, and a window to the outside.

After some initial questions to assess my background and interest in the commune, he asked me why I was traveling.

"I wanted the whole dream, to experience new feelings, and see for myself what I watched on TV through someone else's eyes." Always a different answer.

I reversed the questioning process, eliciting from him that he fought in Vietnam and afterwards worked for a chain of hotels, making enough to retire comfortably.

"After Nam," he said with a smooth Boston accent, "I constantly asked myself who I was fighting and why. Osho explained that the rebellion was within me. That was twenty years ago. I've been with him ever since."

"In Oregon? What did you do in Oregon?"

"Building a commune—the city of Rajneeshpuram."

"I'm curious, what were the Rolls Royces all about?"

"Ah, that! Osho liked to piss people off, you know. To flaunt American materialism and expose Christian hypocrisy. He never believed in eliminating all desire. He liked women and creature comforts."

"How about the robes? Must have gone over great in Oregon."

"Like poison!" He snickered. "Cowboys and farmers."

"So what caused the exodus?"

"The women fucked it up," he said matter of factly. "Guys like you and me were burned out. We wanted to drive the tractors. The women ran the commune. You have no idea how spiteful they can be. Lots of jealousy for Osho's attention. We made a lot of mistakes—the robes, lots of sex. But we've learned since then. HIV tests, no drugs, robes only on campus, male and female interaction in the administration of the campus."

"I guess men and women need to work together."

"Like a lock and key."

"What does meditation mean to you?" I asked, getting on to the subject I wanted to explore. Eric remained relaxed as he scanned me closely for about a minute.

"Meditation allows me to look inside, to forgive myself for the times I'm an asshole. That's not me, but it's in me. We are many people."

"That idea of many people inside seems to be a theme in India," I observed. "Is yours a typical explanation of meditation?"

"Osho said meditation opens doors to light, and suddenly what you were doing in darkness becomes clear. He said modern people try to understand the world but forget its most influential ingredient: our selves. They put the childish 'I' in charge of the spiritual crowd within us. The 'I' feels superior and separates from the others, lets thoughts, emotions, and desires control life.

"Osho teaches the human mind is obsessed with activity because the more active you are, the more your ego can be fulfilled. He watched Western aerobics and devised a meditation that is so madly active that the illusion of 'I' is thrown out of the system. He said only after this deep catharsis can you fall down into inactivity and have a glimpse of the world that is not the world of effort, but the world of harmony."

"Very nicely put. Massachusetts, right?" I asked, comfortably changing the subject again.

"Boston. Went to BU."

"You must have gone there around the time I was at Providence College. You guys had a good hockey team. I went to Providence for the basketball team. When I was there, each October, we'd peer through the window of the gym to watch the new basketball recruits. Now Providence students are scholars and the basketball team sucks. I'm not sure it's a good tradeoff."

"I watched hockey players," Eric said. "You like to control with questions."

"Questions were my trade in business and social ally. They allow me to get comfortable. And, yes, give me a certain amount of control."

"I admire your trek around the world. Why not stay for a while, take time to explore yourself?"

"I'd be on the outside looking in. Before leaving California, I washed dishes at Esalen to transition from businessman to traveler. It takes a while to make the adjustment to a community, and a year isn't a long time to see the world. Besides, I'm not used to the stressful energy here. I feel the buzz in my legs and stomach."

"Judging by the ease with which you move, I'd say you could teach us a thing or two."

"The slow pace of India has gotten into my body. I'm beginning to understand the derivation of the Indian philosophy of self-realization. I'm told it derived from the cramped living conditions—obviously not inside this compound."

"I think so," he said.

"I still have a lot to learn, and the road is waiting to teach me. Maybe I will learn silence and watchfulness instead of questions.

"Oh, by the way, Eric," I asked, sensing the interview was at an end, "why do you say Osho's spirit didn't die?"

"Osho said the body begins the process of dying when we're born. But that the spirit continues to grow after the body dies."

I rose and I walked to the door.

"We beat you guys in hockey in '66!" Eric added as a playful farewell.

At 5:35 a.m., I passed through the Buddha Hall's metal detector and joined the dynamic meditation. Four hundred of us fit easily into the pavilion, which was the size of a high-school gym. A large picture of the white-bearded Osho was centered on a gray altar at the front. While at the sides, insect lamps flashed bright blue as they fried bugs. Naturally, I couldn't resist a slide on the marble floor.

Dynamic meditation consisted of five fifteen-minute segments designed to start the day by releasing stagnant energy. *First*, we breathed chaotically and rapidly through the nose, infusing fresh oxygen and energy, hyperventilating, and shaking to the rhythm of drums played by a pair of musicians. *Second*, we expressed the energy: laughing, screaming, crying, jumping, dancing, whatever came to mind. *Third*, we jumped up and down to drums, yelling "hoo" on each landing. *Fourth*, we raised arms straight into the air in silence. *Last*, we rejoiced by dancing to a piccolo, light drums, and guitar.

The counterpoint to the dynamic meditation was the late afternoon kundalini meditation. Its four fifteen-minute segments were deigned to relieve tension built during the day. At 4:15 p.m. sharp, one thousand barefoot seekers shook their bodies for fifteen minutes to loosen up, and then danced independently for another fifteen minutes. The drums beat gently for the first segment, and vigorously for the second.

I love to dance, to move fluidly to each beat. The drumming reached into my limbs, making them strive for balance in movement. And the rhythms motivated my arms and hands to draw patterns in the air. At first, my movements were awkward, but then a sense of integration arose. Around me, the Westerners swayed, while the Asians jerked stiffly to the beat. The music stopped, we closed eyes, and stood absolutely still for the third fifteen minutes. Continuing in silence, we lay down motionless for the final fifteen-minute segment.

After a dinner of Western vegetarian food, I joined two thousand people, mostly women from the affluent cultures (no Indians or blacks), attending the White Robe Brotherhood. The women proved that the white robes need not be dowdy as they showed off their silk, lace, and fine cotton. As we waited, many people sat, kneeled, or meditated. While others, including me, danced to drums and the sound of the harp. A few sisters set up a video and large screen.

Suddenly the drums began to crescendo. As they peaked, everyone threw their hands in the air and shouted "OSHO!" The verbal orgasm was hokey I thought, but I yelled nevertheless. They began chanting: "OSHO! OSHO! OSHO!" Not me. I was prepared to dislike this guy. Gurus had too much ego, I thought, whether corporate, religious, or political. I enjoyed discourse and preferred to think of myself as equal to anyone. I marveled at how women fussed over gurus. By thirty, you'd think they would have had their fill of all-powerful men.

Osho looked out from the monitor seemingly to catch all eyes individually. In the Buddha Hall, the present-day Brotherhood folded hands in prayer, invoked his name, and bowed to his video reincarnation. Osho looked like an Indian Santa Claus, except that his lips and cherubic face displayed passionless rigidity. Oh great! Another guy with a frozen face.

On screen, an adoring woman stepped up to Osho, who sat on an ornate throne. She took a question from a golden platter she carried like a waitress and read it aloud. It concerned conditional love.

"Other masters, Jesus and Mohammed, required conditions for love. I accept you unconditionally." Osho spoke slowly and precisely, as if each word had special meaning. He was charming. And I observed his face was pliable, not rigid after all. He talked for a while about love, then with a subtle impish look began to relate a story.

"A proud father gives his son twenty dollars and says, 'Go to the whorehouse and spend this.' The kid stops off at his grandmother's on the way. She says, 'Where are you going?' He tells her. She says, 'Take me and save twenty dollars.' The kid returns home with the twenty dollars and tells his dad how he saved money. The dad becomes enraged and screams, 'You made love with my mother?' The kid says, 'Hey, why not? You make it with my mother all the time.'"

Two thousand people in white robes exploded into laughter. Three years after he left his body, he had everyone in stitches. What a guy!

"Sometimes when you speak," the woman in the video read another question, "I get a vision of living a kind of Zorba the

Greek life—eat, drink, and be merry, lusty, and passionate. Other times, I feel you're saying the way is to sit silently, watchful, and unmoving, like a monk. Can we be both Zorbas, moved by passion and desire, and Buddhas, dispassionate, cool, and calm?"

"That is the ultimate synthesis," the guru spoke, "when Zorba the Greek becomes Zorba the Buddha. Zorba is beautiful, but something is missing. Eat, drink, and be merry is perfectly good in itself. But it is not enough. It is repetitive. Only a mediocre mind can go on being happy with it. Sooner or later the question is bound to arise: 'What is the point of it all?' The question is always there, persistently there, pounding on your heart for an answer.

"Buddha himself was Zorba. He had all the beautiful women available in his country, the most beautiful palaces, all the luxury that was possible in those days. Hence, when he was only twenty-nine he became utterly frustrated. It is repetitive. He escaped from the palace, the women, the riches, and the luxury.

"So, I am not against Zorba the Greek, because Zorba the Greek is the very foundation of Zorba the Buddha. I am all for this world because I know that the other world can only be experienced through this world. I will not say to you: become a monk. A monk is one who has moved against Zorba—an imitator greedy for the other world. You can earn the higher, only by going through the agony and ecstasy of the lower. Before a lotus becomes a lotus, it has to move through the mud."

My mind spun trying to grasp the meaning of Osho's words: Zorba was the foundation of Buddha. I recalled how Eric had said meditation allowed him to look inside, opened the doors to light, clarity. It was a kind of focus. Then I saw that there was nothing intrinsically wrong with the controller in me. His focus on family and money allowed me to travel. He was the foundation personality, the Zorba that needed to be synthesized with the others in me to achieve change.

18

BARNEY IN GOA: PIECING TOGETHER HOW VISIONS WORK

NO MORE FUCKING BUS RIDES! I'd endured a terrifying night driving over mountains, thrown one way then the other as we careened around narrow curves and passed gear-grinding trucks. Fortunately, by the light of morning—and following a change of driver—our bus was gently weaving along a red dirt road in the lowland plains on the other side of the mountains towards Goa. We safely passed the horse- and oxen-pulled wagons amid fields of coconut trees and pineapple bushes. A fresh breeze drifted inland from the Arabian Sea, carrying with it sweet smells garnered from the fields.

Legend had it that Goa was created by Parashuram, an incarnation of the god Vishnu, who in search of a completely pure piece of land shot an arrow into the sea, commanding the waves to retreat to the point where the arrow landed. I believed the legend.

In a little town that reminded me of my childhood—oak trees and the smell of roasting nuts—I rented a small motorbike and drove to Anjuna Beach. I spent the day simply walking along the clean golden sand. By nightfall, the gruff cough that had been with me through dusty India had miraculously disappeared.

I breakfasted on porridge (oatmeal), roasted bananas, and a mango yogurt lassi with honey at a comely open-air cafe overlooking the ocean. Da-licious! Then got chatting with an engaging young Englishman at the next table, who eventually carried over his chai, ashtray, and smoking cigarette to join me.

He stood tall, maybe six-five, gangling like a Great Dane before filling out, and had the broad shoulders of a whooping crane. With a goatee, his wide, round face looked caught between teenager and adult. Aware of his size, he moved with English formality, careful not to knock things over.

"The name's Barney, mate. But if you like formality, you can call me Barnaby."

"I'll stick with Barney."

"I couldn't help noticing that you're a people watcher."

"My favorite hobby. People are interesting."

As with other travelers I met, our conversation quickly bound us together. We spent the day motoring through northwestern Goa along one-lane roads through coconut tree-lined lagoons. We munched peanut brittle while watching a cricket game, and chatted to helpful people in thatched-hut communities. Their huts may have been small but their smiles were broad. We marveled as a dark-skinned Indian climbed a coconut tree to chop down palm branches. He had circled his legs and arms with ropes to shimmy himself up and down the towering trunk. The locals must have thought the white guys on motorbikes equally exotic.

We boarded an old ferry that looked like an oyster dredge. Our destination was a stretch of soft white beach. All the while we talked—about everything from politics and psychic phenomena to making love, nipple rings, and the effect of hugging. We exchanged stories such as the time Barney's mother caught him getting a blow job in the back seat of a car during his uncle's wedding.

"What did she say?"

"Driving home from the wedding, without even a ruddy glance in my direction, she said, 'Interesting way to uphold the family honor, Barnaby!'"

Barney spoke a hip version of middle-class English and mixed different accents with a grossness of speech that somehow stayed within the bounds of propriety. He flashed a natural charm, smoked incessantly, and struck me as an extremely intelligent individual—moments without discussion or laughter were remarkable because of their rarity.

The soft white beach was home to meandering cows and Goan men staring at Western women, who bared their bosoms despite local customs. Meanwhile, Goan women swathed in vibrantly colored salwar-kameez carried bundles of clothes or pineapples, coconuts, and mangos in baskets on their heads to sell to tourists.

Barney told me he'd struggled with boredom and grades and was very disruptive at school, so his parents sent him to a private one where he skipped two grades and graduated early. "I thought about attending Harvard. I had loads of ideas but too little ambition. I decided to travel." He'd been on the road for eight months so far.

"At first, I was afraid to leave home for Thailand. How would I bloody well survive? Two days in Bangkok and I thought to myself: 'I reckon I can do this.' The fear left." The travel had given him some insight into the world and he was thinking about going to school to become a political journalist.

"The great empire is buggered," he complained. "Political parties are so polarized they play tug of war rather than functioning as a unit. They groupthink! One accuses, the other refuses, and then they switch sides. The system needs to get rid of the nobles and get fresh new gobs—that means mouths, squire. We need understanding.

"For instance, drugs won't go away because the heavy users are taking them to escape their wretched lives. Organizing a committee of people that have never taken drugs to fix the problem is like mounting an assault on Everest dressed only in thongs. They might as well play with their tallywackers all day.

"But I feel positive about the future. We're making brilliant progress on recycling."

Then Barney posed the same question everyone had: why wasn't I traveling with my wife?

"When my girls left home, I guess the little boy inside got lost."

"So you're traveling to bring back the little boy?"

"Maybe! When I was young I had an old, leaky, blue boat with a fifteen-horsepower Evinrude outboard motor. If I wanted to escape, I'd whisk away at full throttle down the creek and into the bay, wind rushing in my face, my hair flying in all directions, smells of salt and seaweed filling my lungs, the boat fucking bouncing from wave to wave. I felt an intimate sense of freedom in that boat that I never forgot."

"I read this book, squire, *King, Warrior, Magician, Lover*. The author talks about when men were men. He says we've lost our role model for maleness. Growing up, we blokes can't wait to shed the little boy who creates fantasy, so we bottle him up like a genie until the right time. We spend our lives being proper and by the time we look for the genie, he's gone. But I'm never going to lose that little boy."

Barney then, as everyone did, asked the *other* question.

"So have you remained faithful to your wife during your sojourn around the sphere?"

"How do little boys and faithfulness relate?" I answered elusively.

"One life, one love!"

"Ah, the freshness of youth."

"Out of the mouths of babes."

"Okay. The answer to your question is that for one year of travel I have placed no limitations on what I do. My wife knows. After twenty-five years of being the faithful servant to the queen and ladies-in-waiting, I deserve to let the genie out for a while."

"While I ponder that nugget of potentially flawed wisdom on my journey for truth, perhaps you can educate me on what it is like to be married for twenty-six years?"

"Let's see, we fell in love and our brain chemistry only had one purpose."

"I'm with you, pal."

"After a while, the brain chemistry settled down a bit and we were *in love*. We had a ten-year honeymoon. I couldn't wait to go to bed, wrap myself around my wife, and lose the cares of the world in her softness. Then we began changing as people and the opposites that attracted us began to grate."

"Fascinating! We work like the universe!"

"We're still in that vast ocean called love—we do love each other! But I don't exactly get love. People say it all the time, but what does it mean? Do you really love someone if you don't commit to work out issues, to keep your sex life vibrant, to spend time together with friends? Kundera said love is an interrogation."

The brightly garbed Goan beach hawkers spotted us from fifty yards away. They must have sensed I was hungry for a pineapple.

"To answer your question precisely," I continued, "after all this time we are friends with lots in common and lots of issues. There's lots of damaged trust, but also a kind of trust that becomes more flexible as time goes on. That's it in a nutshell."

"My mom and dad had issues, too," Barney offered, "and somehow had the tenacity to work through them. Someone said there are only a few human stories, they just get repeated over and over. Hey, do you believe that old saying: 'Absence makes the heart grow fonder?'"

"Yeah, I do."

"Old sayings are fuck-in' wicked! They're honed by centuries of experience."

"On that subject, what do you Brits mean when you say, 'Bob's your uncle'?"

"Bob's your uncle, Fanny's your aunt. You know, like 'Voila!' There you go."

"Educate me on British idioms, O magician."

Barney tossed a handful of sand in the air and sat up with his legs crossed. Words poured from his lips in rapid fire. "Well, there's *bollocks*, which means bullshit. *Cheers* is thanks. *Geezer* is like your Mac in America. Good-looking women are *babes* or *robo babes*. *Sorted* is when things are tickety-boo. And then there's—"

"Nah, you don't say 'tickety-boo,' do you?" I laughed.

"*Dicksplat* is a really stupid bloke. What you call a piece of ass we call *chassis*. And when you say someone's an asshole we'd say *knobhead* or *twat*, which technically speaking is a pregnant goldfish. That's just a few. I'll educate you more as we go along, Yank."

"Thanks!"

"Twenty-six years," he said, returning to my marriage, "that's the *dog's bollocks*. In this context, it means simply the best. Do you still make love as much as you used to?"

"That's a relative question," I said with a grin. I was refreshed by his directness. "I still have lust for my wife. But time and familiarity definitely affects lovemaking, don't you think?"

"I'd offer my left nut to be qualified to answer. Your Yank basketball players are *my* heroes in that department—the male equivalents of queen bees."

"Isn't there a little of the queen bee in all of us?"

"The guys that exaggerate their sex life bugger me. They ought to get a slap in the face for the insecurities they cause others."

"You are so funny, Barney. What do you believe in?"

"Let me think. Balance. And staying awake to notice little things like flowers jutting from decaying walls."

The women hawkers (and a few cows) had surrounded us. One of the women wore earrings that cascaded to her neck and a gold-plated nose ring the size of a silver dollar.

"You do business with me!" she commanded, flashing her impish brown eyes. "How much you give me for hat? Your best price!"

Was Goa where the Dahab girls migrated after they turned fifteen? Those young Egyptians had charmed and bargained with me as if they were Mae West—all to peddle string bracelets and gamble at backgammon.

"He's got the money." I pointed at Barney.

She didn't fall for it.

"You buy shirt from *me*. Not much, you my last customer. I give you special deal."

Same sassiness as the Dahab girls, same bobbles on their sashes.

"How much?"

"Five hundred rupees."

"Are you kidding?"

"How much you pay? Your best price! Good for you, good for me."

"This real silk?"

"Yes, yes!"

"Why does it smell?" Laughter.

"Sell me that small bag for eight rupees. I will give to your sister as present."

"Ten rupees!"

I bought the bag and a pineapple. Then we hung out with the saleswoman and her younger sister who wore yellow and red pants with stars. The sister was fifteen and had been working the beach for seven years. She was getting married in three months to a boy she had never met. Did she want to marry this boy? It was the family's decision, she said, marriages were a joining of families. But she also added she was excited to be getting married.

The night before I left for Calcutta, Barney and I found a hostel near the airport on the edge of a horseshoe-shaped beach. We returned my motorbike. Barney would take me to the airport on his. On the far end of the beach, a fisherman unloaded the day's catch. And two busloads of Indian tourists rolled up their pants and saris and attacked the aqua surf. I was always amazed at how people massed together. My inclination was to separate from the group.

Barney and I sipped beer in a restaurant swathed in palm leaves as crimson and pink rays illuminated the heavens. As night descended, the sea rumbled, crickets rubbed legs, frogs croaked, and flashes of distant lightning torched the darkness, lighting up the sky and water as if it was daylight. We chased crabs under the moon and stretched on the sand.

"Yesterday, you talked about a boy's dream," Barney said. "You believe dreams come true, squire?"

"I think dreams and visions are live energy fields created over eons by people who have passion for the same desire," I explained. "Think about this, Barney. It's been just forty years since the invention of the integrated circuit. We've just scratched the surface of energy. It manifests itself in radio waves, electricity, and force fields like planets and plants—or humans. What we know is a nit at the end of a dog's tail compared to what we will know a thousand years from now. So why not visions as their own energy fields?"

"Cheers, I love it! But what about the view that desire is bad, that it masks the real self? Wasn't it that bloke Tom Robbins who said, 'If a person forswears pleasure in order to avoid misery, what has he gained?'"

"Maybe it's not bloody desire," I said, borrowing Barney's vernacular, "but the proliferation of desire that trashes us."

"So you think visions are alive! What a delicious concept."

He smiled. We paused to listen to the crickets that nearly drowned out the pounding sea. Then I shared some of the conversations and observations I'd made in India, such as the discussion with Derrick about visions, the view of the old man on the bus about multiple spirits within our host body, the chance meeting with the German couple at the Taj Mahal, and my thoughts at Osho's ashram about focus and change.

"I've got pieces of a puzzle that I'm trying to fit together," I concluded. "A vision I believe is alive, a body that is host for multiple spirits, an energy that seems like coincidence, and habits I want to change. I know this from personal experience: if a person focuses their passion long enough on a simply stated vision, they can achieve it."

"Check this out, dude, let's say that desire creates energy compatible with an existing force field, which itself is created by others with the same desire! Too many desires probably dissipate or scatter energy. But let's suppose that to achieve a vision, the desire needs to be simple and focused. For example, when I was twelve I knew I could train my mind to levitate, but decided it would take a bloody lifetime and I had other desires. I couldn't focus. In order to make a vision come true, we need to focus, really focus, to the extent the desire dominates your life."

"That's a mouthful," I said with a laugh. "But it's not *bollocks*! That's exactly how entrepreneurs think."

"Cheers. Now let's say for discussion's sake, that our lives can have as many doorways leading to our future as we have desires. If we focus on a particular desire, it becomes a vision that reduces the number of doorways we can walk through—"

"And the doorways all lead in the same direction!"

"Spot on! Now how do multiple personalities or spirits fit into the equation? Assuming you and I have one dominant spirit with its own set of talents, then multiple spirits living together would have a smorgasbord of talents. It makes perfect sense to me, that the spirit inside your host body with the talent to achieve a particular vision would dominate the other spirits."

"Or they would work together to achieve a common goal, like a company. The executive staff concept with the CEO as leader."

"Spot on again. Now, what about coincidences like meeting the German couple?"

"Maybe coincidence isn't arbitrary. Maybe it's energy that connects things. You know, nudges us towards certain doorways to the future, puts a light on them, so to speak. And the stronger and more focused the vision, the bigger the light, no?"

"So, squire, to get it sorted out and put the puzzle together, let's say that focus on a particular vision taps the shoulder of the spirit within our host body, among many spirits perhaps, that has the talent to achieve the particular vision. This spirit becomes the CEO. Then, what if the CEO's *focus* creates this *connecting energy* that illuminates doorways in life leading to the vision's energy field, thus, connecting the CEO to the power of the vision?"

"Fucking-A, that's brilliant, Barney. So practically speaking, I can change from being a controlling person to a traveler by focusing on a vision of the person I want to be. The secret of changing habits, then, is to visualize who you want to be and practice being that person. The energy will lead us to the right doors."

"Change the energy, change the person!" Barney said with a flourish.

Early the next morning with the sun shining brightly, Barney took me on his motorbike to the airport. Riding on back, I told him there'd been four airline accidents in India that week. "I calculated," I said, "that based on airports I'd visited, India operates no more than eighty commercial domestic jets. Four accidents and eighty planes. Suddenly traveling by bus is beginning to look appealing."

"Relax, mate," Barney said, "you're a lucky bloke. Things will turn out tickety-boo."

At the departure gate, we hugged goodbye. Barney bent down looking a bit lost. We were two travelers faced simultaneously with the loss of friendship and looking forward to the thrill of the next adventure.

"I have the feeling," I said, "that you will be in my life for a long time to come."

19.

OH! CALCUTTA! PROSTITUTES, LUNCH WITH A BEGGAR, KIBITZING WITH MOTHER TERESA

OH! CALCUTTA! ITS GRAND BUILDINGS and wide streets, once the epitome of colonial elegance, were decaying relics in a human jungle. Stand on any street corner for an hour in Calcutta and you'd see something you'd never seen before. "Visit Calcutta," my nephew had advised. "It's the soul of India."

I took a room in a cheap hotel on dust-laden Sudder Street. The street was a microcosm of the city. On the sidewalk, a mother with sagging breasts and cascading black hair suckled an infant pestered by flies. A depleted woman fingered clothes that hung from a line stretching along the face of a redbrick building, while below a pavement-dwelling family hand-pumped water. Each member in turn stood wide-legged to bathe and brush their teeth using their fingers. Nude children loitered, fiddled, and practiced handstands.

Brushing off defeat from trying to fix a leaky toilet in my room, I stepped out into the stillborn air. A boy of five sauntered close by asking for rupees. Competing for space on the hard dirt street were kiosks, beggars, scarred dogs, trampled garbage, forties-style black taxis with orange roofs, human-powered rickshaws, and vendors hauling rice and coconuts in wooden wheelbarrows. You couldn't spit without hitting someone—and everyone seemed to spit. Sudder Street connected to hundreds of streets just like it. It was how I imagined medieval Paris in summer must have been—but maybe a little more worn and with a few more souls.

I took a begging mother and her baby to a food stand to purchase dry milk. Some of my most satisfying moments were giving away tired clothes, money, and leftover restaurant food to beggars. What were a few rupees? In past years, I was too busy making money to have time for charity.

A skinny old man with gray hair, dull brown eyes, and sallow skin casually walked up to me. He was pimping women, hash, and black market money. I refused each offer, but he quietly persisted. A sudden impulse overtook me. Some might call it a sleazy thought. Such is the nature of curiosity.

"I'll tell you what," I said. "I do not want a woman, but I will pay you twenty rupees to show me the places you take people."

"Take people?"

"Yes, take me to bordellos where the women stay. I want you to be my guide. I am only interested in seeing."

"One hundred rupees," he said with a shrug.

"Thirty!"

A deal was struck.

We set off along narrow back streets. I kept a wary eye out for danger, mentally mapping the direction from Sudder Street. Two guys squatted on their haunches, one plucking a needle from the other's arm and wiping it on his pants. It was the first time I saw hard drugs in the Third World. We dodged a herd of rank-smelling goats. A white dog with pink skin chewed raw over half its body and a cord of sticky saliva hanging from its mouth moved like a slug in the middle of the road, as if awaiting the impact of a careless taxi. Was Calcutta the overcrowded future African cites were destined for?

A half-mile later, between corners of a tenement complex, we came to a ramshackle wooden staircase that looked like a fire escape. I nervously followed the creaking old man, looking around for escape routes and lurking thugs. What the hell was I getting into? And how far would I go? Fear and curiosity had obliterated sexual desire for the time being, but what lurked in my unconscious?

We opened the door at the top of the stairs and a madam wrapped in an emerald sari, smiling to please, showed me into a neat room with a small cot covered by a clean red woolen blanket. She patted the bed for me to sit as a jolly, plump lady came in and settled alongside me. The coquettish new arrival poked and pinched me playfully, giggling at my surprise. She made me laugh and her charms began to titillate.

"You like me?" she asked, pointing to her bosom.

"Fifteen dollars," the old man said. "Top of the line."

"Tell her she has captivated my heart," I said, determined to remain on my mission, "but unfortunately I cannot afford her." The price came down, but my resistance held. She pouted and ran her fingers through my hair in a last, fruitless effort to relieve me of cash.

The old man and I found ourselves back on the streets of Calcutta, which now echoed to the sound of firecrackers. The city was celebrating Kali Puja—a festival in honor of the goddess Kali. I was still curious about the sex trade and asked if there were brothels for those of more meager means.

As we maneuvered through a host of kiosks towards our new destination, a couple of kids scared the shit out of me by flipping a cherry bomb at my feet. I went straight to one of the kiosks, bought a handful of firecrackers, and, to cheers and encouragement from onlookers, ran after the little buggers lighting and tossing the fireworks along the way. Boys will be boys.

The old man led me to a single-story fenced-in tenement of huts. A place of serious faces where the women were thin. He delivered me to a dark, humble cell. A prostitute in a simple sari stood by a tortured mattress and cot. A frail wooden table stood next to the cot. On top was a condom.

Although fragile-looking, she was attractive—with long, jet-black hair, a thin, elegant face, big brown eyes, and small firm breasts. Avoiding her eyes, I felt like a voyeur, peering into her life. How society's tastes can vary—in India plumpness meant wealth and greater attraction. Thinness signified "poor," and thus less attractive. However, my blood burned with a desire that surprised me with its intensity. She had aroused me without a word.

I tried to keep to my original objective: to see, not touch. In the end, that proved impossible. I couldn't just leave. I felt obliged to respect her quiet dignity and her job. I didn't want it to look like the white man didn't think she was worthy. And, this might seem silly, I felt very unsure of the etiquette in the situation. So, without going into details, I received the minimum, paid the woman her small fee, and terminated the walkabout.

Over the years, conversations about prostitutes with well-off friends never got past AIDS and abuse. I found their views degrading to prostitutes and often inaccurate. Their line was that no prostitute would *pick* her profession—she must have been coerced. I remembered a discussion I had with a Dutch woman and her boyfriend.

"No man I know would ever have sex with a prostitute!" she proclaimed.

"How many men have you asked?" I inquired.

"One!" she answered defensively.

Her boyfriend gave me a "How else could I answer?" shrug that she missed.

"And he said?"

"No! Have you ever been with a prostitute?"

"Yes," I replied matter-of-factly. "Have you ever met a prostitute?"

"Why would I? I don't know why a perfectly healthy man would ever go to one."

I didn't tell her what I was thinking: sex with a prostitute was exciting and a natural rite of passage for most healthy men.

I do not defend the evils of prostitution. However, I do believe the profession provides a livelihood for many women and their families *and* fulfillment and intimacy for many men who otherwise might live a life of quiet desperation.

I like the way George Carlin put it. "I don't understand why prostitution is illegal. Selling is legal. Fucking is legal. Why isn't selling fucking legal? You know, why should it be illegal to sell something that's perfectly legal to give away? I can't follow the logic on that one at all! Of all the things you can do, giving someone an orgasm is hardly the worst thing in the world. In the army they give you a medal for spraying napalm on people! In civilian life you go to jail for giving someone an orgasm! Maybe I'm not supposed to understand it ...."

On my second day in Calcutta, I invited an eight-year-old beggar to lunch. I'd ordered too much at a restaurant near my hotel.

(I kept forgetting that my stomach had shrunk.) So I walked outside to the street and asked him in. He accepted with a smile. At the table, I pushed my spare bowl of hot and sour soup over to him.

"How about a Coke?" I asked.

"Yes, Coke."

Clad in orange-colored rags, his body was all bones and no fat, but his eyes were street smart and expressive. With a little meat on his body he would have been handsome.

While the owner brought the Coke, we talked about his living conditions. He spoke English quite well, explaining to me that he slept in a burlap bag on the street, beside his friend. The owner treated the little guy quite well, considering his appearance. I asked the boy how he learned to speak English so well.

"What kind businessman you think I am?" he responded. "My customers, they speak English!"

He told me he "no like India because no money for school," and he "no like asking tourists for money."

"What about going to Mother Teresa's for a place to stay?"

"You see something wrong with me?" he said with an incredulous look on his face. "Maybe I no have arm? What is wrong that Mother Teresa take me?" In between wolfing down an ice cream and another Coke, he said school would teach him how to achieve his ambition—to drive a taxi. Already at eight, this kid could sell dust to a street sweeper. And, sure enough, the little feller was soon hitting me up for school money.

"No way!" I said firmly. "I just bought lunch. What can you do for me? I need a guide."

"You give me, I give you," he bargained.

His first act as a guide was to take me to a bank so I could change a traveler's check.

He directed our rickshaw (complete with collapsible hood) to Mother Teresa's. The ninety-pound, seventy-year-old driver pulled us like a long-retired mule. I naturally felt sorry for him, but people needed jobs to survive. Straining meager muscles, he maneuvered in and out of traffic and negotiated one-way streets the wrong way. Finally, he trotted up and stopped in front of a wide entryway to the only clean building I'd seen so far in

Calcutta. "Mother Teresa," he exclaimed, and motioned he would wait.

"Can I help you?" asked a nun at the entrance, dressed in a white habit with blue trim.

"I'm just looking around," I answered with a smile. "Is that all right?"

"Yes, of course, walk around at your leisure.

"Perhaps you would like to see the chapel?" She pointed to a stairway to the right of the entrance.

Climbing the stairs, I wondered where the children were—the only sounds disturbing the quiet came from birds and occasional traffic. I came to the chapel entrance, but before I could enter my attention was taken by an old nun who stepped out from one of the other rooms. She had bloated bare feet and a face cracked and soft like sun-baked clay after a drizzle. A space separated her two front teeth and she wore the same striped habit as the nun downstairs. She might have been Mother Teresa. But I banished the thought as too unlikely.

She walked slowly towards me, asking in a nice quiet tone: "Can I help you?"

"I'm just looking around," I said with a smile. "Is that all right?"

She nodded with an equally friendly smile. We talked for ten minutes discussing where I came from, where I was going, and why I was traveling alone. Those sorts of things. All the time, I was thinking, "This can't be Mother Teresa. I must be in a home for retired nuns." Nevertheless, there was something about this "retired nun."

Her eyes attracted me most. They revealed strength of character and inner calm, eyes that had a sparkle of curiosity and liveliness that age sometimes makes more prominent. There was something else. A real humility gave strength to those eyes. It also came through in the ease of her smile—a smile that said, "I am no better or worse than anyone." That was the first time I considered the power inherent in humility. To be no better or worse eliminated ego in a pure kind of way.

In the end, of course, curiosity got the better of me. I bent down to her height, and looked into her eyes.

"Hey, what's your name anyway?" I asked nonchalantly.

"Mother Teresa."

"Nah! You're kidding!" I said, absolutely startled.

"I am not kidding!"

"This is wonderful to meet you!" I shouted, delighted and excited. This was a lifetime thrill. We shook hands as I would an old friend, my right hand in hers and my left on her clothed arm. She returned the gesture—with both hands. In my peaceful mood, I felt in harmony with her.

In answer to my question about how she'd started her mission, she said faith in God's plan for her brought her to Calcutta. (I didn't know at the time, she was born Agnes Gonxha Bojaxhiu of Albanian descent in what is now Macedonia, but was then the Ottoman Empire.) I was impressed at her courage to travel so far and to such a difficult place.

She asked if I had seen her children. When I said I hadn't, she told me to be sure to see them.

"Do you have a rickshaw?" she asked.

"Yes."

"Tell the driver to take you to Nirmala Shishu Bavan," she said emphatically. "Shishu Bavan! It is my children's center. Shishu Bavan!"

I bowed goodbye and walked downstairs to the rickshaw driver and gave him Mother Teresa's instructions. At the Nirmala Shishu Bavan, a ragged beggar sat in the shade of the closed wooden entrance door. I worked my way round him and knocked. A middle-aged volunteer opened the door. She might have been Scandinavian judging by her accent and the white, pimply pallor of her skin.

"Mother Teresa sent me over to see the kids," I said.

"Mother Teresa?" she responded, a little dazed.

"Yeah, I just saw her." I loved the feeling of disclosing this coup.

"You saw Mother Teresa?" Her jaw dropped. "She must be back from Italy. I've been here for six months and still have not seen her. How does she look? She's been so sick."

"She looked okay to me!"

The pallid volunteer asked me in, carefully closing the door on the beggar. Another woman showed me around the several wings of the spacious compound, which appeared to be divided by type of ailment and degree of abandonment. Before long, one of the skinny, playful kids handcuffed me, sticking like glue. Another rode me piggyback. I felt so natural with kids. They could be so easy to please.

As I climbed back in the rickshaw, I reflected on Mother Teresa. This simple woman was really an entrepreneur who risked traveling to an unknown and scary land to build a worldwide community based on a vision from God. Visions could come true. Mother Teresa was proof of it. But what about my eight-year-old guide sitting next to me wanting to be a taxi driver? And the poor prostitute I met? Did she even have a vision of a better future?

THAILAND

THE TRAVELER

20

TRAVELERS: WHO ARE THEY?

SHE PLUCKED HER BACKPACK EFFICIENTLY from the suitcases spinning around the baggage claim carousel at Bangkok airport. In her early thirties, I guessed. Compact body, pretty, thin traveling face, and red, curly hair spilling from a dusty bandanna. She was coming from India, like me, had the sturdy walk of a long-term traveler, and wore loose-fitting clothes and rubber sandals. I passed through immigration and went to change American Express traveler's checks into baht, the local currency. *Thump!* I turned around. She'd dumped her backpack on the shiny marble floor behind me as she joined the sparse line. She smiled.

By this time, I had learned that in each new location I'd experience something I never had before and meet *someone*. Was she the one?

"Where ya headed?" I asked.

"Khao San Road."

Aha, American, judging by the accent. "Me too! Maybe we could share a cab?"

"Sure! My name's Laurie."

Laurie had been in Bangkok before, so I followed her. She'd been on the road seven months and was traveling alone. *Alone* meant you hooked up with other travelers but could get off at the next stop if there was conflict. In "real life," she lived in San Francisco and made videos on a freelance basis.

"Have you figured out where you're going to stay?" she asked, once we got comfortable in the cab.

"Well, actually I haven't decided."

"If you care to join me, I'm going to the Apple Guest House. I've stayed there before. Good location. Inexpensive."

"Sounds good to me!"

I always liked to get the first night's accommodations settled early. After that we exchanged stories about our travels in India. She came across as pleasant and efficient. Being pretty didn't hurt.

Twenty minutes later, we were crowding along with other cars and three-wheeled tuk-tuks, which looked like motorized hansom cabs, in Bangkok's evening rush. Khao San Road felt like a diminutive Haight Street. Just six blocks long with a Buddhist monastery behind a white wall at one end, it thronged with an even greater diversity of people and activity than the San Francisco road. At 9 p.m., it had closed to traffic and come alive—pulsing with Western music and videos to attract the swarm of colorfully dressed travelers to a multitude of open-air restaurants. Fried-food vendors cooking pad thai noodles on makeshift grills and in steaming cauldrons lined the road. And you could buy almost anything else you wanted to eat—chopped pineapples, noodle coconut soup, banana crepes flavored with condensed milk, roasted and flattened chicken legs and gizzards, even fried grasshoppers. The whole atmosphere created my first impression of Southeast Asia—one of mystery and magnetism.

Laurie knew exactly where she was going. She reminded me of Sweet Sue in Egypt, who took control of our bike ride through the Valley of the Kings. We slipped between a food stand and sarong shop, headed down an alley, and crossed a street convulsing with honking traffic. A couple of turns past a huge Rolex sign and we were walking along another alleyway—this one full of closed shops smelling of fish—past a row of small flats, then through a busy kickboxing gym. As we lugged our backpacks past smoky stands selling satayed chicken, noodle soup, and beer in yet another thoroughfare, we agreed to share a room. A natural and innocent enough arrangement, although sharing a room with a woman was accompanied by natural if not innocent thoughts.

"Mama," a heavyset, tank-faced old woman with a baked-in scowl, met us at the entrance of the Apple Guest House. She explained curtly she had only one room available. We asked to see it. Mama led us through a small concrete courtyard where three travelers sat around a long weathered table in front of an ivy-covered brick wall, which gave the establishment some privacy. There was a movement at the base of the ivy. Rats! Laurie was blasé. But, Jesus, I thought, rats!

Mama agonizingly lifted her bulk up rickety stairs to show us the second-floor room. Laurie and I peered in. We slowly looked at each other. Surprise! Just *one* double bed.

"This is the only room left?" I asked, eyes still riveted to the bed.

"Yes. Four hundred baht," Mama growled.

"What do you think?" Laurie said.

"It's okay with me if it's okay with you."

"Sure!" she said with a shrug. "Twelve dollars, I like the price. You take the right side. I'll take the left."

What a woman! This was another first. I had slept in the same room with a female traveler, but never in the same bed. I didn't know what to think. In fact, my main thought was should I strip to my underwear or not? And I considered little else during the next two hours. What was first-night-with-a-stranger-in-the-same-bed etiquette?

Before climbing in to bed for the night, I sought the sanctity of the downstairs toilet to ponder this question. In my absence, she had gotten into bed wearing a peach-colored, silk nightshirt; the lower part of her body was covered with a sarong. What was she wearing underneath?

Outside crickets chirped and low voices murmured at the communal table. There was no breeze and the air hung hot and humid—the kind of humidity that deposited a light film of sweat on your forehead and caused you to kick off the covers. The kind of humidity that hatched wicked thoughts. I stripped off my shirt, and modestly decided not to remove the pajama-like pants I'd acquired in Egypt.

"Did you see those rats?" I said. She turned to me from reading *The Dancing Wu Li Masters*, a book on quantum mechanics. Her gestures carefully did not cross the imaginary Maginot Line that separated us.

"Those rats are big, aren't they?" she agreed. "Look in the kitchen in the morning. Mama feeds them in bowls like cats."

Lying back to back, we read our books—nary a word spoken except for "Goodnight" when she switched off the light. I felt her next to me, struggling to sleep in the humidity.

In the middle of the night, I woke and looked across at her. Sarong tossed aside, just her green silk panties hugged her derriere. A moonbeam penetrated with enough glow to light up her body. She moved ever so softly to the rhythm of her breath.

As I watched her in the dim blush of a crescent moon, I felt the stirrings of manhood. Can a man resist the inherent beauty and grace in a woman's body? That demanding *Lust* that nature has embedded into our chromosomes. My admiring eyes followed the sleek lines of her freckled body—from feet to flowing red hair scattered on her pillow.

I lay there wanting to touch and find out who she was. But she had been right to trust me beside her—I wasn't going to touch, although I still desired to know more about her. The exciting surprise to my journey was how interesting travelers turned out to be. I could not learn local languages traveling the world in one year. Contacts with locals added spice, but it was the travelers who provided the main meal—the deep dialogue and closeness.

The next morning, we ate breakfast at one of Laurie's favorite hole-in-the-wall restaurants on Khao San Road. The street was quiet as the travelers slept late. After sleeping together, we had formed a quick bond and she talked easily about her personal journey. She had dropped out for a while because the real world became too formidable. The decision to travel had begun when she nursed her father for a year before he died.

"I really didn't know him most of my life. My mother divorced when I was ten and he just, um, you know, he really never came around much. My mother made it difficult. She hated him. Said she loved me while poisoning my mind with hate!

"Dad drank a lot, was gruff. But in the year before he died I developed a fondness for him. He made me laugh. And he made me cry when he died. Cancer's a bitch. He smoked all his life."

She paused to drag on the cigarette between her slim fingers. The sun gently illuminated the restaurant. The air was blessed with a light humidity. The still sleepy street was now open for cars, and the makeshift grills of the night before were gone. Sidewalk shops began the process of opening for the new day.

"Well, anyway, afterwards I moved back in with my boyfriend in San Francisco," she continued. "The lapse of time was enough for me to see that our six-year relationship was going nowhere.

"You know what it's like. I had to get out. I made up my mind to be strong and healthy, and scraped together every dollar I could lay my hands on. Traveling was scary at first, but now I love it!"

"Why Third World countries?

"They are so much cheaper. I'd always wanted to go to India. And I'm very interested in massage, especially traditional Thai massage. It's part massage, part philosophy. So I contacted a massage guru who lives near Chiang Mai, which is about a hundred miles north of here. He's an older man. When he learned I made videos for a living, he suggested I make a video about Thai massage—featuring him, of course. Both of us will market the video and split the profits. That's why I'm back in Thailand. Besides, I love this place."

"What happened with the six-year relationship?" I asked.

"Don't you think that's a little personal?" A teasing smile rippled through her freckled face.

"Well, of course it's personal, but after sleeping with you I feel ... a certain intimacy."

"We *didn't* sleep together!"

"What would you call it? We shared the same bed. At night! Alone! In the sex city of Bangkok! It was rather nice, but tonight please cut the chatter in your sleep."

"I don't talk in my sleep," she said, leaning over the table to slap my arm. "You asked me about Bill?"

"That his name, Bill?"

"He's a lawyer. Works too hard. The rare times I saw him, he had a habit of making decisions that impinged on my life without consulting me. Mostly we just didn't fit. We always seemed to be debating—and the lawyer was mostly right.

"Bill is ruled by the clock, and sometimes he can be hard as nails. Sometimes he made me feel really low. We just couldn't find a way to communicate after a while."

"The ravages of communication. What part did you play?"

"You know by now men are always guilty," she said with a laugh.

I let her comment pass, although I recognized a certain truth in it. In any dispute, I always felt I was the guilty party—no matter how much I was right. I could never be the innocent one.

"How do you feel now?"

"Now I make myself feel whatever I want. I'm in charge of me, no one else," she replied. "But what about you? How come you're here?"

As Khao San Road filled with late risers, I told Laurie about my friend Frank Zolfo, the Big Z, who I would meet in ten days. I recounted how Frank set the stage for this journey ten years ago. He told me to visualize the future I wanted by suggesting I imagine myself as an eighty-year-old looking back on my life. I had known Frank throughout my business career. He restructured large troubled companies and, in one case, a city—New York City. He was dynamic, powerful, and used to luxury.

"I told him, 'Frank, buy a backpack. We're staying at twelve dollar-a-night hostels, not your five hundred dollar-a-night palaces.' He said, 'Denny, this is your trip, whatever you want we do. I'm just along for the ride.'"

"Does he know how rough the ride can be?"

"I doubt it!"

She leaned forward and zeroed her hazel eyes straight into mine—clearly she had something important to share.

"I'm thinking about wandering over to Patpong tonight to film one of those sleazy massages and contrast it to the real thing. Want to come?"

"Sure. Why not? Do you think they'll let you film it?"

"I don't know. I've never been in one of those places."

"Who's your subject going to be?"

"I'm looking at him."

"No fucking way!" I said, taken completely by surprise. "I'll take the video, *you* be the subject."

"Oh, come on. I'm the expert," she countered, blushing. "I have to take the film. And besides, they don't give those massages to women, do they?"

21

Laurie's Porno Movie

A VIDEO WAS IN THE making, but we were still missing its star. However, strong desires attract connecting energy. Back at the Apple Guest House, we met Werner. He was sitting around one of the courtyard tables showing off the pictures he'd drawn during his cycling trip through China. We began to chat as Werner flipped through his sketchbook of Norman Rockwell-like pencil drawings. A six-foot Austrian, Werner looked about thirty and had handsome features: wide face, straight nose, and clear complexion. A strong, muscular physique was constrained by his heavy, formal posture.

"That village scene is terrific," I said. "You must have seemed like a giant to the locals."

"Yes, they were small compared to me."

"Did you worry about your bike being stolen?" Laurie asked.

"Only in the cities. The Chinese were honest in trains and in the countryside. My major concern was cycling up the mountains."

An hour and a couple of beers later, Werner finished showing the sketchbook, and Laurie asked him if he wanted to go with us on a tour of Bangkok. A threesome was born. It amazed me how easy it was to find mates traveling. Like minds and compatible personalities came together naturally. Perhaps the connecting energy I had discussed in India also connected spirits from former lifetimes, spirits familiar with our energy because they loved us or even inhabited the same body as us. The origin of déjà vu? I liked that thought.

The three of us decided to tour the outskirts of the city by boat, and then head to the center. We hopped a fast, slim commuter boat made of teakwood, and navigated the army-green *khlongs*, or canals, that snaked into the city proper. The waterway widened as we rolled past gold-tipped pagodas and emerald and crimson temples with golden spires and perfectly geometric gardens. Statues of the Buddha ran the gamut from powerful through meditative to soft and gentle, almost feminine. Shaven-headed Buddhist monks in orange robes wandered mellowly about the temples or sat on mats in contemplation. Although I'd read that Buddhist philosophy arrived in Thailand perhaps two thousand years ago with traders and settlers from India, and, today, ninety-five percent of Thais were Buddhists, I was still unsure exactly what Buddhism was.

Laurie explained that the Buddha was an Indian sage who, like Christ many years later, preached non-materialism, love, and the golden rule that everyone has total responsibility for what happens to him or her because God was within and part of everything. When you found your "self" you became God. He'd left his family and possessions to seek this enlightenment and truth. On the way, he met all sorts of people and experienced all sorts of situations.

"Sounds like a traveler," I said. "I bet he had fun."

"He was probably the original traveler," Werner agreed.

Although Laurie and I knew of the plan for the Patpong "massage," we had yet to tell Werner. The first stage was for us to be filmed having an authentic, traditional Thai version. We picked a simple building filled with thick floor mats and professional masseuses. Laurie thought these treatments looked appealing but didn't compare to those up north. It would provide a good contrast, she thought, and arranged with the management to record Werner and me on video.

Relaxed from the massage, we supped on chicken satay, vegetables, and shrimp in coconut sauce at a riverside restaurant. The romance was offset by a Coke bottle holding a lighted candle placed under the table to discourage mozzies. Werner told us he graduated university as an architect, but hadn't yet plied his trade because he hated the personal characteristics of architects, who, he said, were like empty rooms. In the meantime, he worked as a carpenter, earning money to travel.

Werner did things by the book. He was unable, for example, to see the logic of Laurie inviting our petite waitress to share a drink with us.

"What's the sense of it?" he asked impatiently. "She's not going to do it."

"Oh, come on, Werner!" Laurie chided. "Don't you do anything just for the hell of it?"

I tucked that thought away, it struck me as important.

"Sure!" he said softening slightly, "but there seems to be no point to asking."

"Look at her face, Werner," Laurie said. We turned to observe our shiny-haired waitress. "Look at her giggling through her hands and looking straight at us!"

"Look at how she's talking to that other waitress, gesturing towards us and laughing," I added enthusiastically. "She loves the attention she got from us."

Blushing, the waitress brought a tray with three Bintang beers and two glasses of Coke. A half bottle of Mekhong whiskey lay hidden among the three brown Bintang bottles. She poured the beers out for us very carefully. Bending over giggling, she thanked us for the whiskey and Cokes, which we were surreptitiously buying her and the other waitress. Looking supremely innocent, she then strode with the half-filled tray to her station, out of sight of the restaurant manager. Her colleague joined her. They broke the Mekhong seal, hunched their shoulders together as a shield, and poured the whiskey into their Cokes. All the while, they stole glances and giggled. Finally, they raised their glasses to toast us.

We clinked bottles back to them.

"*Prost!*" Werner said with an embarrassed laugh. "I give you credit. Not so much for the succeeding, but for the trying."

I was taking a liking to this chap.

Perhaps sensing a change in the otherwise conventional Werner, Laurie chose that moment to tell him of our plans to videotape a sex massage. Did he want to join us?

"Sure, why not?"

It was the perfect time to untuck the thought I'd stored away earlier—and to get myself off the hook. "She needs a subject," I said. "Someone to receive the massage just for the hell of it. How about it? Are you interested?"

"Sure," he answered without a moment's hesitation. "That would be fun. Why not? I have never done that before."

We jumped a tuk-tuk to the flashing lights of the infamous sex extravaganza—Patpong. But we did not complete our mission on that notorious street. For no sooner had we stepped out in front of the gleaming red arches of one of the nightspots than a smiling tout jumped in our faces.

"You want famous Thai massage? Most famous in Bangkok!" he cajoled us, pointing to another tuk-tuk. "You come! Come!"

Werner favored a walk down Patpong to, as he nervously put it, "gear up for the challenge ahead." But Laurie insisted the tout was heaven-sent and we followed dutifully. Seasoned travelers, we scanned the neighborhoods we traversed. The surroundings looked fairly safe—lots of locals milling about. At this juncture in my travels, I could feel the energy around me. It was as if I was in an energy bubble that subconsciously attracted good energy and repelled bad. Ten minutes later, we stopped in front of a modern, brightly lit hotel.

To describe the left wall of the lobby as eye-catching would have been a gross understatement. The "wall" was a titanic glass window, about the length of a basketball gym, behind which groups of pretty, young women sat on three separate bleachers. Each group wore different colored, sensuously clinging silk uniforms with numbered tags hanging on their chests. Some sat smiling, others chatted a mile a minute and laughed together, while a few remained bashfully silent.

Our mouths were still agape when a chunky gentleman dressed in a light gray suit and red tie that fit the décor stepped in front of us. "How much for a massage?" Laurie managed to spit out.

"We do not offer massages by themselves," said the pimp. "The girls in blue, to the right, give blow jobs and a massage."

Whoa! That was blunt, I thought, exchanging stunned glances with my partners in sin. "And the other two groups?" I asked.

"The girls in pink, in the middle, give 'the works.'"

"What do you mean 'the works'?" I persisted.

"A massage, blow job, and make love," he said as if he were a waiter routinely listing the night's specials.

"Oh!" Laurie said, her blush overwhelming her freckles, "And on the left, the girls in white?"

"They also give the works but these girls are superstars."

"Aha!" she said. "How much for a superstar?"

"Three thousand baht," he said. It was about eighty dollars. "For three, that would be nine thousand."

"Far too much," I began to haggle. "How about fifteen hundred for one of us?"

"But the three of us want to be in the room," Laurie added.

I couldn't believe I was doing this. Three days before, I'd been chitchatting with Mother Teresa!

"This very unusual," the fat man said, though he didn't seem surprised. "I give you deal—four thousand for three. Last offer."

"This is a special day," Laurie explained, pointing at me: "It's his son's birthday. We want *the works* with a superstar. And the two of us watch."

"That's my dad's girlfriend!" Werner earnestly added, pointing at Laurie.

"Yes," I pitched in. "We want to make sure that my boy has a good time. You know what I mean?"

We settled on twenty-eight hundred baht.

"I like number eighteen," said Laurie, who was paying the lion's share. "She has such beautiful hair. What do you think, Werner?"

I was curious to be a voyeur, but wondered at the advisability of a woman picking another woman for a guy. Werner nodded zombie-like.

The woman Laurie chose looked about twenty-one, with long, glistening, black hair. On the fat man's signal, she came out into the lobby. A surprised look flashed across her perfect round face when *three* of us followed her down a cream-colored corridor. We entered a large, elegant room with a double bed and a white Formica table with matching leather armchairs on either side. Armchairs for voyeurs. A three-person, rose-tinted oval bathtub was visible through a wooden latticework panel.

An elderly maid entered. She turned down the rose-satin bedspread, poured oils in the tub, and shot us a "what's going on" look before leaving. The masseuse sat on the meticulously neat bed and glanced nervously at us. She instructed Werner to strip, and proceeded to do the same—her white silk nightgown slipping to the floor revealing her lovely naked body. She then removed a barrette, and her silky hair dropped around her brown shoulders and swollen nipples. Stunning!

"It is okay," I said slowly and softly. "This our son, and you his birthday present. Okay?"

"Okay." She smiled demurely.

"We're very proud of him. Thank you," Laurie added in a sensitive tone. She slowly placed the camera on the white table. Again, a nervous glance. Laurie indicated "no problem" with her hands palms up. The scene reminded me of the movie *The Electric Horseman* when anchorwoman Jane Fonda surreptitiously flipped on her video camera, while a passionate Robert Redford explained why he was freeing a five-million-dollar horse he had stolen. Laurie switched the camera on and slowly pointed it at the bed. Unobtrusively peering down the viewfinder, she very carefully made adjustments. Laurie's hazel eyes met mine. We smiled, co-conspirators.

Werner was trying to act cool but was clearly nervous about being a porno star as the naked masseuse straddled him. She massaged the bulky but yielding muscles on his back. It was as if she was fumbling with a hot potato—fast and clutchy. Werner appeared to be enjoying it, though.

The hostess donned a white shower cap, making sure every strand of hair was covered. Then she gently grasped Werner's hand, and walked him over to the tub. She leaned in to swirl the water, worked up heavy suds, and then they both slid in. The masseuse lathered herself first and then slithered sensuously over Werner, paying special attention to his seriously protruding part. I felt stirrings myself and looked at Laurie. She was too intensely absorbed to notice me.

Laurie adjusted the camera while the couple dried off and returned to the bed. Bathing cap still on, the prostitute knelt in front of Werner, applied a condom in businesslike fashion, and moved on to the blowjob. Werner winced and looked to the heavens for guidance. The rest of "the works" followed. There was some confused choreography as the woman maneuvered for position on top of the muscular Werner. Laurie glanced at me, eyes wide open.

However, I wasn't excited anymore, just uncomfortable for the woman and poor Werner. She looked so young and inexperienced at her trade. What was her story, her family life? I knew the moral pros and cons of Thailand and women, but my traveler's desire was to experience and not judge. To mull over a slice of life's pie without bias.

Without warning, the girl stopped her pumping motion and apologized for her performance.

"He drink alcohol?" she cried crestfallen.

"Yes," I answered, as Werner lay silent.

"No good, liquor," she said, miming a rocket sharply rising into the air and then crashing. "No good."

Werner looked dazed and his face was red. Laurie and I meanwhile reassured the young woman that it was okay, that she did just fine. But she kept repeating the Cape Canaveral disaster. I didn't know who to feel more sorry for—the woman or poor Werner. Up, up the woman's hands went, then a swan dive. With each dive, I could feel her disappointment at screwing up the birthday present—not to mention Werner's embarrassment.

During the tuk-tuk ride home, Werner also apologized profusely for the performance, his agonized face in his hands. We attempted to soothe his ruffled pride as we motored past stands selling fruit salads, fried rice, curries, and sizzling with crab and fish on spits.

"Werner, don't apologize," I said. "I could never have done what you did in front of an audience. Relax about it. Laurie got her massage film and that's all we were after. You did good!"

"Denis is right," Laurie said sympathetically. "But Werner, I'm puzzled by one thing. Did it occur to you to remove the shower cap? She had such beautiful hair."

22

Brush with Death on
a Dream Island

Unfortunately, I missed seeing Laurie off. Keen to pursue her quest, she headed north the next day to meet her massage guru in Chiang Mai. I'd met a couple of American businessmen and, hungry for news from back home, spent too much time with them. They monopolized the conversation from the get-go with dull details of their business drama. The contrast between their miniscule attention spans and the listening skills of travelers was stark. By the time I returned to the Apple, Laurie was gone. I was left feeling disloyal for staying with people I didn't care about and letting her go without a goodbye.

I still had a week before Frank Zolfo arrived in Bangkok, so I joined Werner to travel south by van with a group of other travelers. He appeared to have put the previous evening behind him, but was quieter than usual. From the sleepy town of Chumphon, we embarked on a grungy fifty-foot fishing boat to sail seven hours east to the island of Koh Tao in the Gulf of Thailand.

Boarding in the black of night, I felt *risk* creeping up my spine. Between eerie movements of cloud cover, stars glittered deep in space. A few backpackers chose to sleep in the security of the boat's cabin next to the staccato grinding and moaning of the engine. The rest of us climbed a narrow wooden ladder to the slippery upper deck. We preferred thin bamboo mats under a poorly patched canopy and a glimpse of the midnight sky. A warm tropical breeze blew briskly, bringing the occasional heavy burst of rain from a series of squalls.

Werner and I talked into the early morning with John, a lanky Australian with curly, blond hair, a bird-like nose, and mischievous eyes, and Angie, an attractive Irish woman with a soft lilt to her voice. Angie was offering her take on James Michener's *The Drifters*, a novel about travelers in the sixties, which I had also recently read.

"Michener's characters seemed so lost. They were running away and using hard drugs to travel even further away. I think today's travelers are seekers. They use soft drugs to embellish what they find."

"Travelers probably reflect the times," I put in.

"Exactly," she said.

"Sixties travelers have similarities to us," Werner said. "For instance, they took a big risk to venture into the unknown and be responsible for themselves. They wanted the same freedom as us—to speak honestly and look for meaning through shared experiences. Fantasies became their reality. I am looking to find who I am, and so maybe were they."

"We have many reasons to travel," Angie concluded, "but we all come to be with each other, to communicate about ourselves to someone like us. In that sense everyone can be a traveler."

About four hours into the trip, red, white, and blue lights exploded and flared below us—like some twisted Fourth of July. An electrical fire had suddenly broken out in the cabin towards the bow. The power shut down and we drifted, rolling ominously in the dark, heavy seas. Danger lurked, and the unknown pricked the senses. A squall hit us. As the pelting rains and high winds attacked, we dived for protection inside our sleeping bags.

However, the great advantage of traveling in the Third World—and one I experienced over and over—was that the local guys were mechanical geniuses. With a couple of basic tools—a screwdriver, stick of gum, rags, and wire—they could fix anything. As we drifted dangerously in stormy conditions, the crew chatted away and made running repairs. Then just as suddenly as the squall came it left, and we were under full steam.

Somewhere along the way, there always arose an ordeal that provided the glue to bring a group of travelers closer together. This time it was danger on high seas.

On Koh Tao, our small troop of travelers packed into the back of a pickup, and bounced through a palm-tree jungle for three miles to Rocky Resort, a cottage haven at water's edge. The manager showed Werner and me to our accommodation—one of the itsy-bitsy A-frame cottages built on a boardwalk, which waltzed this way and that into the bay. The boardwalk was on stilts hammered into the barnacled rocks and also acted as a front porch for the cottages. A three-foot railing in front of each building ensured you did not fall into the sea or, at low tide, eight feet on to the rocks. However, until you reached the cottages the boardwalk lacked this protective railing—an incidental that nearly cost me my life.

Inside the cottage, I was faced with a familiar situation—just *one* double bed. Only this time, it was shrouded in white mesh mosquito netting, and Werner was by my side staring, not Laurie. We tossed our backpacks into the minute space available on the floor. Through slits in the wooden flooring we could see water sloshing below.

"Are you uncomfortable sleeping with me?" Werner asked with Germanic bluntness.

"Only if you snore and don't behave yourself."

"Good! Which side do you want?"

In fact, I was nervous about sleeping with Werner. Homophobic? I don't know, probably. I flashed to the movie *Yentl* and Barbra Streisand (dressed to look like a guy) climbing into bed with a man babbling something about it being written that two men in bed together must sleep back to back!

Nine years before, my business partner and I snagged the only room available at the Waldorf Astoria in New York. We also opened the door to one double bed. I worried then that, in the dead of night, thinking he was Kathi, my arm might slip around his shoulder. Women shared beds easily with other women. And men in underdeveloped countries didn't have an issue either. So where did the homophobia come from?

Four days in paradise allowed our little group to grow close. Meals together, exploring the island, snorkeling beneath the turquoise, palpitating waves. At night, we shared Mekhong whiskey and fruit lassies and swam naked in the warm ocean while choirs of insects and animals sang loudly in the jungle. Once, lying in sweaty half-sleep next to Werner, I heard wild dogs tearing apart an animal they had cornered. Most likely a monkey.

On the fourth night, my accident-free seven months' travel came to an abrupt end. We were sharing a fish barbecue with a couple of Swedes and a few Dutch travelers on the white sands of the nearby horseshoe beach. Sitting around a crackling fire in the middle of palm trees, we played hangman and talked about UFOs and energy. Angie's boyfriend, Paul, a charming New Zealander of Japanese descent, stoked the fire and tended the Thai snapper and potatoes hanging on sticks. Strumming a ukulele, Aussie John sang a few funky songs he wrote. No radios or earphones on this beach. The food looked delicious and its aroma danced through the air, tantalizing us as we lounged under the stars.

I was talking to Wadgi, a good-looking, enthusiastic Australian of Lebanese descent in his mid-twenties. As usual with travelers, we quickly entered the inner sanctums of our lives. His brown eyes narrowed as he revealed a secret that had been on his mind—how he'd lost his virginity to the mother of a boarding school roommate when he was sixteen.

"I felt this incredible attraction to her," he said, "Like I'd known her before. We were alone in the house by chance and I spilled it all. I confessed I was in love with her and felt bloody miserable. She gave me a Mona Lisa smile I'll never forget, took my hand, and, without words, led me into her bedroom."

He described her body language—very gentle yet hungry—and smell—lavender perfume. She'd closed the curtains to darken the atmosphere but left enough light for them to see each other. Then she removed her clothes, and instructed him as to the ways in which he could excite her.

"It's interesting," he said after a pause, "how detailed sensory data and whole sequences of events are stored in memory like a video."

"And can be accessed years later if you really concentrate."

"Spot on. What's been on my mind is that maybe my friend's mother and I acted out an age-old drama. That our attraction was more than merely hormones, but spiritual."

"Kindred spirits you mean."

"Yeah, mate."

"What a wonderful way to lose your virginity. Another perspective is that you related your innermost feelings to her—you were honest—and, when you think about it, honesty is the ultimate intimacy. She's what, in her thirties, married fifteen to twenty years, maybe an aging relationship with problems? And here you come along—young, muscular, and *honest*."

"I never thought of honesty and intimacy being linked."

A pack of scrawny wild dogs interrupted us. Maybe ten in number, they'd been lurking under the palm trees at the edge of our gathering. These were not pets with tails swishing. I disliked them immediately. They probably killed the monkey the night before. My and Wadgi's attention was drawn by a couple of more intrepid dogs who'd begun to shimmy their way between the humans. Eyes serious and concentrated, they were drawn ever closer by the scent of skewered fish dripping fat into the fire. They flashed wary eyes back to the main pack. No one shooed them off. Suddenly, they made their move and tried to grab the fish. We sprang into action, whipping our sarongs in the air and chasing them away. Still the pack waited in the gloom. I wouldn't have wanted to encounter them alone on a dark night.

"Hey, mate," Wadgi said, resuming our conversation, "while those dogs were plotting, I was thinking. Maybe the experience with my friend's mother is resurfacing because travelers are people you don't know? We don't judge each other's actions or argue about what we think or say or believe. We're just interested people, who bloody listen."

"That's my experience. How did the story end?"

"We were never alone after we made love. She was very careful of her eye contact. But as I was leaving for school, she pecked my cheek in a formal way but squeezed my hand unobtrusively and warmly. I think it was to tell me she cared. Her son and I drifted apart soon after and I never saw her again."

After eating the snapper and potatoes off palm leaves, Angie, Werner, Wadgi, John, the two Irishmen, and I moseyed back to Rocky's for a late-night snack of mango crepes and lassies. We lounged on the wicker chairs, chatting and passing joints of particularly potent ganja.

As the midnight hour approached, a cooling sea breeze came in and we decided to play cards around the long Formica table.

We realized immediately we needed a second deck, so I volunteered to retrieve the one in my backpack.

"Have you got a torch?" Angie asked.

I shook my head.

"Then be careful, mate!" Wagdi warned.

"*Ja!*" Werner yelled, "the tide is out!"

I crossed the soft grass and sand to the boardwalk. In the shadows of night, I would have to rely on my memory. I counted six paces straight ahead, and made a ninety-degree right turn. Then, very carefully, another three paces, during which I leaned cautiously away from the unprotected side to my right where the railing was missing. Safely into the cottage. The cards were easy to find as moonlight broke through the clouds.

Outside again, the other cottages loomed with a shadowy menace in my altered mind. Extra wary in my stoned state, I turned right and again carefully avoided the dangerous unprotected drop, now to the left. I took three paces forward, but had committed myself to a fourth step. Mistake! I saw my right leg and sandaled foot extend from the boardwalk into a dark abyss.

"darkness!" my mind screamed. "i don't remember darkness!"

In slow motion, I began to fall. I felt helpless panic, and had time for one lonesome thought: *I could die.*

I crashed on to the rocks below.

Silence.

I lay spread-eagled face down on the granite. No movement except in my mind: *I'm alive!* A chilly dew formed on my skin. Not immediately, but suddenly, pain shot through me. Pain so intense it made me dizzy. My left shin, both knees, ribs, chest, a finger on the left hand, all hurt like hell.

My mind took over. It had been trained to take control in crisis, a well-oiled machine.

Boardwalk above. Tide out. On rocks. You stupid fuck. Bones broken? Your hips—at the very minimum. Asshole! never, never lose control traveling! Check the joints. Move them!

I methodically flexed each joint.

Right toes work. Left toes work. Right ankle works. Okay! Left ankle works, left knee ....

My head lay frozen. I saw a stick next to me. Three inches away, sticking straight up, rose two granite spikes each about a foot long. I had avoided impalement. I moved the fingers of the left hand. They worked! The one next to the pinkie hurt like hell.

You lucky fuck! No major breaks. Ooh, the finger hurts bad. Not good! And the ribs. Everything hurts. But no major breaks.

Since nothing was broken except maybe a few ribs I could still travel. Yet I berated myself once more for being stupid enough to get this stoned and walk without a flashlight in a dangerous environment.

You lucky fuck! Must have been the ganja. Positive energy maybe? Karma? Whoever is traveling with me, thanks!

Lying under the heavenly stars, feet caressed by the incoming tide, I felt alone. Just me, rocks, and water. I knew I might have died and no one would ever have seen me alive again. Destiny. The tide could have been coming to take my corpse out to sea. I lay there a while longer.

I struggled to rise. Adrenaline ignited a body that was having trouble breathing due to pressure in the right of the chest. I retrieved the room key and deck of cards. Then I looked around. Bamboo shoots and brambles blocked the route back. Protecting the wildly throbbing finger, I pushed aside the brush and jumped about a foot to grab hold of a concrete bulkhead shoring the boardwalk. I hauled my battered body up, feet working against the bulkhead and uninjured fingers assisting. The climb was difficult and I had doubts whether I could pull it off in my weakened state. Swinging my right foot up and over the bulkhead like in the movies, I cleared the wall and lay relieved on the grass. Then I got up and staggered to where the others were still playing cards.

I placed the deck on the middle of the table and dangled my injured left hand in front of them.

"How bad is it?" I asked.

Angie screamed.

I felt nauseous.

"Sit down, Denis," Angie said gently, quickly taking charge. "You look faint, probably in shock. Put your head between your knees."

"So stupid," I muttered. "This is not the place to walk stoned without a light. *Never* again!"

Werner volunteered to retrieve the medical kit from my backpack.

I issued a groggy, and at this stage obvious, warning: "Take a torch."

Then the crew went to work like a MASH unit. Angie, Werner, and Paul worked the right side, with Wadgi, John, and the Irishmen on the left.

"How's my finger?"

"I don't see the fingernail," Angie responded. "It's gone!"

My hands and arms quivered, but my mind was clear, even playful.

"I'm a terrible patient. If you touch that finger, I'll scream, Angie. aaghh!"

"Now, Denis, be brave!" she said, flinching as she cleaned and gauzed the finger. The extent of the bruises and cuts only became clear when they slipped off my bloodstained pants and shirt. They must have washed and bandaged for an hour. Then Werner and Wadgi put my arms around their shoulders and carried me to bed.

Feeling ethereal after a strong painkiller, the last words I heard before surrendering to sleep were Wadgi's from outside. He must have been shining the torch over the side of the boardwalk.

"Bloody hell! Lucky Denis wasn't killed. Look at those fucking rocks, they're like daggers."

When I woke up the next morning I felt as if my body had been used as a battering ram. I could barely move. My right hip was bruised, knees swollen, pain in the chest, right wrist hardly able to bend, left hand badly scraped, but it was my finger that felt worst—like it had been mashed in a blender.

I needed to find a professional to look at the finger and to call Zolfo to confirm his arrival date in Bangkok. Lanky John graciously offered to take me to a small village near the docks on his rented Yamaha 200cc dirt bike.

"Be careful, John, I feel like the Tin Man in *The Wizard of Oz* before they oiled him."

He laughed as he maneuvered around the dangerous, post-rain ruts in the road. The journey was easy enough—apart from jumping a two-foot ravine—and we followed the single-lane dirt road into a humble seaside village. To our surprise, we found a phone and the sweetest nurse on the face of the earth.

She carefully washed and re-bandaged the finger and checked the myriad of wounds. The finger would take a month to heal and four months for the nail to grow back, she said. She also gave us medical supplies, antibiotic pills, and instructions on how to clean the throbbing, red stump. It dawned on me how strong the impact of the fall must have been to blow out the fingernail. Not a sliver remained.

On the way back, we jumped the ravine again and all was going well. I was humming "Summertime" when a local kid seeing his motorbike and ours were on a collision course tried to rectify the situation. We crashed head on. I flew gracefully through the air and landed on top of John, gouging his ribs with my elbow.

We wheeled the bike to the nearby shop where John had rented it, then limped arm-in-arm towards Rocky's. A group of islanders were using little gray monkeys to collect coconuts from tall palm trees. The nervous-looking monkeys, leashed to collars around their necks, scampered up the trunk and then began to twist the coconuts free. It looked as if they were removing lug nuts from tires. When the coconuts finally snapped off, the monkeys dropped them down to the ground where they landed with a heavy, dull thud. Whether or not it was true, the oft-repeated statistic that in Thailand seventy people a year die from falling coconuts became immediately more vivid.

At the guesthouse, Angie and Werner had come back bruised from snorkeling. They pointed at us and we all laughed hysterically at our slapstick injuries.

23

BIG Z TRAVELS LIGHT

FRANK ZOLFO WAS BORN IN the Bronx, second-generation Italian. His side of the family were honest, hard-working people, but there was a dark side he rarely talked about. He needed only four hours sleep during his business life, yet he shone like a lighthouse compared with everyone else's sixty-watt bulb. He was a force of nature.

We first met as young business consultants in New York City at a company that is now called Deloitte Touche. Frank was a senior consultant with a photographic memory, and I was a fast-track associate, a nice phrase for the lowest level. We were terrific working together, had similar curiosities and passions, and both had young families. We philosophized about everything. You couldn't shut us up. If we were driving in a car together, we'd get lost—too busy talking to mind the road.

Frank went on to build a powerful consulting firm specializing in corporate reorganization, the same field I later entered after working in Silicon Valley. He restructured the mega-companies of the eighties that were ravaged by junk bonds and mismanagement. The business allowed Frank to retire at forty-nine with enough money to live many lifetimes in grand style.

Despite Frank's success, he could always talk and laugh with anyone, no matter what their social status. In business, he was *the Don*, but another spirit sharing his body was a very likable tough kid from the Bronx, with a natural sense of humor and charm.

I often called Frank *the Z*, or just plain Z. It fit his Sagittarius, dominant-aggressive, fun-loving personality. This combination could be explosive. So it was with no little trepidation that I met Frank at the airport to begin sixteen days of travel together in Thailand and Vietnam. My experience meeting up with friends had not been sterling, and although Frank and I agreed on most issues, he had become hardened against liberals. I was a moderate with liberal leanings. The challenge would be to keep the traveler's energy and empathy even when my persona was threatened.

There were problems starting off. Frank had undergone extensive knee surgery eight days before. He decided to make the trip anyway. Also Frank stayed at five-star hotels and I didn't even get to those neighborhoods anymore. I'd tried to warn him on the telephone about the level of luxury, but with his Bronx-accented exuberance he responded: "Denny, I go where you go! Anything you want! I'm just hitching a ride."

Long after midnight, a tired and spaced-out Frank walked out of customs on to the sparkling marble floor of Bangkok airport, his eyes searching. When they met mine, a smile creased his face. He'd put on a little weight. Even so, he still looked trim from working out with a personal trainer in his basement gym. I chuckled sympathetically as he wheeled an airport pushcart—the Z with backpack and aluminum cane. We hugged and kissed Italian style. Then he pinched my ass, a gesture I had over many years learned to accept as pure Frank.

I steered Frank away from the official taxis queued up outside to a cheap taxi at the poorly lit end of the airport. I toyed with acclimating Frank slowly, poshing it on his first night, but settled on the Khaosan Palace, a high-end budget hotel priced at four hundred fifty baht for two, about eighteen dollars. What the heck? He might as well jump into the stew.

Flooded with light, the white-tiled outdoor lobby of the Palace sat smack in the middle of Khao San Road. Even at this hour, the street was still very much alive as travelers watched movies at restaurants or sampled delicacies from the portable food stands. We opted to settle in our room.

"Hey, Denny!" Frank yelled, emerging from the shower wrapped in a towel, "How do I get this hot water to work?"

"You don't. There isn't any."

A few howls later, he stepped back out of the shower chuckling and limped on to the brown-tiled floor. Water dripping from his nose, he stared at me. "The room is fine," he said approvingly, "and you can't beat the price. But I have to tell you, I don't know how long I can go without any fucking hot water."

"Ah, don't be a sissy, Frank. Be a man!"

In the morning light, Frank unpacked, flipping me the guidebooks for Thailand and Vietnam I'd instructed him to buy. He hadn't cracked either book, except to read the history section. "Whatever you wanna to do, I'll do!" he said, looking refreshed and lighting up a Camel non-filter. "Wherever you wanna to go, I'll go! I'm here to experience a piece of your trip, and I'm excited. In fact, I was hesitant about Vietnam, now I'm hot to go. I was against the war, you know. Now I realize I don't know a fucking thing about that country. First, I got married, then had kids. There was no threat of me having to fight, and I was too busy to understand what was going on."

"Me too. I was ignorant of the history. The first couple of years in college I was pro war. Love your country right or wrong. Then in graduate school I traded that concept for Muhammad Ali's view: 'I ain't got no quarrel with them Vietcong.'"

Frank shrugged, took a deep drag, and combed his charcoal hair straight back, the glare of his crown more pronounced than a year ago. I told him to stand still while I wrapped a hair band around his curls in back to form a piglet-tail. He continued unpacking, tossing the contents on to the bed while telling me exactly what he brought. "Look, I even got these Patagonia shirts, just like you asked."

"I'm impressed," I said, sketching a rough itinerary in my notebook. "I thought we could fly north to Chiang Mai tomorrow, spend five days and maybe take a trek in the jungle to visit hill tribes, and then come back to Bangkok for a day or two before flying to Ho Chi Minh City. That's the new name for Saigon. We could spend a week there, then come ba—"

"And here!" He threw me a brown paper bag. "I brought some of those Good & Plenty candies Kathi said you liked, and the silk underwear you asked for." He laid a pair of swirling emerald-green and sea-blue silk boxers on his bed. "Actually, they're mine. Maddie bought them to make me look sexy."

"Thanks, Frank. Did you hear what I just said? Other than that, I haven't planned a thing. Nothing! We're not booked anyplace, we'll wing it."

"Sounds great!" he said, mainly admiring his sparkling-blue backpack, which smelled of fresh vinyl. "Hey, aren't you proud of me? I got everything in my backpack. This is the lightest I've ever traveled on vacation. Ever!"

"You're definitely a hot shit, Frank. But I suggest we take half of what we have in our backpacks to go north, and use this place as our base of operations. I don't want you to overload yourself with your leg the way it is."

24

JUNGLE JOHNNY, Z, AND UNDERSTANDING WOMEN

FOUR HUNDRED MILES NORTH OF Bangkok, Chiang Mai was the second largest city in Thailand, home to numerous golden temples, and the perfect starting point to visit the surrounding tropical jungles. The taxi driver picked out the Central Guesthouse, situated on a neighborly alley not far from the famous Night Bazaar. Frank loved it. Red bedcovers inscribed with Disney characters compensated for thin mattresses. The shower was downstairs at street level near a quaint seven-table restaurant. The bar was all teak woodwork and wide-leaf potted plants. At the entrance, a blue motorized rickshaw with painted gold safety bars waited for passengers. Frank immediately charmed the manager, and then instructed the bartender on how to put enough vodka in orange juice to make the drink fit for a New Yorker.

The bartender, Lucky, also had a second job—assistant to Jungle John, a trekking guide who conducted business out of the Central Guesthouse. Jungle John told Frank he was of Tibetan lineage and that his people had migrated south to form part of the hill tribes. His face differed from local Thais—his cheekbones were higher and his street-smart eyes had a more intense quality. His mustache had the softness of infant hair and his beard consisted of a just few long strands. Jungle John and Frank took to each other like the Starsky and Hutch.

"Hey, Denny!" Frank bellowed above the click, click, click of his cane striking the shiny, tiled floor. "This guy, Jungle John, says he can take us on a three-day trek in the jungle, elephants and all. We would leave tomorrow morning. I like him! What do you think?"

"How much?"

"Twelve hundred baht apiece. What's that? Fifty bucks for three days, including food. And we can stay at tribal villages. What do you think? If you got it flaunt it, right?"

"Alright, let's take what fate dishes out. But let's make sure this guy's an authorized guide. We should also find out how many people are coming, and if he speaks the language of the tribes we visit."

We dined on the street corner, literally—our table, dressed in white linen, was carefully arranged on the sidewalk, next to the kitchen and a freshly painted one-room bar. Our waiter wore a formal black tux. Frank wore a brand-new pair of white socks and sneaks, perhaps figuring the whiteness would blind the mosquitoes that hunted under our table.

"I always wear fresh socks," he said, sipping a pre-dinner martini.

Despite using chopsticks, we inhaled the food and were soon into our inevitable after-dinner discussion.

"Lust is a feeling," Frank stated emphatically, tapping the ash off his cigarette. "Love is a decision. It's more organized than lust, needs a modicum of communication."

"I fought falling in love with Kathi for a long time before throwing in the towel. At twenty-two, I wasn't thinking of love or marriage. Didn't even want them on the griddle until twenty-six. How old were you when you got married?"

"Twenty-one when I married Carol." An easy smile.

"Twenty-six, that was my dream. Fuck as many women as possible, and then settle down. You're right, though, once the thought of Kathi as a mother took root in my subconscious, I definitely made the decision to fall in love. Lust began to grow stronger after the commitment. Then I couldn't get enough of her."

A young Thai couple sauntered by, shyly sending each other flirting glances. I fished for money to pay the waiter. "I miss the passion of those early years. The touching and the absolute trust in each other."

After an early breakfast at the guesthouse, we loaded backpacks, food, and ourselves into a covered pickup heading north. Jungle John and Lucky had assembled a disparate, maybe desperate, group of voyagers eager to visit the hill tribes. Six Germans—two couples and two single women—a smiling Italian (who was not Frank), a rare uppity Australian, and an English stockbroker living in Singapore. Because of Frank's bulging knee wrapped in an Ace bandage, Jungle John insisted that Frank and I squeeze into the cab. Everyone else climbed in back. After an hour of driving north in the direction of Myanmar, the paved road gave way to a bumpy dirt trail along a river gorge.

We pulled over when the swell of bushes began eating the pickup. Jungle John grabbed Frank's backpack and gave it to Lucky. "You don't carry a thing Mr. Z!" he cried. Relieved of that burden, Frank, blue bandanna across his forehead, was free to wield his cane like an English duke. He engaged people and they liked it.

I worried about whether he should have been here at all. The swelling in his knee had subsided to a point where the outline of bone was barely visible, but the bulging white flesh around his calves and ankles looked like puffed rice. If Lucky hadn't carried Frank's stuff, I would have.

We followed a path that led to a bridge over the river gorge we had been skirting. Frank and I immediately threw each other worried glances. The bridge was constructed of thin, weather-beaten bamboo slats tethered together with twine and then fastened underneath with rows of bamboo poles and old rope. Missing slats left dangerous gaps. And although the river below couldn't be called raging, it wasn't docile.

Our elephants were waiting for us—roaming the bare brown earth near the river's edge, wading in the swift current, or standing patiently while local tribesmen doused them with buckets of water and scrubbed their rubbery bodies.

Tentatively venturing on to the bobbing bridge, I grabbed the rope handrail, glancing down at boulders far below and sunlight ricocheting off silver rapids. *This is fucking dangerous*, I thought, as

I stepped cautiously over a wide section of missing slats. "Careful, Frank," I cried, hearing his *click, click* and worrying that he would slip or catch the cane in a gap between slats. He poked at the planks with his cane, like a blind man, and miraculously made it to the other side.

Next, we had to mount our elephant. We climbed steps to a platform made out of hewn trees. At the top, a handler instructed us to walk on to the massive, wrinkled head of an Indian elephant with a sawn-off tusk, then along its back to a bamboo cradle. This looked far more dangerous than the bridge. Traversing those few steps from the platform across the leathery head of the beast was like balancing fifteen feet up on Jabba the Hutt. Attempting to ignore the height, I stepped along with my arms out. What did the elephant make of it? Finally, I could gingerly turn around and plop into the cradle next to Frank, who somehow had maneuvered the distance with his swollen leg. Sitting side by side, we laughed nervously, legs dangling from the cradle on to the elephant's back.

The beast set off into the jungle—delicately, like a ballerina, tip-toeing down a red-clay path no wider than the length of a child's arm. High in the air, we clung to each other, staring at the middle branches of trees and looking down at the path. It was like being on a moving four-story bridge. The elephant's eyes were small, unlike those of horses. For some reason, that made a difference, made me feel more trusting. I don't trust horses—their big eyes unnerve me. When the dips were particularly treacherous, Frank and I yelled and screamed like kids on a roller coaster, clutching the rickety cradle and each other. We shouted our fears and wild instructions to the elephant and the guide riding on its neck. My New York accent, which had lain buried under layers of Northern California propriety, blasted its way out to mingle with the Big Z's in a coordinated opera of profanity.

Frank knew how to say "fuck" naturally, with perfect inflection and tone. He wielded it like an artist wields his favorite brush. You had to have New York-Irish or Italian blood to use the word properly. It was definitely nurture over nature. The fetching flexibility of the word was lost in the gentility of California. Fuck cut through the bullshit. It created meaningful dialogue between Frank and me, helped us relate and identify with each other, to get in touch with our feelings.

As we shouted, the twelve-year-old guide took a different approach and Frank got his first taste of how another society treats animals. The boy beat the head of this noble beast with a wooden truncheon, until blood trickled down its forehead and into its eye. I yelled at him to stop, and he did. Elephants were beasts of burden, and dogs and cats a barely tolerated evil. Remembering the magnificence of elephants in Africa, I couldn't help but think how we had enslaved so many millions of animals on the principle that they were inferior. Our egos must need this distinction.

Two and a half hours into the jungle, the caravan halted at a clearing. We then trekked by foot another two hours, emerging into a primitive settlement of thatched huts. Chickens and small pigs meandered about the garbage. Jungle John escorted his troop to an elongated hut made entirely of bamboo. Colored gray-white like aged hair, the thatched roof came halfway to the ground. A weathered picnic table sat awkwardly outside. Inside was dark and humid with a hard dirt floor. Thick woven bamboo mats covered the wooden-slat bunks. Clearly not incorporated into the village, this hut marked us as outsiders.

Frank, however, thought the place was "fuckin' great." Discarding his cane for the first time, he limped along on a pre-dinner excursion, discovering that men worked in the fields until dusk. He saw women with babies strapped to their backs balancing buckets on both ends of a pole running across their shoulders. With joy, he listened to the sound of music coming from a strange-looking bamboo pipe, sniffed the aroma of cooking herbs, and observed dirty kids laughing as they kicked tin cans and threw kittens into the air (or at trees). This was his first sense of the old way.

"People go to bed when the sun goes down, and get up when it rises!" Frank exclaimed with amazement. I'd had that exact thought in a little village in Zimbabwe at the start of my journey. His enthusiasm was renewing my own sense of seeing, tasting, and feeling.

After dinner, two long-haired, somber young men walking barefoot entered the hut. One of them carried a long opium pipe and asked for volunteers. Angelo, the Italian in our group, quickly offered to be first. The New York Italian meanwhile paced up and down the dirt floor puffing furiously on a cigarette, struggling with his conscience. The rest of us waited our turn with the pipe.

The villager with the pipe had a characteristically sparse mustache and wore blue sweats with a yellow line down the sides and a smudged white T-shirt. He gestured at Frank to be next to sample nirvana. "No way," said the Z, speaking to the group. "I just don't feel right about drugs. But I don't mind if you guys try."

In case anyone else succumbed to guilt, the young tribesmen told us of the positive medicinal effects of opium. Their solemn countenances attested to the fact that opium sales were serious income for this hamlet. While drug sales were illegal in Thailand, that stricture did not apply to the hill tribes.

From a process perspective, smoking opium started with a bamboo mat, which served as a workbench, and tools: a candle, a long needle that looked like a hatpin from the thirties, a lighter, and the pipe, consisting of a foot-and-a-half-long stem connected to a singed green, metal container. Slouching forward, the young villager mixed the poppy with aspirin granules for bulk and consistency, then, using the long needle, shoved the resulting black gunk in the pipe. To smoke, you lay prone and inhaled while he applied the candle flame. The black mass undulated and bubbled to the dancing flame as you puffed away.

I didn't find the opium overpowering, more it felt like the lingering lethargy of lying on a beach in a daydream, watching sunlight flicker off waves. Afterwards still in that state, I wandered around the hamlet. Opium was right in these hills—a place devoid of television, movies, video games, city activity. Here was only nature and basic life activities.

"What time is it?" asked Frank.

"5 a.m., on the dot!"

"I don't fuckin' believe it," he bellowed, "sounds like a zoo outside."

"And the pigs aren't even up yet."

"I know! I know!" he snorted and let out his infectious laugh. "Ha ha. I haven't gotten any sleep!"

"*I'm* the one who hasn't gotten any sleep. I know for sure you've gotten sleep, Frank. Because your snores sounded like pirates dragging treasure chests across a tin roof."

He guffawed to the point of choking.

"Then the rooster relieved you at three o'clock."

"I know, I know! The 'alarm clock'! Then the hens clucked, the crows crowed, dogs barked, toads and frogs rumbled. And I haven't even gotten to the fuckin' insects. No wonder they smoke opium, it's the only way to get some sleep."

We were literally pained with laughter. The pigs began to oink and snort at whining dogs. Birds screeched, crickets chirped, babies screamed, and at least five other sounds that I couldn't name joined in the cacophony. Frank sat up on the mat, stretched his aching body, and breathed deeply a few times to clear the pain.

"Can you believe that Jungle John woke me up last night to ask if everything was okay?" he said incredulous as he pulled a pack of Camels from his pants. "And then I went to take a piss and stepped in pig shit. My bare feet! Had to run around looking for water to wash it off. Can you imagine, pig shit?"

"You should step in human shit. I did that in India."

Frank could barely contain himself. When he recovered he abruptly swung off the bunk, straightened up to the extent his knee would allow, put on his shorts and sneaks, grabbed his cane, and hobbled outside. An hour later, I staggered out to join the crowd at the picnic table for breakfast.

"You missed something this morning," Frank greeted me. "Old women were grinding corn by hand and teenage girls were feeding their babies. A little kid came over to that there hut, grabbed a chicken, and broke its neck. Killed it!"

As we were preparing to continue our trek into the jungle, I asked Jungle John why he wore army fatigues. He puffed out his bare chest like a rooster and recounted to anyone listening how he fought for seven years as a mercenary in Cambodia in the 1980s.

How was that possible, if the war was over in 1975?

"Your American CIA," he said, "they finance. I kill many enemies."

Frank and I were given a one-hour head start from the rest of the group, with Lucky leading the way and carrying Frank's backpack. We hoofed leisurely through heavy ferns and overgrowth, the beauty of the mountains and flora enrapturing us. At first,

Frank and I parried about his favorite subject—the advantages of capitalism and free-market economics. Our disagreements about capitalism weren't that fundamental, we just enjoyed taking time to joust. However, soon the rigor of the trail called for less confrontational topics.

"Say, Denny, what did you learn on this trip of yours?"

"Well ... I've learned that if you're positive, whatever happens, happens for the best. And that there are always two sides of a coin. Possessions inhibit personal freedom, and that traveling is the essence of freedom.

"Also, I'm learning a lot about what's happening to families today, and I'm beginning to see that it's possible to balance family, money, and personal freedom."

"Have your cake and eat it."

"If that's what balance is, yeah."

"What do you think is the biggest impediment to that balance?"

"Open communication, I reckon, along with being able to blend personalities."

"I guess the decline of the patriarchy puts a premium on communication, doesn't it? But people rarely change, Denny. You know that."

"Relationships change and we have to do the same, or risk divorce. Kathi and I need to figure out how to communicate."

"Yeah. Maybe you're right. Most relationships get their initial spark from two people trying to communicate to understand the other, don't they? Then we get lazy."

We were three or four miles into the trek, struggling for balance and breath on awkward angles that cut across never-ending hills. There was no breeze, not a leaf in motion, as if the wind was in hibernation. I worried about Frank's leg. The operation had sliced through an assortment of muscles and tendons. It took courage to take this trip. I felt proud knowing I was important enough for him to risk injury.

"What kind of changes did you go through living with a much younger woman?" I asked, thinking of Frank's girlfriend, Maddie, who was more than two decades younger.

"Tough question! Well, as you know it caused a lot of problems with my family, my oldest daughter being older than Maddie. The fights I've had over innocent communication would make you laugh with sadness. On the other hand, a younger woman causes me to think younger, feel younger. Gave me the opportunity to change. I like knowing I can change.

"Most times I don't notice the age difference at all. Never give it a thought. It's how you relate that counts. However, I've noticed with the operations on my shoulder and knee in the last year that I've been more conscious of physically aging. I gained some weight because I haven't been able to exercise."

"The weight looks good on you. You were too gaunt last year."

"You really think so?" he said pleased. "You know, I'm not a handsome guy. Sometimes I worry about how attractive I am."

"Takes more than a pretty face to attract most women. Look at you! You're a powerful personality and good-looking guy. Besides, our older bodies aren't meant to compete with younger ones."

"Yeah, maybe you're right."

"Still," he asked shyly, "what do you think of my smile?"

"I like it."

"Would you remind me to smile? I've been told that I'm often too serious."

"Sure! I'll also remind you to start walking without a limp."

Two hours into the trek, the rest of the troop struggled into a clearing where we were enjoying one of our many rests. Claudia, a stout German in her mid-thirties, was battling heatstroke, trying to keep up on what she called "a forced march." So Jungle John assigned her and her dark-haired friend, Meggi, to our smell-the-flowers troop. With the change of pace, Claudia soon regained her composure.

Even at our speed, the trek wasn't the proverbial walk in the park. We helped each other negotiate the slippery sunbaked hardpan of the steeper slopes, often having to grab long bamboo branches to use as railings. And most bridges we had to cross were no more than a bunch of bare saplings strung together with twine. Frank, meanwhile, was intent on bringing Claudia and Meggi into the conversation.

"*Women*," he proposed, "don't realize how powerful they are. They use tangible data because they know things, feel things. Whereas, men use intangible data because emotion has been drummed out of us. We build a case by applying logic to incomplete data. The result: our conclusions are well thought out, but often faulty. Women have power. But they don't need to be anti-men to use it. What do you women think?"

Frank liked to dive into issues and get under people's skin. He began to fire off comments like rifle shots, such as, "Politics and finances have enslaved women since the beginning of time, because women find them boring." And then, "Women have the ability to make relationships work. Men don't. If a woman sours on a relationship, it's got no chance. The opposite is not true." The two women were shy at first, but gradually they participated—as had been his aim.

When the sun began to cool, the slow and fast groups met again at a spectacular waterfall, which dropped its thundering load into a clear, deep pool. We set up camp by the water, downing liquids and relaxing to its soothing sound. While the guides whipped up a curry dish, Angelo stripped off his shirt exposing a husky, muscular frame that drew veiled glances from the women. He rolled a joint and smoked it himself. It was not that he was selfish; he smoked a joint at every available opportunity and probably got tired of asking people if they wanted a hit. The same way, I guessed, that Frank didn't constantly offer his non-filters, which had more initial punch than Angelo's reefer. I hadn't smoked cigarettes in twenty-five years before sampling the sharp buzz of his Camels. It struck me immediately that cigarette smokers were equally druggies.

After apparently voting to spend the night by the water, we were inexplicably moved on towards the next tribal village. Frank was not happy, and neither was I. He had just soaked his leg in the pool, washed, and changed his sweaty clothes. For him, it was martini time. We lagged behind the group, sulking. We only buried the subject when we reached our destination.

The new hamlet was much more affluent than the previous night's. Its huts rested high on stilts amid the hazy shroud of dusk and the smoke of smoldering wood fires. Though there was no electricity or indoor plumbing, the prosperity was also apparent in the physiques of locals and condition and numbers of livestock, including water buffalo, all of which exhibited more bulk and vigor.

I wandered around the village alone and met a family with six children. Using broken English, I learned that their nineteen-year-old son lived and attended school in Chiang Mai, at a monthly cost of two American dollars. The muscular father conveyed that the village had a resident schoolteacher for younger children. A daughter, speaking English passably, said the huts were built on stilts so that the bare ground under them could be used to socialize. Other family members and neighbors came over unobtrusively. It was unlike India and the Middle East, where people wearing big grins introduced themselves by inquiring: "What your name? Where you from? Are you married? Where your kids?"

Arriving back at the visitors' hut, I found Frank rearranging and repacking his backpack, a traveler's fetish, and gabbing to the Germans at the same time. "Can you believe it? I came with all these clothes and I don't need 'em. I keep packin' to leave more behind." When he saw me, he grabbed my arm and walked me downstairs and outside.

"Listen," he whispered, "I've been trying to avoid those bathrooms with the holes in the ground. Now I'm desperate. I'll never make it back tomorrow without burying the van in shit."

"Let me personally escort you to the communal crapper," I said, leading him up the hill arm-in-arm. "This will be another first for you."

Papaya trees and mammoth bushes with shiny green leaves, reminiscent of elephant ears, added a mysterious shadow to the descending darkness. Corralled water buffalo stared with menacingly black eyes, a pig grunted, and a chicken sat in the crook of a tree branch. We sidestepped the fresh mud created by water trickling down from the town pump at the top of the hill as we approached the outhouse.

"Is it a regular toilet?"

"It's a hole in the ground, with stirrups for traction. You back into the stirrups, place your feet directly on top of them, drop your drawers, squat down, and aim slightly in front of the hole. That's all you need to know."

"Ah, *no*! I have a problem squatting. My leg. What if my aim is off?"

Before entering the loo, Frank grabbed me: "I just want you to know I can't believe I'm doing this. The trip, I mean. *This is so exciting!* All of it."

The group ate outside by candlelight that night, around a bamboo table. Only then did it become clear why we'd moved on from the waterfall—this was Jungle John's native village. He and a few boyhood buddies chitchatted and laughed near a small wood stove in the far corner, as they cooked our supper of noodle soup and a peanut-vegetable dish. But for Frank's ebullience, it was a pretty dull scene among the Westerners. Meggi and Claudia were nice, but quiet and shy. The Italian smiled a lot. He was happy, stoned, and silent. The two German couples spoke seriously among themselves. While the young English stockbroker and dainty Australian talked to each other with affected accents, without the slightest interest in anyone else.

Things livened up when John showed us a dead rodent. He held it up by the scruff of its neck, its four little legs and pink nose dangling. Then, to our amazement, he skinned, gutted, and minced the creature, sautéing it in a spiced sauce. To cries of disgust, he offered us a taste. I gave it a go, feeling revolted at the same time. The "meat" had a soft texture, but the spices were so overwhelming that I gagged. Nevertheless, Jungle John and his friends ate the rest of the varmint, their standing among us Westerners at a low ebb.

Deigning to finally speak to someone else, the Englishman and Australian began to question Jungle John. However, they ignored his answers, babbling to each other as if he was invisible. Seemingly oblivious to their attitude, he explained how village elders ran things. With age came respect. I decided it was time to use my rank of elder, so I politely asked the two elitists to listen to our guide or at least let me listen to him.

Jungle John's people were Buddhists. How was it then that with the discovery of self you become God, I asked. He gathered three rocks, and lined them up. "This rock is God. The middle rock is ego. The third is you." He removed the middle rock. "Take away ego and you are God. Buddha says humility comes from this supreme knowledge: You are God and have no ego to win or lose."

Meggi was listening closely, but in the background, Frank was holding court with the German couples. "Women expect men to do the right thing, but they shouldn't. Men are stupid. Women should teach them. What do you guys think?" I wished that Frank didn't give the answers first, that he would ease into the conversation more. That was what I was used to, but Frank had his own way and I couldn't disagree with the results. He got people involved and smiling.

"So tell me, John," I asked, "isn't it true that Buddhists aren't meant to kill anything?"

"Yes, if everything is God, you need to submit to God."

"But you killed soldiers in Cambodia. How do you explain killing if you are Buddhist?"

"Aha, you listen to me," he replied with a laugh. "The Christians come to Vietnam and Cambodia to kill people who do nothing to them. What Christ said is difficult to do. Same same with us Buddhists."

We bedded down on thin goat-hair mats in the loft. Frank worried about the burning candles and the flammability of bamboo. He lay belly-up on the mat with a thin sheet and equally thin blanket neatly draped over him. His hands and arms were tucked into his body and he wore black eye patches.

"Hey, Frank," I whispered. "With the air so chilly, and with babbling roosters and a hard floor, do you really need eye patches?"

"Ha ha! Yeah, it's freezing!" he snorted, "But what I hate most are the roosters. I'll never feel bad eating a chicken again."

Since I didn't get to sleep right away, I wound up joining Meggi who was staring at a sheet of paper creased with age. She put it away as I approached. We listened to crickets in the blush of a crescent moon, elbows on the table and hands clasped firmly under our chins. As we talked, Meg bemoaned her lack of confidence and self-esteem.

"Women and self-esteem!" I said, as much to myself as to her. "Jungle John would probably say that lack of self-esteem relates to ego."

The early glow of sunrise peeked through missing bamboo slats in the loft and woke me. I retook my place alone at the table outside. The villagers were still inside their huts. In the distance, a smoky mist settled over mountain peaks. In the peaceful quiet, I felt as if I was the only person in the world.

25

Third Challenge: Z in Chiang Mai

Inevitably, the blowout came. Frank and I were just back at the Central Guesthouse in Chiang Mai with the rest of the trekking group. The evening started innocently enough. Most of the group were sipping drinks and lounging in wicker chairs. The scent of flowers wafted in. We might have been in a mountain chateau. Then, slicked up and ready for a night on the town, Frank entered and limped across the tiled floor towards us, great bursts of laughter erupting from his throat.

"This one's a beaut," he said describing the shower. "Finally, I get hot water, which is like gold around these parts. But with every glimmer of sunshine there's a little rain. Do you guys know that I had to push a red button for the hot water? That was okay. Who could mind that? But once I let go of the red button, the hot water stops comin'.

"So now I'm trying to keep one hand on the red button and wash with soap with the other. And that was a lot easier than shaving. A professional juggler would've had a tough time with the button, the razor, and the soap! To make matters worse, there's this here tiny shelf for toiletries near the shower spray. I used it to hold my shaving gear.

"If I'm not screwing up keeping my hand on the red button, I'm hitting the tray and knocking my shaving gear all over the floor. And that's not all. A renegade spray from the shower is aimed right at my dry towel. Ha, ha, ha!"

Third Challenge: Z in Chiang Mai

That laugh was infectious.

"Hey, Lucky," Frank called to our assistant guide behind the bar. "Would you mind mixing a couple of those screwdrivers I showed you how to make? Don't forget to be generous with the vodka." Then he motioned Jungle John over and put his arm around his shoulder.

"Hey, John," Frank said, as they both flicked ash off their cigarettes in unison. "This was a wonderful, wonderful trip. When my girlfriend and I come back we're going to trek with you. Only thing is that your village could do a lot more business if they had a better toilet."

"Mr. Z that is good idea. Tomorrow, we drive to my village and you tell them how to build this toilet you are donating," the guide said, knocking back a shot of Mekhong whiskey. "Outside the toilet, we nail a sign: 'In honor of Mr. Z, Adventurer.'"

The gathering eventually dwindled to Frank, Meggi, and me. She and Frank were engrossed in a disagreement about capitalism and the treatment of poor in America. Meggi was outgunned—water pistol versus bazooka—but she stuck in there, squirting at Americans.

"You see, the economic concept of communism has proven to be a disaster," Frank said, leaning back in his chair as if he were a professor with a student. "People need to be *incented*, and the best system to accomplish that is capitalism. There is no benefit to society when the government pays people who don't work."

"If America works so well," Meggi shot back, "why does it have so many people living on the street, so much violence?" Her eyes gleamed righteously behind her black-rimmed round glasses. The absence of lines on her face and willingness to fight a losing battle with Frank were testament to her youth.

"We don't have a true capitalistic system in the US. The liberals spend money paying people who don't work, and on layers of bureaucracy that make and enforce laws that often restrict free trade and business growth. With less restrictions and more money in the hands of business, there would be more investment and growth, and less people on the streets."

"Why is one system the best? Maybe we need a variety. Not all people are the same."

"Because, you see, one system—capitalism—means growth

and jobs," Frank continued, relishing his professorial role. "And with a growing worldwide economy, countries compete with each other for a piece of the pie. Socialist systems create government jobs to keep unemployment down. As that structure grows, fewer and fewer productive people support the whole. There's no incentive for anyone to work harder than the least productive worker. In a global market, that means your goods are not competitive."

"Frank, not all societies are ripe for capitalism," I interrupted. Although I didn't essentially disagree with him, I wanted to level the playing field for Meggi. "In fact, the very nature of capitalism is often destructive to the growth of the society. For instance, Russia at the turn of this century had no middle class, either monetarily or in terms of education. The rich would have gotten richer and the poor poorer under capitalism. Communism prevailed because the vast majority of citizens were poor farmers. There's a good argument to say that communism brought the people to the point where they now have an educated middle-class ripe for capitalism and democracy. Was it the wrong system?"

We went back and forth. Meggi pounded on Americans' propensity for arrogance, shallowness, and societal violence. Traits, she felt, they exported in films and videos. Sometimes I agreed with her, sometimes I didn't. Frank steered clear of challenging my comments. I didn't do the same. Frank's face was placid towards me. Too placid.

When Meggi left to go to a popular nightspot Frank turned to me icily. Barely controlling his voice, he sneered: "Don't you ever, *ever*, do that to me again! You and I should keep our disagreements in the family, not spread them on the fuckin' table for all to see."

I was shocked. Only my father ever talked to me like that. I responded too quickly. "Frank, if you'd asked me nicely, I would probably respect your request, but not when you speak like that." I knew it was a stupid response for the circumstance. An ego reaction to a button pushed. Why couldn't I let someone blow off steam? Apologize, then discuss.

A glazed look filled his eyes and the Frank I loved disappeared. He had the look powerful people get when they lose control.

I wasn't in the same space as Frank, but I also wasn't the traveler persona either. What was this pride that rendered even

Third Challenge: Z in Chiang Mai

the best of friendships as fragile as an eggshell? Frank's shoulders stiffened, color drained from his face. His chin jutted forward stretching the muscles of his neck, and even the three-day salt-and-pepper growth on his face now looked threatening. I felt a chill when he looked at me.

"What did you say?" he said sternly before the volcano blew. "I WANT RESPECT BETWEEN US. THAT'S ALL I'M FUCKING ASKING FOR!"

"THEN ASK FOR IT IN A FUCKIN' RESPECTFUL WAY!" I shouted back, throat tightening.

We were two rams locking horns, acting out a primeval drama for supremacy. Two people who rarely felt the yoke of domination, familiar with any opponent wilting in front of them.

Normally, I was spared this type of confrontation because my body language already gave fair warning to tread easy, which I'd inherited from my grandmother. But I had triggered Frank's submerged dynamics. His struggle with his family lasted for years after he separated with and finally divorced his wife. Now he was trying hard to reassemble the pieces.

It was an all too familiar dynamic: talented male rises through the ranks in business, augmenting his natural power with logic and pragmatism. He becomes an infallible machine, with no "off" switch when he walks through the door of his home. Wife and children become "losers" because logic makes him always right—even when he's wrong. Who can argue with the power of logic? The spouse and kids eventually guard their self-esteem by taking the opposite position to whatever philosophy comes out his mouth. They're tired of losing, of not being heard because of different logic. They lose trust in his motives. They have no choice; they're dealing with a machine. But the machine is sensitive too, needs understanding, a pat on the back. He's just doing his job, supplying wealth to the family the best way he knows how.

I learned from Frank's experience. His pain probably saved my marriage. Now, in Thailand, I tried to concentrate on *seeing* Frank. His Italian culture required that the father receive respect above all else. And here I was taking the opposite position to him, the father, by teaming up with Meggi.

Frank shot out of the chair, which was hard to do with the bum leg, and started to leave. I didn't want our friendship to slip away down some drain in Northern Thailand. It was déjà vu—losing a friend because I couldn't find that awareness to communicate. *Change the energy,* the voice inside said. *Get rid of the ego!* As my energy changed and I softened, I noticed Frank's inner reluctance to leave. He stood there, undecided. I saw in his face that part of him wanted to say, "Fuck you," and another was asking, "Hold on, Frank, what are you doing?"

"I'm sorry, Frank," I said exasperated. "I didn't mean it. What I said was stupid and childish. You're right. We're good friends. We shouldn't quarrel in front of other people. And if you want to keep it in the family, that's okay with me.

"It's true, I didn't like the way you dominated the conversation. I felt you patronized her, gave her the answers. *Your* answers. I've been trying to avoid giving advice and answers on this trip."

It felt so good to address his problem with me in a constructive rather than defensive manner. Deep down I was honored that Frank considered me family.

His stance eased noticeably, but his face retained harshness. He reiterated that he wanted our disagreements kept "in the family." If I agreed, it would close the matter for him.

His words and manner stirred up an old, old feeling, one buried deep into my sub-conscious following violent arguments with my father. It was a button that had been pushed again and again in my youth. There'd been no handling me after that button had been pushed. The predecessor to the controller was the uncontrollable.

I slammed my vodka and orange juice on the table and began to stride out. Memories of the incidents in Greece and India haunted me. At the doorway I turned and saw my friend looking irate but not moving from beside the table. Lucky caught the corner of my eye. He was cleaning up as fast as he could to get the hell out of there.

"That's great for you, Frank!" I said on the verge of exploding. "But what about me? What about my issues with you? Friendship is a fucking two-sided coin.

"I SAID THAT YOU GIVE PEOPLE ALL THE ANSWERS. THAT'S NOT WHAT THIS TRIP IS ABOUT FOR ME. NOW, I WANT YOU TO ADDRESS THAT!"

Stop and change the energy! Try to see him, the voice of the traveler entreated. We looked into each other's eyes. Our demeanors softened. We slowly walked towards each other and stood face to face for a few seconds, silently trying to sort it out. Then we both went into the street. Two Western women in their early thirties, with large Indian daypacks slung over their shoulders, passed us. We didn't know them. Unbelievably, they smiled and nonchalantly invited us to join them. They were going to the same bar as Meggi.

Still vulnerable to anger, Frank and I walked and talked. We concentrated on the positive, buying time to heal. Frank asked me to repeat my issues.

"You know, there's always something else that causes us to explode," he said after I'd spoken. "There's always something behind our statements that we're not saying." This was Frank's nature—to articulately sum up and analyze both sides of a discussion. "And look, this is your trip. I'll keep my mouth shut. I won't say anything. I'll just listen."

I put my arm through his, feeling something major had happened to me—my traveler personality was here to stay.

"Don't get me wrong, Frank, I love the way you get people involved. You show interest in them. That laugh of yours lights up your entire face and puts us all at ease. It's just that I'm out of touch with conflict and I'm in between new and old ways of handling it.

"But hear what I'm saying, because I mean every fucking word from the bottom of my heart. I love the way you are with people. If the price I have to pay is that you control the conversation more than I would like, I would gladly pay it! I swear to God I would.

"Besides, you couldn't keep your mouth shut even if you wanted to."

"Do you really think I dominate?" he asked with laughter in his voice. He looked across at me warmly, the twinkle returning to his eyes.

"You're a powerful man. You don't need to say much. People get your drift just looking at you. Everyone on the trek knew you were pissed when we didn't stay at the waterfall the day before last. And you said very little."

"You think so? I'm never able to gauge the effect of my personality on other people."

"Me either."

"Let's have a drink with the ladies," he said, pressing my arm with his hand. "Can you believe they invited us to join them?"

Shaky, but smiling inside, I realized I had blown off steam and made it back to mellow. It was true that, unlike Joe Reilly and Janet, Frank was a person doggedly determined to discuss the issues. He needed to get conflict out and not harbor it. But still, I witnessed how the voice inside me could change the energy. It might take a lifetime to take away ego, as Jungle John said, and easily switch personalities to match all kinds of circumstances. But for now I felt confident that the traveler was in charge.

26

WOMEN'S FOUR
PHASES OF NEEDS

I MARVELED AT THE JUXTAPOSITION OF old and new in Thailand. In the past five days, we had gone from Bangkok, with its modern airport and roads, rush-hour traffic, and gorgeous waterways, to jungle and tribal villages with scarcely the bare necessities. Somewhere between was Chiang Mai filled with flowers, parks with waterfalls, and gleaming golden temples that spiraled into the sky. All these Thailands were within a radius of five hundred miles.

After touring the charming city during the day on rickshaw, the Piccola Roma Palace beckoned us to dinner. The owner, Angelo, was old Italian. He led us to a table by the window, beyond which merchants were closing up for the day. Frank spoke with Paolo in Italian and ordered a bottle of Chianti Classico.

Paolo doted on us, carefully selecting the wine and pouring it himself for our approval. A waitress with shiny, black hair down to the small of her back brought mussels cooked in an outstanding red sauce. We toasted to friendship.

Paolo came by and proudly introduced his pretty, much younger Thai wife. After they left, Frank said, "Young women give an older guy the chance to do over right what he did wrong the first time."

"Many people would think you're with a younger woman because of a midlife crisis," I said.

"Jesus," he gasped, almost choking on a mussel, "I went through that in my forties. People like to put things in neat little boxes. Look at you: long hair in a ponytail, strange clothes. They might say you're going through a midlife crisis. But traveling with you for five days, I think you're on an adventure of a lifetime. So fuck them!"

Frank lamented how hard it was to get back the respect of kids once you've lost it. "Kids are hard judges on divorce. They have no experience of what it takes to keep up a long-term relationship—especially in these times when it's hard enough to maintain a relationship between friends, much less spouses. In the end though, blood really is thicker than water. You can have only one biological dad and mom."

The evening developed into an exquisite meld of good food, wine, and stimulating conversation. A feeling of unexpected, Old World elegance permeated the place: white linen tablecloth, matching napkins, the flicker of candlelight. The carbonara was remarkable and Frank approvingly declared the pasta *al dente*.

The subject we settled on was one of our favorites: differences between the genders. I described the island in Lake Naivasha, Kenya where a brutally scarred male eland guarded a territory in which his troop of females and young felt secure. I was alone on this island and had felt his frightening power.

"Men and women have different roles designed into our genes," I said. "All of a sudden, faced with a six-fold increase in population growth this century, massive environmental damage, and a nuclear button that could destroy the planet, nature came up with an elegant solution: equalize the genders. Balance man's desire to build and conquer with woman's desire for security. The result is gender equality, which led to birth and arms control. But let's face it, equality means individualism, and individualism is hard on relationships."

"You have an interesting theory there," he said in his business voice—no Bronx accent. "I read this book recently. It said women progress through four phases of needs. First, security. Second, family, and third, sex. And number four … Oh yeah, is baubles. You know, things to buy. It said women are designed to be receivers and men givers."

"That last part would get you crucified, but it's an interesting concept. And it applies to our most basic need and programming in life. Men give the seed and women accept it."

"That's it! Relationships will work as long as men give and women receive. The problem is that men don't always know what they are supposed to give, and women don't ask directly. Communication! And even if the man did continue to give, the woman might not acknowledge it. So he stops giving and she stops receiving—scratch one relationship.

"This book also said that people use different languages to communicate needs, and that each of us is usually most fluent in only one of the languages."

"What are they?" I asked, wishing I had Frank's memory.

"Touch, gifts, chores, words, and feelings. Denny, you, for instance, predominantly use *words* to communicate."

I was thinking "touch."

"The problem is that while one communicates love through words, the other doesn't get it," Frank continued, "because that person can only hear love through touch or gifts. The challenge is to be sensitive to each person's dominant form of communication. It's incredibly frustrating to try to communicate love, and the other person doesn't get it."

"Kathi uses gifts. She's always giving me these nice little cards and gifts, especially around holidays. She loves holidays.

"Christ, the levels of communication! First, there's nature with its confusing gender interpretations. Then oral language with its innuendoes, hidden meanings, and multiplicity of words. There's each individual with their stored memories, feelings, and body language. Then there's the family system we grow up in, with its own pitfalls. Now you've tossed in the language of need. It's amazing how many ways there are to communicate!"

"And we generally don't!"

"It's like crossing the Bermuda Triangle in a storm," I said, "navigating gender, family systems, and all these personal characteristics. We all have Bermuda Triangle relationships. And listening is the key to navigating them, my man, cos we ain't ever gonna remember all this other stuff in the heat of discussion."

"Amen to that."

Back at the hotel, Frank dug into his pocket, pulled out a faded piece of paper, and handed it to me. "I ran into Meggi this morning before they left. She gave me this to give to you. Said she and Claudia were staying at the Mandarin Hotel in Bangkok. She said it was a poem. You figure it out."

We poured over it as if it was a treasure map, trying to make something out of the foreign words.

"Looks French," I said. "What's the meaning, do you think?"

"A young woman, romance!"

"Let's try to have it interpreted."

27

Love Me Two Times, I'm Goin' Away

Frank had gotten heavily into budget traveling, so by the time we arrived at the Bangkok airport, *he* led me past the tourists paying full price for the official taxis and grabbed a rogue cab. Crowds were everywhere. The traffic was so bad downtown that we could leisurely observe the locals playing mahjong on rugs in their small flats. Bangkok's traffic jams might be like the West's, but you get to (slowly) pass heavenly golden temples and sidewalk food stands sizzling with all sorts of delights. Today, in the stuck traffic, there were also revelers leaning out windows waving banners.

"What is happening?" I asked the driver as firecrackers blasted.

"Today, king birthday."

"Well, you have a beautiful country," the Z said slowly, speaking through an unlit Camel. "And a very good king, a very good king."

"Our king good to us. He very wise king. Two million people come Bangkok. Celebrate birthday. Many games and much celebration," he said smiling broadly.

Thais, I'd noticed, got turned on by their king, as well as celebrations, fast boats, food, the outdoors, beauty, women with child-like voices, kick-boxing, and, sometimes, cleanliness. I particularly liked their broad smiles.

"Why not try the honest approach?" Frank said, going back to the poem we were unable to translate. "Call Meggi to make arrangements for dinner—just the two of you. I'll lie low and leave our room free till early morning. Remember she gave you that poem for a reason."

"Calling for a date! Jesus, it's been a long time. Does 'date' even exist in the vernacular anymore?"

"I have no fuckin' idea."

The conversation didn't go as smoothly as the rehearsal with Frank. "Ah, Meggi. Hi! I got your poem. But I really need an interpreter. Would you like to join me for dinner, ah, an intimate—"

Bzzzz! The pay phone went dead.

Fumbling for change, I hadn't been quick enough feeding in coins. Christ! Did the phone have to cut off at "intimate"? What will she think? "Tell her you two have only one night together, and you'd like it to be intimate, just the two of you," Frank had advised. "Why not?"

Right, why not! Why should I be afraid of a young woman I will never see again? Because I fucking hated rejection. But I liked Meggi—serious, sense of humor, pleasant smile, intelligent. Not bad legs either. And why would she give Frank that poem to give to me? Oh well, hoping she'd read *Fear of Flying* and was familiar with the concept of the zipless fuck, I dialed again.

"Yes, I'd love to," she said in reply to the dinner invite.

How sweet it was! Things looked good. A mature man like me, poetic atmosphere, dinner on the river! How could I miss? The clunker was dealing with the mind of a woman. It was a thousand-piece puzzle with most pieces blank. But romance beckoned.

I picked up Meggi at 8 p.m. on the swank side of town at the palatial Mandarin Hotel. What a metamorphosis! From baggy pants and pullover to silky, black slacks and colorful, form-fitting, flowery blouse. Her clothes accented proud, firm breasts and rounded, heavenly hips. Raven hair dangled in curls down her delicate neck. The big circular glasses were gone, better to see brown, pensive eyes and long eyelashes, and shift the emphasis to her moist, full lips. She looked terrific, and smelled like fresh lilacs. Women never ceased to amaze me.

The plan was to go to the cozy riverside restaurant near Khao San Road where Laurie and I bought the waitress whiskey. I felt in control, a man of the world, sophisticated traveler. I was wearing the blue sport shirt I picked up in Greece for just such an occasion—opened up to expose blond chest hairs. Maybe a little gray, but so what, a guy uses what he's got! Hair slicked back, face smooth as marble, missing-nail finger bandaged anew, and shave lotion from Frank. I was cool.

Unfortunately, I wasn't destined to remain quite so cool. Crowds were celebrating the king's birthday with the kind of frenzy reserved in the West for an eighty-percent-off sale at Walmart's. People were everywhere, dressed in colorful flowered silk costumes that brought visions of the days of Siam. They loved their king.

To make life easier for our cabby, I magnanimously suggested he drop us off "near" the restaurant. But neighborhoods here looked the same at night, and there was nothing I was familiar with when we exited the taxi. After twenty minutes of shuffling down back alleys and asking directions from lounging, no-English folks, I shrugged and suggested we take a rickshaw to Khao San Road.

From the fresh start of Khao San, I took what I thought would be a shortcut to the restaurant through the grounds of the aging, golden-topped Buddhist temple. Meggi stayed close at hand and trusting. I knew that on the other side of the temple was the river. No dice! The shortcut became a long cut, dead-ending at a faded white concrete wall eight-feet tall with a locked gate. The only other route I knew to get to the river was the alleyway that Laurie had led me down to get to the Apple Guest House.

My confidence was fading with each errant step. I felt stupid.

This was definitely not a route to impress any date, but it would get us to our destination. *My* date trailed slightly behind, not speaking, but her eyes still soft and trusting. In the daytime, the alleyway had been innocuous, but at night, it became a dark concrete jungle, threatening danger. A mangy dog barked in the distance. A half-moon pierced the darkness to light our steps. We walked two blocks, past the empty kickboxing gym to a gate that led to the road the restaurant was on.

Son of a bitch! The gate was locked. Meggi looked at me

with a face I couldn't read—adventure struck or dumbfounded, I couldn't tell you.

Sweat dripped into the blue shirt, and my face reddened from embarrassment. The mature man had faded. Meggi made matters worse. Still cool and patient, she didn't offer any advice. She was relying on my judgment. And all I was thinking was, "What's she thinking?"

We retraced our steps and took an alternate route through the dusty kickboxing gym. The leather punching bags hung in the gloom like gargantuan roosting bats. From between the bags, a wiry, battle-scarred fighter suddenly appeared.

"This is a dangerous place to take such a pretty lady," he growled, deep and raspy like you would imagine Jack the Ripper.

"I agree, buddy," I said, feeling disgusted with myself after stumbling around for over an hour. Romance had withered like a green salad left out overnight.

Finally, we arrived at the restaurant. It was 9:40 p.m. A petite hostess showed us to our seats—a table for two at the edge of the gurgling water. A warm romantic breeze blew in from the river and dried my nervous sweat. A long narrow boat motored quietly across our view, hardly disturbing the water. I took a deep breath and tried to change the energy.

"Sorry! No wine!" the waiter said.

Another deep breath. "Meggi, do you want beer?"

"Beer is good, thank you." She was showing a warm sensitivity, which comforted me after I'd muddled through the streets. And I began to compose myself.

"So, what does the poem say, Meggi?" I asked with a smoothness of delivery that surprised even me. It was clear from her answer that she'd expected the question.

"The poem reflects the tug of war between the harshness and joy of life," she said with a slight lisp, probably from being Portuguese living in Germany and speaking English. "It's the constant battle to maintain a balance."

Soft lights twinkled like distant stars on both sides of the river. Water gurgled. We shared shrimp and vegetables in a delicious coconut sauce, along with a large brown bottle of Bintang beer. Most of the other customers had drained from the restaurant to celebrate the royal birthday. The king was the furthest topic from my mind.

I asked her what the poem meant to her. She brushed her hair back from her forehead and played with a silver and jade earring. Her sad eyes focused on me. "It's my favorite poem. I see myself in that struggle. I'm a twenty-six-year-old woman who has the same problem I had when I was sixteen. I don't know where I'm going, and the perfectionist in me cries for direction." If Meg didn't look so serious, I would have thought she'd thrown in the confused female to make me feel better. She said how hard it was to visualize a satisfied future without confidence to see it through.

"*So*, why did you ask Frank to give me that poem?"

"Why do you think?" she responded, her despondent eyes changing to coy and mysterious. I loved it when women gave that deep look.

"I think you wanted me to know something about you. I think you wanted me to contact you in Bangkok."

Without taking her eyes from mine, she nodded.

"Why did you want to see me?" I asked, leaning forward to revel in the response.

"I like the way you treat your friends. And I like the way you and Frank laughed and talked about so many different ideas. The way you included Claudia and me in discussions," she said smiling, but then caught me by surprise. "Denis, sometimes you ask too many questions. It helps to question less, feel more."

We left the restaurant and walked in the direction of the celebrations. Feeling like a boy on his first date, I grabbed Meggi's hand. I wasn't from Podunkville, but I felt more comfortable manipulating a troubled company than I did reaching to hold her. Hand-in-hand, we meandered through dense carnival crowds. Slender revelers, shouting and laughing hung out of cars in traffic that crept like a caterpillar. People in celebratory spirit filled every square inch of the grassy park near Khao San Road. Half the seven million residents of Bangkok must have been on its streets—not to mention those two million visitors from all over Thailand. What a bash! People smiled and joked, firecrackers blasted, lights dazzled night into day, little kids looked round wide-eyed. And vendors sold the normal variety of barbecued meat, pad thai, and roasted insects.

We watched a Thai-style beauty pageant. Pretty women promenaded gracefully across a stage, very shyly smiling at the crowd. They were all dressed in artistic satin costumes recalling eighteenth-century Siam. While across the street, the boys were showing off too. In a brightly lit field, two opposing teams—one in brilliantly colored yellow shirts with blue stripes, and the other in blue shirts with yellow stripes—tried to kick a soccer ball fifteen feet up into a rope basket. I marveled at the skill of the players in this combination of soccer and basketball. The ball never once touched the ground.

After the romance in Russia, I felt more comfortable as a single man, confident in my looks and charm. I put my hands on Meggi's shoulder, turned her to face me, and kissed her gently on the lips.

She responded to the kiss, then looked around. "Oh, Denis, I don't think Thais like this kind of open display."

"Let's go to my place."

"I'm scared."

"It's a moment in time, Meggi. It won't happen again. Grab it with me!"

Meggi sat on Frank's bed looking shyly across a deep chasm at me on my bed. Two people trying to figure out what to do next. Such a simple room, I thought. Newspaper-sized window on the far side, Formica table loaded with the contents of backpacks, two single beds on a tile floor. No hot water, no air conditioning.

"I feel like a virgin," she said, exhaling a deep breath. "I've been with someone for six years. We only broke up three months ago. You're the first 'other man' in all those years.

"Do you think you could get me something to drink?"

"Do you mean a Coke or water?"

"Whiskey, I think. I guess. I don't know why. I never drink it!"

I left the room on the verge of panic, not wanting to lose the moment or the woman. Here I was, a guy who'd been through a lifetime of corporate intrigue, who'd traveled three-quarters of the way around the world in all sorts of dangerous conditions, and I was being such a ditz with a pretty woman! I ran across Khao San Road into the first store I saw.

"Can I have one of those bottles of Mekhong? Some Coke too?"

"Sorry, we closed," the attendant said.

"This is an emergency! I wouldn't ask otherwise. It's not quite a matter of life and death, but it's close." He shrugged and reached for the Mekhong.

After Meg and I had downed a shot of Mekhong and Coke, I leaned over to her side, took her hand firmly, and pulled her into my bed. As our bodies pressed against each other, building heat, I relished the first moments of a new passion. I looked into her eyes, dark, mysterious pools. She retreated from the intensity of my gaze, and lay back on the pillow in surrender, her black hair flowing like a deity's. She moved her tongue in the corner of her mouth, wickedly, invitingly.

I felt heat rush into my loins, each of my senses immersed in the intensity of the rush. Leaning down, I answered her invitation, nibbling at her moist lips and tasting more vigorously the fragrance and wetness of her mouth.

Then we undressed each other ever so slowly, starting with my shirt and her blouse. Each button savored. As she felt my face tenderly, she ran her other hand up the firm muscles of my stomach and through the hairs of my chest. We pulled off each other's pants. Her bra followed.

How I loved to undress women!

I felt the contours of her firm, milky-white breasts as they were unveiled. Then I kissed her neck and eyes and ran my fingers from her breasts, across her flat stomach, and under tight white cotton panties that clung to her shapely buttocks. Meggi searched my eyes as my fingers massaged her clitoris, moving with the rhythm of her body. My heart was bursting.

"Do you have a condom?" she whispered urgently.

"Yes"

"Oh, Denis," she moaned relieved, "no more worries!"

We gently removed the last of each other's clothes. I was naked and hard and she stroked me until I could hardly take it anymore. In the humidity of the tropical air, our tongues hungrily explored every inch of the other. I tasted the salty beauty of her smooth body.

As I entered her, we moaned in unison. I delighted at the ecstasy in her face, the look of intense satisfaction. I held back my own pleasure, like a dam with a rising, swollen river. Our energies became one. I countered and flowed with her rhythm. We switched positions and she rode me, back arched, straining for the sweet spot, breasts wonderfully poised. I don't believe there's anything in the world quite as exquisite as a woman leading up to orgasm.

Watching me watch her climax excited her all the more. A voyeur to her own ecstasy. Stoked by her cries and the stimulating rhythm of her pelvis, I let out a primal scream of passion and exploded into her. The moment lasted forever. Our months of abstinence were over.

We clung to each other, like vines.

We wanted to prolong this sweet evening. She nestled her head in the crook of my neck, and the passion of lust evolved to tenderness and laughs. Lying naked, we probed each other's thoughts. What did we like about each other? Did I ever make love to a prostitute? How did making love to an older man feel? When would Frank get back? One thing led to another and she pulled me on top of her for more.

At 3 a.m., Frank knocked gingerly on the door and whispered he'd be in the lobby. "What should I say to him when I see him?" asked Meggi while we dressed.

"Take a deep breath, give Frank a kiss on each cheek, and say goodnight." It was only then that my bandaged finger began to throb again.

Meggi and I never exchanged addresses or last names. She left the next day with her friend, Claudia, for the southern island of Koh Samui. Two days later, on the eve of my flight to Vietnam with Frank, I received a phone call from her. She'd had a loving time with me and requested I buy a specific music tape, *The Best of the Doors*. "Listen to song number six," she said. "Don't forget! The album cover shows Jim Morrison and his hands." Her voice faded, overcome with static, and she disappeared from my life.

A person could buy just about anything on Khao San Road—silks, cassette players, tickets to travel anyplace (in Thailand or the world), and music tapes. You name it, this road had got it. Frank and I followed her instructions. We scoured the music stands until we found the tape. Back at the guesthouse, song number six blasted out of my tape recorder. It was "Love Me Two Times."

What a romantic. She left no address—Cinderella without leaving the shoe.

28

God, I Love Traveling!

Our last day before flying to Vietnam saw us experience two contrasting sides of Bangkok. After a Khao San Road facial—complete with cucumbers over the eyes and a full fruit salve—we rented a boat to tour the khlongs. Made of varnished teakwood, the vessel was partly covered by canvas awning to protect passengers from heatstroke and its bow was so thin it could have doubled for a needle. Sitting at the very stern of the boat, the captain fired up a powerful outboard motor and steered off between other long, narrow boats down the dull-green waterway. Once we reached the center of the city, the river widened and we rolled past the elegant picturesque pagodas, temples, and gardens I'd seen with Laurie and Werner.

On the other side of the center, back in the suburbs, the river narrowed once again as we navigated through garbage-strewn neighborhoods, then neat, well-kept-up ones. People bathed in front of thatch-roofed docks, picket fences, and V-shaped homes that rose on stilts. Swamp reeds and telephone poles merged and willows hung over the water. Neighbors chatted with each other as they shopped at the floating markets. Protected from the sun by hats shaped like lampshades, the vendors served freshly cooked fish and noodles from tall pots and pig-iron woks. A colorful array of vegetables and fruits were stacked in the hulls of the boats, while more delicate stock was kept in aluminum boxes.

The statue of a goddess in an ancient triangular temple with painted golden flames sparked a resumption of our favorite dialogue.

"Long-term relationships are so much harder to maintain these days," I said. "Society is so fucking complex. The family structure is fragile and the workplace makes it easier to find lovers. Now the individual is king and we are less willing to perform traditional roles that kept us bound to family in the old days."

"I agree," Frank said. "The difference is that in the old days—and I'm not saying it was better—people stayed together because it was expected.

"Getting married's a big risk. I can see why older societies used matchmakers. Before people get married today they should ask these six questions.

"Number one: Do they accept each other for who they are, and do they acknowledge their bad habits? Number two: Are they committed to each other's commitments, and can they empower each other? Number three: Can they communicate vulnerability without it being used against them?

"Number four is, Can they live through bad times? Five: Will they make good parents? Did they consider each other's genes, take a hard look at each other's family and how they related, and—"

"You marry the family, don't you?"

"You bet your sweet ass. Now, wait a minute, there was one more. Oh yeah, number six is, Do they have similar interests?"

Frank then took a break from marriage counseling to point out a bunch of boys hanging on a rope. It was attached to a steel railroad trestle that crossed the river. The lads swung three at a time, pushing and shoving to maintain their position on the rope before letting go and plunging into the water below.

In a mirror of my day with Laurie and Werner, after another excellent dinner on the river, we rickshawed to the bright lights of the notorious Patpong. We began by walking down the middle of the street checking out booths with silk scarves, watches, and colorful pens. But the main action was away from the market. In the sidewalk bars, troupes of beautiful women—some girls of just sixteen or so—danced in scanty bathing suits with number tags. They danced like their legs hadn't quite caught up with the tempo of Western music.

I often tried to assess the happiness quotient of people I observed. I watched their smiles, glances, nuances, and worked out stress levels from the suppleness of their bodies. Were these young women from the jungle areas I'd just visited? Although in some of the villages life appeared easy going, often it was harsh or just boring. Was it the bright lights and thrills that attracted them to the capital, or had they been forced by family for economic gain? Most likely all these reasons. And their happiness was hard to gauge—the smiles looked genuine enough on most of the younger women, only among the older ones was there a harsher face or two.

A tout urged Frank and me to follow him, have a beer, and see "girls do *everything*" on stage. He shoved a "menu" at us with fifteen numbered acts. Number one on the list—*Man and woman fucking*.

"How much for the beers?" I asked.

"Four dollar."

"Are you crazy? We're not tourists." Frank and I began to move on.

"Okay, okay. One dollar!"

He led us up a narrow stairway into an intimate room, with a stage elevated to the height of the bar. Young women immediately came over and rubbed their bare skin against us, encouraging us to fondle them. Frank sent them away. On stage, a woman stripped to pounding rock music and then popped table tennis balls from her vagina across the room.

"I can't believe that, can you?" said Frank. "How can they do that?" Soon another was pulling razor blades on strings from her vagina. And a third held a lighted candle over her head dripping hot wax on to her face, lips, breasts, and genitals.

"Ow, Denis! That's got to hurt. Who gets off on these things?"

Another woman flirted with us from stage while an artist painted her as if she were canvas. Across the oval bar, a middle-aged couple watched and teased each other. What was the woman thinking? There was nothing erotic to me about the painting or a woman pulling razors from her body.

The couple went to leave through a door by the stairway only to find their way blocked by a hefty, gray-haired woman in her late fifties. They bickered with her for about ten minutes. Finally, the couple paid. A single man went through the same routine—also eventually dipping his hand into his pocket for money before the madam opened up.

"Hey, Denny, have you noticed the commotion over there?"
"Yeah! What do you think's going on?"
"I don't know!"

We'd reached our limit of degradation and requested the bill. Two thousand five hundred baht, almost a hundred dollars! I looked at the itemization. The beers *were* a dollar each, but napkins, twenty dollars each .... That was as far as I got.

"Let's get the fuck out of here," I whispered to Frank and slammed two hundred baht on the bar. We bolted for the door. The portly madam was in the process of turning a key in the lock when I grabbed her hand and yanked the door wide enough to jam my foot.

All hell broke loose behind me. Frank caught the brunt of the frenzy. Every working woman in the place must have been pounding on his back and arms. We squeezed through the door and headed downstairs as fast as we could.

Two touts stood between us and the exit to crowded Patpong. Women were yelling and screaming above us. Someone tossed a chair down. I caught a glimpse of the madam waving our bill in righteous indignation. Her sheer gall pissed me off and I began to run back up the stairs intending to grab the bill, crumple it, and fling it in her face.

"What the fuck's the matter with you?" Frank yelled, before I'd managed three steps. "Didn't you learn anything where you grew up in the city? Let's get the fuck out of here!" I turned quickly, and close on Frank's heels, fled past the touts guarding the door.

"What are you?" Frank screamed, red with anger, "Fucking crazy? You never go back! You don't know who those guys are!"

I grabbed him around the shoulders, and laughing, pulled him to me and kissed his forehead. Of my friends growing up, I was always the one in control. The one who kept *them* out of trouble.

"You're absolutely right, Frank! But what a fucking time we've had, huh? Look at the trouble you get me into! God, I love traveling!"

VIETNAM
TWO SIDES OF A COIN

29

THE MAN, THE HOLE, AND THE RAT

I WASN'T THE FIRST AMERICAN TO fly in over Vietnam. And probably also not the first one who realized he understood nothing at all about the country. What it looked like. Its history. Religion. How people thought. Why during the war Buddhist monks doused their orange robes with gasoline and set light to themselves. Who were these people that beat the most powerful war machine ever assembled, and had such a financial and moral impact on America?

Vietnam brought back memories of Johnson and Nixon "bombing for peace," Rambo, and US Navy air cadets singing "Cos napalm sticks to kids" in the movie *An Officer and a Gentleman*. It was the other half of George Carlin's observation on the absurdity of prostitution being illegal: "In the army they give you a medal for spraying napalm on people! In civilian life you go to jail for giving someone an orgasm!"

In Calcutta, I'd heard a BBC program that said there were more bombs dropped on Vietnam than the entire Allied tonnage during the Second World War. I tried to picture what it must have been like for those souls on the ground as a different kind of airplane from the one I was in roared overhead day after day, year after year. The program spoke of the millions of landmines still lurking in the ground—ready to blow limbs off humans and animals alike—how Agent Orange had defoliated the forests and caused genetic malformations, and the three million Vietnamese killed. I avoided making eye contact with the delicate flight attendant handing me chicken curry.

I remembered the blasé statistics on the nightly news in the sixties. war dead today: 50 americans, 100 south vietnamese, 1,500 vietcong. Images of farmers leaving their homes and rice fields to jam roads. Thirty percent of the country being made refugees. I recalled I was too busy with my young family to get involved, except for bitter arguments with friends who supported the war. How Jane Fonda boarded a plane to seek the truth in Hanoi. Who was the greater hero: the one risking life and limb fighting, or the one risking loss of livelihood and everlasting scorn to find the truth?

"Jesus," Frank said, flipping through a travel guide while balancing an icepack on his knee. "Look at the topography of Vietnam. It's like an elongated barbell. Look, a narrow 1,700-mile corridor along the country's coastline connects landmasses in the north and south. I'll bet anything the setting of those boundaries contained seeds of war."

I told him about the BBC program. He considered silently, and then gave his take on it. "The domino theory got us into the war, right? If Vietnam fell, all the countries in Southeast Asia, including Australia, would fall."

"We'd be fighting communists on the shores of California!"

"You have to admit it must have looked a lot different to anti-Communists in those days. They wanted to make the world safe for democracy, figuring the enemy would crumble in a year."

"Yeah, and a strategy once adopted is sometimes impossible to scuttle. I remember a comment by a captain interviewed after the Tet Offensive. It pretty much summed up our reasons for involvement: 'We had to kill them to save them.'"

We began our descent, the plane's shadow crawling along the Mekong Delta as we followed the muddy, meandering river between luminous-green paddy fields, past palm trees and rust-colored tin roofs.

We filled out entry forms at the tiny airport in Ho Chi Minh City while the passenger in front sweetened the hand of a customs officer to ensure certain parcels went unchecked. Then grabbed a cab to a guesthouse that only had an address: 42, Pham Ngu

Lau, Q1 (which stood for Quan, or District, 1). The weather was hot and sticky.

At reception, we met a businessman who'd fled the country fifteen years before and only returned when the business climate became favorable. He acted as interpreter for us with the innkeeper. During a brief conversation in the lobby afterwards, which was in fact the proprietor's living room, he told us that the industrial strength of the country was in the north. The south had been predominantly farming except for Saigon, which the French built to administer their colonial plantation system and military. He also said that Americans were thought of as a big brother in the south, and that people were waiting for them to return when the MIA issue was settled and embargo lifted. Life wasn't repressive, as many people outside the country thought, although search, seizure, and detainment laws were tough. I'd become increasingly aware through my travels that the outside perception of a country was created by those who'd left it, controlled it, the news media, and groups with an ax to grind.

Frank was ecstatic about our spacious corner room on the second floor, with pale-blue curtains and a balcony looking down on to the street. The room had a fridge, wall clock, air conditioning, and fresh, multi-colored flowered sheets. But most important to Frank—hot water!

We looked out from the balcony on a busy food market clogged with motorbikes, bicycles, and petite men and women wearing traditional *nón lá* hats, which looked like umbrellas at half-mast. Whole families squeezed on to Vespas, girls laughing and jabbering while riding sidesaddle with crossed legs. Boys, cigarettes dangling from their lips, zigzagged through street traffic like eels.

When Frank emerged from the bathroom wrapped in a towel, he was quite pleased with himself. "For the rest of my life," he said with a laugh, "I'll appreciate hot water." He'd kept his week's growth.

At the Vietcombank, we cashed traveler's checks at ten thousand dong per dollar. Frank traded a hundred dollars for three inches of bills that he stuffed into his money-belt and bulging pockets, his gestures and snorts drawing laughs from employees and customers. "Feels like drug money," he whispered.

207

Rivulets of perspiration were crawling down the gully of my breastbone by the time we began our cycle rickshaw tour of the city. My immediate impression was there were an abnormal number of cripples on the streets. We took in the war museum and the American embassy, from where the US airlifted nervous evacuees during the '75 exodus. Amid the seriousness, we were invigorated by the laughter from a group of velvet-haired young women. I admired how they looked in their traditional *ao dai*—a sheer outer tunic that dropped sensuously to the hips, with slits exposing underlying nylon pants.

Following a short fight with the Vietnamese postal bureaucracy to mail home exquisite teak boxes, Frank and I walked to the Saigon Café to arrange transportation to Dalat in the mountains and Nha Trang at the coast.

The outdoor hole-in-the-wall café was the size of a carport, accommodating six small picnic tables partially shaded with umbrellas. We negotiated with Doan (pronounced Dwan), a young intermediary representing the absentee driver. Doan reminded me of the seemingly innocent young man Robin Williams' character befriends in *Good Morning, Vietnam*. Frank left me to seal the deal and struck up a conversation at a nearby table with a handsome, middle-aged man whose eyes were blue as the sky.

Once Doan disappeared to make the final arrangements, I pulled up a chair and ordered beers. The handsome man was Mike—about fifty, with a strong build, refined, freckled face, and a neat, sedate countenance. Speaking with a cultured English accent, he told us how he wound up fighting in the American War, as he put it.

"I lived in New York in my twenties and had dual British and American passports. So even though I was a British citizen, I was subject to the draft.

"In order to avoid being sent to Vietnam, I joined 'Special Forces' in '69. In those days, it took eighteen months to train an elite soldier. I reckoned the length of time would be sufficient to avoid Nam. The war had to be over by then. That's what the big wigs were saying, and I believed them!"

A mist of perspiration blanketed his face. His lips quivered gently as he spoke, like the mouth of a feeble old man. He had a need to talk, so Frank and I listened intently. Mike's great stall had backfired and he'd been shipped to Vietnam.

"During my first tour of duty, I was hit by shrapnel and hospitalized. But that wasn't the worst."

"What happened?" Frank asked.

"I was captured on patrol. Spent my time at the bottom of a fifteen-foot hole, with a rat as a companion. I named him Archimedes."

"You were a prisoner of war?" I asked, dumbfounded. "How often did they let you out of the hole?"

"Twice a day, they would haul me up to take a shit or piss. Occasionally to whack me across the back with bamboo sticks."

"Why?" said Frank.

"No apparent reason that I could think of—maybe boredom. Maybe they were just mad at us for being there."

Mike's face muscles twitched. His demeanor was a curious mix of English gentleman and deeply hidden trauma.

"What did you do in the hole?" I persisted gently.

"I probably mentally rewrote and replayed every book I ever read. Every movie or play I'd seen. It was the only way to remain sane. Many of my mates went mad."

He'd done two stints in that hole and escaped both times. Though my heart went out to this guy, the story was gripping.

"How did you escape?" I inquired.

"On their way home from missions, our bombers sometimes dumped their unused bombs so they could land safely. They saved my sanity by obliterating everyone, all the Viet Cong, above ground. So then we could escape from the holes. We were spotted by US helicopter servicemen who noticed our long beards! Bushy beards don't come easy to Asians.

"As brutal as it was to be in that hole, I don't think our treatment was as bad as that meted out by the South Vietnamese soldiers to their prisoners."

Frank and I sat bolted to our chairs as Mike described how the North Vietnamese decimated the South after the US left, and that the officers from the South were sent to re-education camps.

"In the beginning, Hanoi was very authoritarian," he explained. "They kept strong control over what had been the South, changing the bureaucracy, sending down secret police, and maintaining rigid travel restrictions. There were no jobs for former South Vietnamese officers, except as rickshaw drivers."

"The government loosened up after Russia went bankrupt and it became clear that their communist system left them poor cousins in Southeast Asia. They began to adopt capitalistic tendencies and gave Saigon a longer leash."

"There don't seem to be policemen," I said, "where are they?"

"Rickshaw cyclists are either ex-army officers, or spies working for the government. The authorities know your whereabouts. The guesthouse you stay at is government run. You get checked in on police computers each night."

"What about the MIA problem?" I wondered.

"The US made it up," Mike replied, frowning.

"Why would we do that?" Frank asked.

"I don't mean disrespect, but even the United States couldn't afford to pay war reparations for the damage done to this country. They tried to shift the emphasis to avoid responsibility. The bloody shame is that a million Vietnamese bodies lie buried somewhere out there. I say, let all the lads lie in peace."

Doan returned and interrupted the conversation to tell us the driver would pick us up in front of the cafe at 2 p.m. the next day. Once he'd left, Frank voiced the question we both had for Mike.

"Why did you return here?"

"I know the language, the country. I work for a Viet trading company and teach English as a hobby. And I love these people. This is my home now."

That night, Frank and I dined in style at a three-star hotel. Waiters in starched white jackets brought us French wine, pouring it into large, finely made glasses that sat on a rose-colored tablecloth with matching napkins.

"A toast, Frank, to adventure!"

Clink!

"Smell the cork, Denny! Bordeaux—475,000 dong, a quarter of an inch of money. You know, don't you, that this wine was produced in a capitalistic country!" he said with a chuckle, anticipating a reaction. "Capitalism is superior to any other form of economics. And it always will be."

"Spare me. There's a time and a place for capitalism. It's got us growing at breakneck speed, living on credit, and dying with new illnesses because we're running to catch our tails."

"Hey, Denny, let me tell you something. Now don't get excited! This is just an observation. And I know how open-minded you are about observations."

"What?"

"I've heard anti-American in your tone and conversation. I don't like it. There's nothing wrong with America that can't be fixed."

I considered this for a moment as appetizers began to arrive: spinach and beef pastries, cauliflower and chicken, crab claws, egg rolls, asparagus soup.

"You're right, Frank. So many of the locals in places I visit tell me how great America is and how they'd love to go there. And European travelers are surprised by our hospitality. I guess it's natural to see the warts on your own country and forget to look at the other side of the coin—the land of opportunity."

Frank filled our glasses with wine and looked across at me, brown eyes softened by alcohol. We had always had a backlog of topics, Frank and I. And now we had the time to dig into them. I had such fun with him.

"I spent fifteen years with venture capitalists, the paragons of capitalism," I said, tucking in to the main course of chicken and onions. "It's been good to me. Capitalism has given people good jobs and I believe it is designed to self-correct in the long term, when it becomes profitable to clean up the ills it creates. For instance, I can see how computers could drastically reduce paper usage and save trees. However, Karl Marx was afraid capitalism didn't know how to stop growing, that it would chew up the earth's resources.

"He had insight, Frank! How many companies have we dealt with that fucked up because of growth they couldn't control? We said we intervened in Vietnam to make the world safe for democracy, a political concept. Self-determination and government based on the consent of the governed was a noble cause.

"But the reality was that a bunch of rich white people, with devastating machinery, sent a half million soldiers to beat up on poor people in a place the average American had never heard of. Did we do this to protect self-determination, or grow our businesses to supply military needs?

"Americans are creative people who idolize the individual and the future. They use an appropriate system, one that creates wealth with private ownership of the resources by the strongest competitors operating in a free market.

"America itself is about rags to riches, yet there is also the desire to save the world from poverty. We see poor people as oppressed, hungry, ignorant, miserable, and diseased. What do we really know about poor people? Remember how during the war people always said, 'Life is cheap in Asia.' How did we Americans know that? How could we ever empathize? My point is that we may not understand what system is best for poor people, because we don't understand the differences."

"Let me summarize what I heard you say," Frank said, inhaling a Camel and blowing smoke to the side. "Number one: Capitalism gives incentive for growth and provides a nice life, but its Achilles heel is that it creates abuses. Number two: Good and bad are two sides of the same coin and sometimes a mix and match of philosophies moves us forward. Number three: To move forward with more harmony we need to understand differences, rather than destroy concepts. Is that right?

"I would like to add that the Vietnam War brought Vietnam *and* the US into the twenty-first century. Death and destruction cut old strings and both countries could embrace new life."

Frank insisted on paying the bill, slapping a wad of cash on the table. When I reminded him that travelers split the cost, he laughed.

"Listen, Denny, this entire two-week trip will cost what I pay for a single day at a resort."

30

Journey to Dalat and Nha Trang

Our driver to Dalat, Seven, pulled up an hour late outside the Saigon Café. That gave Frank and I enough time for another beer—with predictable consequences. The toilet was just a hole in the floor with more insect company than I wished for. I got out as quickly as possible. But my disgust softened to a smile when I saw Frank anxiously waiting his turn. He entered. I counted the seconds.

Thirteen, fourteen, fifteen ....

"Jesus Christ!" Frank bellowed in perfect Bronx as he rushed out. "I was pissing when this fuckin' giraffe of a cockroach crawled down the wall towards me! This huge guy was comin' right for my cock. And did you see the fuckin' ants? I had to pull out before I finished. Look, I dripped on my pants!"

What could I do but bend double laughing?

Meanwhile, Seven looked nonplussed and scanned us with somber eyes. He had pronounced cheekbones, a ruddy face, and slim mustache. Diminutive by Western standards, he nevertheless appeared bigger than his height. He waited patiently by his maroon, four-door sedan.

At first glance, the vehicle looked moderately new. On closer inspection, the various bumps and scratches of a street-worn ride revealed themselves. Clearly drivers in Vietnam were no less crazy than any other Third World country I'd been in. This had an impact on my seating preference, but I gave Frank the choice.

"I'd like to sit in front, Denny. I like to see where I'm going."

"That's exactly why I like the back, you don't see as much."

Despite my warning he chose the front, claiming more legroom would keep the swelling down. Doan, wearing a red sweatshirt with "USA" written across the front, climbed into the back seat beside me to act as interpreter for Seven, who spoke no English.

Frank and I exchanged wary glances—were they spies?

We weaved through city streets clogged with a variety of motorized vehicles, carts, and pedestrians. Looking out the window, Frank commented to Doan about how lucky the men were to have such beautiful women. Doan enthusiastically shook his head in agreement. It was somewhere near the outskirts of town that Frank began to panic because of the near misses. The driving was familiar to me: hand on horn, jerking in and out of traffic, bumper-to-bumper madness, passing multiple trucks on curves through diesel fumes, a grinding engine, and the rasping of tires on tar. Seven drove flat out on the straights, then pulled up sharply to avoid craters in the road.

"SEVEN! DRIVE FURTHER AWAY FROM THE CAR IN FRONT!" Frank squealed, looking wildly at the driver while gesturing with his arms in a futile attempt to increase the distance between our bouncing car and the vehicle ahead. "FURTHER AWAY!"

Impatient and frustrated, Frank turned back to Doan: "What's the matter with him? Is he crazy? Tell him to drive slower.

"I can't believe all the fuckin' people on the road!" he said to me, rapidly firing his words like a machine gun. "Someone could fall down. What if Seven miscalculates? There's no defensive driving. How can you sit there so relaxed?"

"That's the way they drive, Frank. If you complain too much, you run the risk of damaging his ego. Then we'd crawl."

"Listen! I hate being out of control in a car. That's why I have a driver at home who drives *exactly* as I say! How do you suggest I get this guy to slow down?"

"Try an incentive? In the meantime, yell 'inshallah!' when he's about to pass."

"What's that?"

"In Arabic it means 'God willing.' Might make you feel better." I chuckled.

White-faced and enunciating slowly, Frank began. "Tell Seven, Doan, I am in no hurry. If we arrive in Dalat *alive* and in one piece, we will give him ten extra dollars in dong."

Seven agreed and for the next couple of hours, he and Doan gave their perspective on Vietnamese history. Except in cities, the people in the South were peasants and predominantly rice farmers. Three things were historically sacred to them: ancestral land, the family, and the village. Before the French and Americans came, there was no rice surplus and all people received their fair share. Thus, for the French to acquire wealth it meant others had to go without.

Four hours into the trip, we'd reached the mountains, and we pulled up next to a quiet restaurant similar to the kind in India—meaning a wooden shack open to nature with several excessively aged tables and chairs. But the food and people made up for any lack of polish. We feasted on delicious, freshly made noodle soup and a heaped bowl of rice in chicken sauce—all served by a wrinkled old woman with gnarled hands. Her entire family, numbering in the teens, stared and occasionally beamed brightly at us as we chatted among ourselves. Even Seven smiled.

After three more wearing hours of grinding engine, pounding tires, and Seven's hard rock music tape, we arrived at the former French colonial mountain hideaway of Dalat. Seven found accommodation for Frank and me at the Cam Do Guesthouse where Frank bargained for a large room in the third-floor attic that had three dilapidated beds. We invited the guys to use one of the beds, but they had their own arrangements. Thinking we'd never see them again, we hugged goodbye—an act filled with the camaraderie developed during the perilous drive.

The chilly attic atmosphere reminded me of childhood. In the dead of New York's winter, my parents and my four siblings would pile into the family's '52 Chevy coupe and journey three hours to our converted barn in Long Island's countryside. We always left on a Friday night, reciting the rosary and afterwards singing songs. My dad's "Danny Boy" always brought tears. In our country home, we thawed out around the heat-grate built into the living room floor. Then it was upstairs to the loft to snuggle under old, fluffy quilts.

"I had a headache all the way," Frank said as he brushed his teeth, toothpaste spitting out as he spoke. "I never get headaches. Do you believe the driving? We almost creamed at least ten people. My heart was in my mouth! Denis, there were more people and animals on the freakin' road than ants in that bathroom at the Saigon Cafe!"

"It looks like the tarmac is used for people to socialize and sell their wares, as well as vehicles."

"Yeah, I guess flat surfaces are a rarity."

We crawled into our beds. I curled up in a fetal position inside a bevy of patchwork quilts and rubbed my hands to build up heat. The same as when I was a kid.

"Two things bother me about this kind of traveling," Frank confided. "First, the thought that these beds have blankets and pillows that lots of people have slept in. Second, I hate bugs. And I sense bugs around. Say do you think this place is haunted?"

His laughter lines crinkled as he peeped through the covers to look at me. I felt almost giddy, like I was still a kid sleeping over at a friend's place.

"I feel a breeze in here, Frank!"

"More like a stiff wind."

The source was a mango-sized hole in the alcove window above us. Standing on tiptoes and covered with goosebumps, I peered out the broken window at a rugged, dusty road threading through the quaint houses and shops. A chill mist hung silently over the town. No lights save the glow from the moon and stars, and you could hear a pin drop a quarter of a mile away. The whole scene could have been out of a Dickens novel.

"You know the thing that got me about our discussion in the car was the clash of cultures," I mused, staring out the window. "Individualism versus the collective. Rich versus poor. People sharing what they have as a condition of survival. We never knew the whole story about this place because the news media were so one sided. They only had time for the results, not the story that led to those results."

The town came alive in the morning with outdoor markets selling vegetables fruits and meats. Women in their straw *nón lá* hats carried heavy loads on poles that straddled their shoulders.

An occasional vintage forties DeSoto (automobile) putt-putted among the bicycles and Vespas. I bought bananas and peaches from two wrinkled old women sitting on their haunches. I chatted in sign language as they jabbered and joked with me. The vacationing French were long gone from this town.

We'd planned to travel another three hundred and fifty kilometers to the coastal town of Nha Trang. The only drawback—no buses. Fortunately (or perhaps with some foresight), Seven and Doan were still around and we promptly rehired them to take us. The boys threw in a tour of Dalat before we left, with Doan pointing out villas in surrounding mountains where the colonial rulers relaxed when Vietnam was part of French Indo-China.

Near the Dalat war memorial, we wandered into a Buddhist pagoda. We found ourselves in the middle of a religious ceremony. It was being conducted by monks dressed in white or blue pajama pants covered by lemon, yellow, or gold robes. We were the only congregation. The monks chanted a hypnotic chorus exquisitely timed to meld with gongs, chimes, and what looked like a copper frying pan that a monk tapped at regular intervals with a tiny hammer. The strikes were all executed in slow motion for maximum hypnotic effect.

The music, Frank said afterwards standing under a gingko tree, reminded him of the Gregorian chant. It was only then we discovered we had both been altar boys. Given our personalities, we then competed to see who could spit out the fastest Confiteor—our Latin being of questionable quality.

"I remember standing in a black cassock and a white linen tunic, pouring wine and water from crystal cruets into the priest's gold chalice," I said. "The younger priests usually wanted equal amounts of wine and water from *tiny* cruets. Our old pastor had these *colossal* cruets. And he insisted I pour out every drop of wine, but when it came to the water I managed a single drop before he signaled to cut the flow."

"Ha ha!" Frank laughed. "You sacrilegious fuck!"

The mountainous terrain on the way to the sea was filled with scraggly oaks and long stately firs that sometimes gave way to rich green paddy fields. As in Siberia, boys herded geese with sticks. Occasionally, we'd pass a rickshaw bulging with green bananas. We drove for ten hours, getting to know our companions.

The conversation gradually turned Seven's intense expression to a warm, effortless smile. Now thirty-nine, Seven was in his teens and early twenties during the war. His wiry body looked much younger. Through Doan, he told us the National Liberation Front, which organized peasants in the South against the American-backed government, deserved to win the war.

"I visit the tunnels after 1975," he said impassively, "see how they live. Like moles. Hear how they starve and how they work. I know how they fight."

From the back seat, I gazed out at the countryside through dirt-splattered windows. The Vietnamese insurgents had used this land to protect themselves, while the US strategy was to kill the land these people lived on. It struck me that the courage and endurance of the Vietnamese matched any underdog in history, and was far from the image of the enemy portrayed in the *Rambo* movies. "Ask Seven," I said to Doan, "how the country became divided between north and south."

"Before Second World War, Vietnam was French colony," Doan translated in slow English. "Then Japanese come, occupy country. Ho Chi Minh was hero to Americans during war against Japanese. He fight Japanese on side of the Allies. After war, French come back to claim what they call their property."

Doan used the term Viet Minh to describe the anti-Japanese force who subsequently also successfully fought the French. The Viet Cong had come later, he said. The country had been temporarily divided between the pro-communist North and the South, where most of the pro-colonial forces were, at the famous Seventeenth Parallel.

"After we beat French, Geneva Conference in 1954 call for truce and fair elections in South. Fair elections never happen. We face communist-capitalist difference when Diem become dictator in South and Americans come here."

"You know, Frank," I said. "I always thought of the war as a civil war, but it sounds like a revolutionary war, peasants against colonialists, and inside that a civil war with rice farmers against city dwellers."

"You may be right," he replied. "I'll bet anything the French taxed the villagers and transferred the rice wealth to the cities, which had already become corrupted. As Doan said, that left the peasants deprived."

The next question from my mind was why the Buddhist monks burned themselves in the sixties.

"Bonzes," Doan said, describing the Buddhist monks, "protest oppressive government, say Western ways bring shame. They want free elections promise by Geneva Conference. Also Catholic archbishop forbids them carry flags on birthday of Buddha. Many bonzes killed."

Doan finished by repeating the sacred date Frank and I had heard over and over in conversations—1975. When the Americans left, the North successfully invaded the South, and a new world began. Surprisingly, both our guides agreed they now wanted the Americans and French to return and invest in their country.

Our discussion was interrupted by the driving. Seven had found better pavement in densely populated lowlands and was weaving fast in and around bikes, ox carts, and the occasional car. Suddenly, there was a sickening thud. Seven had hit a dog crossing the road. The body went flying. We didn't stop.

"Seven! You killed a dog," Frank cried, shrinking against the seat. "Slow down. Doan tell him to slow down!"

"Doan," I asked loudly, "would you ask Seven why he drives so fast?"

"Seven say he need concentrate on road. Trip long and dangerous. He not want fall sleep."

Doan admitted excitedly he was seeing these places for the first time. I suspected the same was true of Seven. But Doan's round choirboy face had none of Seven's mental toughness or reserve. His feelings were obvious. He lit up when he was happy and became impassioned discussing subjects close to his heart—such as immigration.

"Why Europeans so against Asian immigration?" he asked, tears creeping into his eyes. "Why don't Europeans like Asians? We have hands. They have hands! We have arms, they have arms!"

I almost cried myself, captivated by the absolute honesty and depth of his feelings.

"I just hope we can last the next two hours without hitting someone," Frank said to me, still preoccupied by road safety. "This trip makes you appreciate what you got—clean pillowcases, hot water, electricity, people that speak the same language, paved roads. You know, it never occurred to me before, but it's clear that countries like this need roads and communication as the first steps towards building economic stability. They need the infrastructure to transport goods and communicate for business. Think about the changes Vietnam will have to go through and the money necessary to get it done."

"Jesus, Frank, how could anyone who traveled to Vietnam and observed the paucity of infrastructure believe in the domino theory? How could these countries facilitate an invasion of the United States? Can you imagine the ships, communications, airports, roads, manufacturing and distribution capabilities, and sums of money you'd need?"

"It would be like us invading Mars."

31

NHA TRANG: THE COST OF WAR

THE VIEN DONG HOTEL IN Nha Trang was modern-looking and clearly valued its guests' comfort and safety, at least according to the sign in English above the TV in our room. It read, "Weapons and objects with an offensive smell must be kept at the reception desk." As I wondered about who traveled with offensive smelling objects, Frank was on the phone to the operator discussing in his loud, clear voice how to call his girlfriend, Maddie.

"Ha ha!" he bellowed, after hanging up. "They're pre-programmed! I said, 'Good morning, how are you?' She said, 'Fine, how are you?' I said, 'Fine, can I call the US?' She replied, 'Would you wait a minute?' I thought, 'Great! They speak English.'

"Then I said, 'I would also like to buy a plane ticket to Ho Chi Minh City.' She said, 'Fine, how are you?' It went on and on. She knew exactly nine words.

"But it doesn't matter," he continued, "because fundamentally Vietnam is teaching me to understand and come to terms with differences. We got our understanding about this place from soldiers and politicians through the news media. We never saw the differences until it was too late.

"It's the level of differences we are able to see that determines the development of our minds."

I never thought of differences that way and I liked the implications of what Frank was saying. Some people distinguished few differences and made decisions on very limited information. Others could see many differences and understand situations more clearly as a result. It stood to reason that bias was treacherous because it limited the ability to see differences. We'd viewed the Vietnamese as evil communists and believed the domino theory as a result.

The next morning, Frank and I rented bikes for twenty-five cents each—complete with baskets in front. We maneuvered out of heavy traffic in the center to a less crowded road along the seaside with predominantly bicycle traffic. Nha Trang was a city of perhaps 250,000. Cyclists must have made up eighty percent of road users. The city's main arteries were lined with mimosa trees and small wooden shops. Butchers sold live chickens—upside down, feet tied and heads dangling.

"You know," I said, trying to pedal and bow respectfully to a seventy-year-old man that rode beside us, "at the height of the war we had five hundred thousand soldiers here for eight years. At a hundred thousand dollars to put the average soldier in the field during that period, that's fifty billion a year."

"You're probably close," Frank allowed. "Add at least half that amount again for administrative support between here and the States, the cost of reserves, the CIA. What's that, seventy-five billion a year for all personnel during those eight years?"

We tried to figure out the rough cost of our country's involvement in the war. To the six hundred billion dollars for eight years, we added another two hundred and fifty billion for the personnel cost of buildup and wind-down, and another hundred billion for the ten thousand helicopters and five thousand planes we'd lost (according to the BBC program I'd heard). We figured an average of seven million dollars for each aircraft. Then we calculated another quarter of a trillion for the rest of the equipment and technology—aircraft carriers, bombs, land mines, chemicals, and so on. We were up 1.2 trillion dollars.

"And add to that," Frank said, "the cost of medical and pension plans for the living and those that died, plus jails and rehabilitation costs for drug addicts and the homeless. And we had to support the Saigon government and their troops for twenty-five years, didn't we? I'd put the total bill conservatively at one and a half, maybe two trillion, by the time we got out in '75."

This was how you made numbers talk.

"And then there's the interest from the beginning of the war until today," I said. "That's forty years." This took a little figuring with zeros. "That triples the number to over six trillion dollars, about the size of our national debt. Let's see, figuring a hundred million households in the US, that's what—"

"About sixty thousand dollars for each household!" Frank intervened, beating me to the punch.

"Can you imagine what we could have done with that money?"

"As long as we are on the subject," Frank interjected, "what are you going to do about making money when you get home?"

"I've been vacillating between going back to my old life for the big bucks and taking some menial job that gives me more time. I've been to three or four fortune-tellers in my life. All of them saw 'big bucks' in my future. So where does that get me?"

"It gets you vacillating."

We parked the bikes and walked barefoot on the soft, golden sand of one of the most picturesque beaches in the world. The tumultuous South China Sea pounded the shore under a low, gray horizon laden with forbidding black islands. The air smelled of impending storm—brash and salty. A few locals milled about.

Almost immediately one of these locals talked me into a massage. Ana, a slightly aggressive woman, worked my back and neck, while her grandson did my feet and legs. As their hands and fingers rubbed oil and maneuvered muscle, I could hear an annoyed Frank in the background. "No, I don't want a massage. No! No beach chair. What's the matter with you?"

The pair massaged me vigorously for an hour and a half. Ana's hands were strong and calloused. She probably wasn't more than a couple of years older than me, but sallow wrinkles and missing teeth bore evidence to a different aging process. Her husband had been killed in the war.

Afterwards, Frank took a picture of us. The eleven-year-old grandson held my hand like a toddler. Both clasped their straw *nón lá* hats by their sides. A middle-aged woman in a floral tunic joined us, flashing a toothy smile and making the peace sign with both hands as the camera clicked. I stood in back, arms around the three of them, feeling at peace with the world.

"You know, Frank, I'm getting a warm feeling about many of the Americans who fought here. The goodwill of these people suggests they made a positive impression."

"Our boys thought they gave their lives for these people. That has to leave an impression."

Frank and I strolled along the beach during the blush of sunset, the tepid water nestling around our toes. He pushed his cane into the packed sand below the waterline, leaving round pockmarks. He looked lost in thought, then suddenly began speaking of the recent death of Maddie's brother and the impact a conversation with her therapist had made on him.

"This therapist and I got talking about extroverts and introverts. Maddie's the introvert."

"Don't tell me, you're the extrovert!"

"Ha ha! Anyway, we were discussing how Maddie dealt with her brother's death. The guy said that introverts generate energy from being alone, and that extroverts generate energy from being with others—kind of like a plug into a socket. He said extroverted behavior drains energy from introverts, and that solitude deflates the extrovert.

"It explained a lot about our relationship. I was always a little pissed with her at family gatherings. She hid out in the kitchen doing the dishes. Shied away from talking with my folks. Seemed antisocial. There are a lot of extroverts in my family. Maddie's energy must have been drained like a car battery with the lights on and motor off.

"She recharges by waking at five every morning and preening herself before leaving for work. Takes a long hot shower, does her face, reads the papers. You know, pampers herself. I knew Maddie and I were opposites, but I never understood the dynamics of our behavior."

"Do you think we need the other's energy to balance our lives, because we don't have the necessary voltage?"

"I don't know!"

As we looked for a restaurant for dinner, I silently worried about how much I had changed and whether Kathi would accommodate me—or the other way around. The heaviest considerations were getting trust and romance back in our relationship, and financial security that Frank had been querying me about. Then, of course, there was Malgosia.

Over a supper of steamed shrimp, noodle soup, and fried calamari in garlic, Frank and I were offered another kind of massage—by two attractive and engaging prostitutes.

"No thanks," I said, "just had one. And as you can see we're eating."

One of them leaned in seductively to assist my hands on the chopsticks. "Make love and blow job," she whispered. "We please."

"Love to, but our wives are waiting. And they are big. You know what I mean." I raised my hand high above her. "They are *big*."

Not put off, the lovely lady next to Frank fluttered her eyelashes, while her friend picked at my food and talked.

"I am twenty-four," she said. "I marry American soldier."

"When?" I asked.

"Just before Americans leave. He go to US in fall of '75. I try to contact him to join him. He tell me he marry again. I left here with no husband."

"So you like join us? We have fun party. We stay in hotel over there. Rooms seventeen and twenty-seven. We have good time."

Her face was stretched too thin, with wrinkle lines scribed around her eyes.

"Let's see." I counted on my fingers. "If you were married in '74, you must have been a real young bride."

"I lie," she said with an impish smile. "I thirty-five. No matter, we have good time. Yes?"

"No!" Frank snapped, just as the first of the typhoon winds and rain attacked. We paid the bill, said goodbye to the ladies, and hit the trail. Tucked under plastic rain capes, we cycled back to our hotel. As the rain pelted us with increasing ferocity, I wondered how many left-behind brides had become prostitutes. How many Vietnamese children grew up fantasizing about an all-American dad?

That night, the typhoon hit with full force. Its wild passion brought mighty talons of lightning and howling winds. The storm pounded the city with gusts hitting a hundred miles an hour. Palm trees bent to breaking point. Some were ripped from the earth. Streets flooded and lights blew out. We lay in our dark room at the hotel with no power—just a pair of candles. Frank quivered under his snow-white mosquito netting half scared to death by the cyclone. By morning, it was gone.

A Western-style breakfast under palm trees at the poolside was followed by some decadent lounging—with an incongruous musical accompaniment. Frank finally had to comment. "They've now played 'Jingle Bells' by James Lord Pierpont four thousand straight times," he said, a tad exasperated. I, however, was curious to check out the source of the music. I followed the sound and discovered a massage parlor in a row of businesses adjacent to the hotel. I noted the location. I liked massages.

After a game of billiards with Seven (who with Doan had wangled a place to stay in the hotel), we all drove along the beach to check out hiring a sports fishing boat. Branches and uprooted trees littered the land along the way, and floodwater created huge puddles and piles of debris. The locals were out in force—sweeping, chopping, bundling cut wood.

"These people are used to calamity and clearing it out of the way," Frank mused, half to himself. On the jetty, local men sat on their haunches. They weren't going anywhere. They told Seven the typhoon meant there was zero chance of a boat leaving harbor today. I was disappointed, but it did leave time for a massage.

The source of the "Jingle Bells" was a small reception room, off which were massage tables (with partitions for privacy) and steam baths. A woman with typically Vietnamese long shiny hair showed me to a changing room and instructed me to take a bath and then lie under a cotton sheet on the massage table.

Lying under the sheet, I wondered if being naked was the proper protocol. My confusion was exacerbated when the same woman reappeared and whispered: "I massage you 'good.' You give me extra? You handsome!"

What did that mean? I wanted a regular massage. She massaged vigorously, smiled sensually. Or was that my male interpretation? Then she rubbed and stroked gently, asking seductively: "Want glasses?"

What the fuck was that? Should I say yes? Before I knew it I was saying, "Sure! Yes!"

I heard a flare and smelled burning phosphorous. The masseuse was inserting a lit match into the opening of a glass she'd taken from a row of similar vessels on a side table. The glasses were the size and shape of the candleholders that glow in silver donation boxes in dark corners of Catholic churches.

Then she positioned the heated open end of the glass—*Christ!*—on my bare back. She repeated the procedure with another bunch of glasses. After a while, she removed the glasses, making a not-so-gentle *whoop* sound. The top of my bum and back had large, red, circular two-inch welts—as if I'd been given hickeys by King Kong.

"How long marks take to go away?" I asked.

"Three day."

I *had* mistaken the smile. It wasn't sensual. It was sadistic.

Back at the room, Frank saw the violation. "Jesus! You look like you've been sucked by a giant fucking octopus," he said with an unsympathetic chuckle. Doan later told me that the glass draws blood to the surface and cured whatever ailed you. In my case, the smallest of coughs disappeared entirely.

We spent the next day entirely relaxing—apart from booking a flight back to the former Saigon.

"The plane to Ho Chi Minh City usually make it. Not to worry!" the hotel concierge—an engaging woman dressed in a pale blue tunic imprinted with peacocks—informed us in a petite voice.

"What do you mean 'usually?'" I asked.

"Most of time it get there," she said, smiling sweetly.

"Most of time," Frank gasped, "It's supposed to get there *all* the time."

"It get there most every time!"

Frank and I looked at each other. His lips tightened. "I'm not driving back," he said.

"We may die, but we must fly," I concluded.

"We all die," she said, and began typing up our tickets.

At nine the following morning, Seven and Doan drove us to a tiny airport with a single runway hacked out of the tropical forest. In a small waiting room straight out of *Casablanca*, Seven puffed on a roll-your-own and listened as Doan, eyes moist, said he loved us. "Frank, you like my father. Denis, you like my uncle."

We took their addresses, profoundly touched. When they left, we sat on the wooden bench waiting for the plane. Possibly for the first time in his life, Frank was wearing the same socks for the second day in a row. "If Doan and Seven are representative of its spies," he said with a shake of his head, "what a great country this is!"

INDONESIA

BALANCE

32

INDECENT PROPOSAL IN BALI

Y TWO WEEKS WITH THE Z were over, and I was onboard a Qantas 767 freshly sprayed for mosquitoes and bound for the exotic Indonesian island of Bali. Air blasted through ceiling knobs, muffling the roar of the jet. No matter how many flights I took, liftoff still sent a shiver through me.

Before Frank and I parted, we had pictures developed. One of them I now held on my lap. I was in Nha Trang, embracing my masseurs, Ana and her grandson, and another broadly smiling local woman on the warm sand along the South China Sea. My face showed a mellow satisfaction with life. Intoxicating! I decided to carry this picture to help me visualize what I wanted to bring home and keep forever.

It was December 19. Indonesia was three-fourths of the way around the world. I was on the homestretch. I could smell the barn. Thoughts shuffled in my mind. I would return from a year of experiencing the most amazing sights and people, equipped with the revolutionary knowledge that I could be happy by myself. But what if people didn't accept me back home? What if I didn't accept them? What if I didn't want to work in big business? How about selling hardware in a small town where people know each other? Did those towns exist anymore? A job would have to be flexible for travel. What about making big money a few months a year? I could enjoy that.

In the window seat next to me was an unusually good-looking Englishman in his late twenties. His shiny brown hair was tousled. A day's growth enhanced his perfect complexion, high cheekbones on a long face, and eyes so green you'd have sworn they were colored contacts. Dressed in conservative shorts, sneakers, and a polo shirt, he kept scratching his calves, then noticed my glance and grinned.

"I rather dislike mosquitoes," he said, in the Queen's English.

"I've found that wearing long pants in the late afternoon helps."

"Thanks. I'm Ken. How do you do?"

I offered him a widely used Asian *muti* for the bites, one that smelled like Ben-Gay, and we got to talking. The normal banter at first: length of travel, destination, weight of backpacks. Eyes weren't the only thing green about him. He'd brought a hairdryer on a year's trip! More indicative of a leisure traveler than jungle-navigating one. Not that I was against leisure. I'd take it where I could get it.

"I quite fancy the idea of visiting Bali," he said. "I was shocked to learn that there are fourteen thousand islands in Indonesia. But Bali is more to my liking than Borneo or New Guinea. I gather there are lots of women. And then Australia is close, isn't it?"

"The thing that amazes me about Indonesia," I said, "is that it takes eight and a half hours to fly east to west and four hours north to south." I had also read that, although Bali was Hindu, most of the two hundred million Indonesians were Muslim. I asked if he knew much about the country's politics.

"This chap, Suharto," he said, "is quite the demagogue, isn't he? Thirty years at the helm!"

"He brought his country out of the Third World, but dictators and capitalism don't mix well these days."

"Which world is Indonesia exactly in now then?" Ken asked.

"I'm not sure, but it's well placed. Its high birth rate is declining and there's an increased emphasis on education," I answered, "Also it has the advantage of low pay combined with a growing skilled labor pool for manufacturing."

Over a scrumptious dinner of duck, Ken told me he'd left his job as a car-leasing agent two weeks ago to travel around the world. His avowed objective was to attend every party in sight and bed as many females as biology and the laws of physics permitted.

"I quite fancy lust myself," he confided. "I don't mind telling you that I'm a cut above average in looks. I'm vain. All my friends say it. No sense denying."

However, he had a point—I'd have to say Ken was the most elegantly handsome man I ever met. Elegant in the sense of fine features, like Peter O'Toole in his youth. And, rather like that actor, Ken came across as an intelligent good-time Charlie, brash but not abrasive. His refreshing, simple honesty could charm the green off a leaf.

We fell silent and I gazed past him out the window. I thought about my dreams of bachelorhood in college, and why men have such a problem with commitment to long-term relationships. Girls grew up playing house and training for family. We trained for adventure and romance. Outside the stars added a surreal touch—as if we were frozen in space.

Ken and I headed off to Kuta Beach, playground for Australian tourists and others willing to fly that far. We shared the taxi there with a pair of English women who were staying at a guesthouse adjoining ours. Chloe and Elspeth were generationally tall and slim—attractive in a dowdy, bookish kind of way. They both recently graduated law school and split for a four-month vacation to celebrate.

The taxi left us to walk in sunshine under palm trees and past bushes with feather ferns and orange flowers. The girls went to their guesthouse and we all agreed to meet the next night for dinner. The streets of Kuta Beach were clustered with trinket vendors, discos, and video restaurants where people greeted the hot humid climate with mixed-fruit lassies and cold beer and munched on guacamole toast, *nasi goreng*, and pumpkin curry.

Unlike many traveler destinations, Kuta Beach was a temporary home to some corporate suits. Men and women from cookie-cutter worlds in which people visited foreign countries they'd read about. But when they got there, they mostly lay on a beach resting and reading about the adventures of someone else. Few Americans journeyed this far, but there were oodles of Australians on holiday and lots of English and Dutch travelers roaming the town's cluttered streets.

The Jakarta Post talked about the great jihad—the war on poverty—while in its business section economists warned of problems that might emanate from the government's double-digit projected growth in the new twenty-five year plan. In Asia, huge inflows of foreign capital had created speculative boom and import surges, and competition was fierce. Projections were always linear. This was the unbridled optimism that sunk troubled companies who organized poorly for growth. In business plans of recent years, I made sure the longer-term projections were wave-like, reflecting realism.

How would Western investors and banks take to paying the accustomed corruption slice off the top when times got rough? They should worry. Growth follows the theory of dissipative structures, which says an organization grows until it can't function properly, and then a painful explosion creates a simple but elegant improvement towards a higher order. This is nature; driving for balance.

After a day lounging on the beach, reading and haggling with vendors, we met the lawyers for dinner and a video at a local open-air restaurant. Restaurants in Kuta Beach attracted customers by displaying a chalkboard out front listing the day's videos. Electronics were changing the face of the world. I liked watching videos, but was uncomfortable with what they represented—'development' and constant entertainment from machines. Over mixed-fruit lassies, guacamole toast, and spicy pumpkin curry, we watched Demi Moore accept a cool million dollars to go to bed with a stranger. I'd been anxious to see *Indecent Proposal* because I heard the movie stirred up a lot of controversy and debate over the value and role of spousal fidelity in the new age.

I was in a strange mental space in Bali—wanting to be alone to contemplate my navel, but unable to resist society. A traveler I spoke to had mentioned a secluded atoll east of Bali that offered *aloneness*. Sounded like the place to spend Christmas. I was lucky to have time to be alone. Time had been missing in my life and I needed it for balance. Kathi always wanted me to balance the playful father and husband with the intense businessman, but I could never manage to integrate the two. Chimene had a knack for balancing. She watched her money and kept her interests simple. When one element got out of sync, she readjusted the time she gave to each. I hadn't given enough time to balancing my ambitions for family and money.

The four of us moved on to a quiet, bamboo-laced bar, where one topic dominated the conversation: "Would you take the money?"

"Well, I don't know," Chloe said, fingering one of several silver rings on her finger. Unusual jewelry for a lawyer, I thought. "How could I be sure he would pay the money?"

The serious-minded Elspeth had the answer. "There would have to be a written contract clearly spelling out the terms."

"And then there is the question," Chloe said, warming to the legal aspects, "of whether the money is tax free."

"Too right," said Ken. "That could get dodgy."

The solicitors discussed all the potential flaws and nuances of the transaction for about ten minutes, but true to their profession couldn't commit to a simple "yes" or "no."

"So would you bloody well go to *bed* with him for that amount of money?" said Ken, tired of the equivocations.

"I don't know," Chloe answered, perplexed. "It sounds so crass, but it's only a sexual act. There wouldn't be any love associated with it, I suppose."

"Only" seemed such an understatement.

"Yes," said Elspeth, "It's not as though you would have a commitment."

"Look, would you take the million dollars or not?" Ken continued. "Personally, *I* would take the million to sleep with Robert Redford. He's not a bad looking bloke."

I laughed. Finally, the lawyers both allowed that they would take the million dollars. "After all, it's only for one night," Elspeth said. "And there would be no love involved."

"How about you?" Chloe turned her eyes on me.

Me? I'd been thinking about the early days with Kathi when the "trust glue" was still hardening. I remembered being jealous of her at a party in Switzerland during our first vacation break from the kids after three years. She disappeared for a half hour—innocently as it turned out—and I was seething with jealousy, thinking the worst.

"I wouldn't have taken the money," I answered. "Not after being married only seven years. But I wasn't teetering on the abyss of financial ruin like the couple in the movie."

The conversation meandered on in a relaxed way till we reached *attraction to the opposite sex.*

"Good looks aren't necessarily the first thing that attracts me about a man," Elspeth said. "Humor attracts me."

When she didn't follow up her statement, I told them

about a book I'd read where the author analyzed ads in monthly magazines. He postulated that magazines selling the most copies represented what men and women desired, while the next tier represented how they got what they desired.

Elspeth and Chloe guessed that for male readers the first tier would be hobby and clothing magazines such as *Popular Mechanics* and *GQ*. Sports and business was their second tier. Ken thought glamour magazines for the women's first and had no clue of the second. Personally, I'd never seen a man reading *GQ*.

"This book was several years old," I continued, "but I think it's still accurate. The author placed *Playboy* and *Penthouse* in the men's first tier and business and sports in their second tier. He had *Ladies' Home Journal* and *Family Circle* in women's first tier and a slew of fashion magazines in the second. I checked it out at the time and was shocked at the extensive distribution of *Family Circle*.

"He contends that most women want family and security and get it by being attractive to their 'hero.' Most men he says dream about sex, attracting the beautiful woman by *being* a hero. Then he proves his thesis by analyzing how advertisers play up to this dynamic."

Elspeth stiffened noticeably, her lips tightening on the straw she was drinking from. The frown on her face indicated disgust in her heart.

"That doesn't reflect very well on men. Does it?" she said with quiet force.

The conversation abruptly ended there. Although we settled the bill amicably—splitting it equally, as was the travelers' custom—the ladies had had enough and packed it in for the night. Ken talked me into trying a bar with a live band. Walking in silence, I was analyzing the evening. Was Elspeth's vehemence towards men's sexual behavior a sign of the times? Was it always a sign of the times?

"What do you think that was all about?" Ken asked, as we stood at the Koala Blue Bar, "I was getting to like Chloe, then, bang, the conversation dies."

"I was just thinking about that myself," I said, pouring beer into a glass. "Cheers! They seem to think that our sex urge is tainted, you know, an inferior 'animal' impulse."

"Women have a love-hate affair with testosterone. Carnal desire is one of our finer qualities, isn't it? Redford followed the script. What was the reasoning that Chloe and Elspeth gave to fuck for three quarters of a million quid? It's only sex, not love?

"Women are as clueless as men when it comes to the opposite sex. The difference, I reckon, is that they don't know it. A guy offers a million dollars to sleep with someone's wife and they think *Popular Mechanics* is on our minds. Elspeth should let her hair down more often. There are so many women like her in England. It's a national tragedy."

"What kind of a woman do you want to marry?"

"A woman who likes being with me. I used to be concerned if my girlfriend had an orgasm, but now my major worry is whether she likes my pub and my football team."

"Come on, give me more. What do you want in a wife?"

"Beautiful, of course. And a good dresser. A poor dresser you can take a point off. Career, so she can earn money. Younger. Sense of humor. Rich, if possible. As clever as me, but not cleverer—don't want the hassle of competition. Honesty and integrity go without saying. I don't want a conniving, lying little bitch."

"Understanding is a must for me, if I had the choice," I said. "Of course, I like beautiful, intelligent, and humorous, but for getting along I'll also take an understanding woman. Without understanding between people how do you deal with a person who puts on a lot of weight when you like thin, or a mate who is apathetic to romance when you think it's the spice of life? 'You should love me as I am' doesn't quite measure up sometimes."

"The way I feel about it, if one spouse wants romance and the other won't give it, then to preserve the relationship and marriage to further development and old age, the one apathetic to romance should let the other get their jollies elsewhere," Ken said, then pointed to a table on the far side of the dance floor. "Do you know why none of the blokes are talking to those two *fan-tastic*-looking creatures? They don't have the balls. Right then! Care to join me and have a go?"

"You're on your own big guy." Although, they were beautiful.

Ken sauntered over and bent down to their level. Suddenly the two women burst out laughing.

Back at our tiny bungalow, I couldn't sleep. I lay sprawled on the faded orange bedspread and rock hard pillow reading Gary Jennings's *Raptor*—the adventures of Thorn, hermaphrodite and right-hand man to fifth-century Ostrogoth emperor Theodoric.

A few feet away stood Ken's empty bed. The table fan provided a welcome breeze in the otherwise stuffy humid atmosphere.

I put down the book and recollected my "seven-year itch"—a delightful lusty experience during a business trip to Guadalajara. I was twenty-nine and deeply in love with my wife. The other woman was struggling to love her husband, a recent Vietnam veteran who had too much on his mind to treat her romantically. I was ravenous for another woman, and she appeared. I didn't feel guilty afterwards. It had nothing to do with my marriage, and I didn't tell either. In retrospect, it was a cherished adventure. But fucking for money with my wife knowing struck me as different somehow.

33

Roosters in Action

In the morning, Ken and I rented small Yamaha motorcycles and toured the island. We motored under fluffy clouds to Bali's southern tip. In Kuta Beach, the well-to-do local women wore short skirts, cosmetics, super-high heels, and cropped charcoal hair. But outside the tourist town's reach, the dress was sarongs and hair was kept long and straight. Women and children spread chili peppers in neat rows on the road to dry in the sun.

The young children lived outside and played games such as hide-and-go-seek. We laughed and acted silly on the bikes. They giggled and pointed at us, saying in the fast singsong quality of the language: "Hell-o mis-ter." We slowed down and responded: "Hello miss-ee." People with smiles high on the gum-line called out: *Selamat pagi* (Good morning), or *Mau ke mana?* (Where are you going?). *Jalan jalan* (walking), we answered—even though we were on bikes. We stopped occasionally to play with the children and connect with adults using eye contact and gestures. They laughed, smoked, stared at us, and played the national card game, rummy. The message I got was *Indonesians welcome strangers*.

Smoke from rubbish fires brought back childhood memories of tossing tinfoil-wrapped potatoes into burning leaves to cook. We stopped to watch a gang of twelve-year-old boys refereeing cricket fights inside match boxes, careful to make sure the insects didn't jump out.

Socially, the absence of police and guns was consistent with what I had seen in the poorer countries in Asia. Smoking was commonplace. Cigarettes were to be found in the mouths of most males over fifteen and a few women over seventy. I noted

Indonesian cigarette boxes did have a warning, but on the side of the pack in very fine print. There were no video restaurants in the boondocks, but we passed one hut with a TV and a crowd in front.

We rolled to a stop at Uluwatu on the southernmost tip of the island. Our intention to visit a famous ancient temple built on rugged cliffs that reached down to the Bali Sea.

"You know," Ken reflected, "Indonesians have little monetarily, but they're millionaires when it comes to time and family life, aren't they?"

"So true, mate. Have you noticed how men and women hang out separately?"

"While in the West we're as close as two sides of a bloody oyster."

Turquoise waves slowly, unceasingly crashed against the rock cliffs, spewing a constant layer of white froth forward like the tentacles of a giant squid. The turquoise reached back towards a coral reef beyond which was the deep blue ocean. Surrounded by nutmeg trees, the dilapidated Hindu temple was populated by gray monkeys—squeaking, growling, and scampering across and down the aged stone walls and over the carved faces of gods. Baby monkeys the size of rats looked like shrunken old men with wispy hair.

As we clambered around the walls—careful not to get too close to the monkeys who even though they were said to be sacred had also been known to bite—I asked Ken what he said the night before to make the two women laugh.

"I asked them, 'Would either of you lovely women like to go to dinner with me tomorrow night?' They said they were engaged. So I said, 'How about the night after, or the night after that?'"

"Did they agree?"

"They humored me, said they had boyfriends. But I'm used to getting my way."

We rocked the motorcycles out of their stirrups and started back. We spotted a steep rocky off-road trail through dense foliage. We took it. I leaned over the front wheel, the wind buffeting my face and my hair flying free. *Yowee! Let the wind rip!*

At the end of the trail, we found women selling sarongs above an abyss that dropped down to a sandy seaside cave. The sarongs were artistic with bright colors and images of fish and geckoes, and we each bought one. Then the women led us down a narrow trail into the cave, which was the size of a basketball court. Engulfed by rock, the cave smelled of fish and seaweed. Its floor was the color of pure gold, washed pristine. The sun shone through an opening in the overhanging rock, directly above the center, showering glittering rays. The heavenly splendor was made complete when, for a small fee, the women gave us full body massages.

Nearing Kuta Beach, we came upon a group of men gathered in a circle in a small field. We pulled the Yamahas to the side of the road and stopped. "Mate," Ken hollered, rolling up the rear, "the travel book says that when groups of people gather like that, it's probably a religious meeting and it's rude to interrupt."

No fucking way was this a religious group.

"I don't think so, Ken, let's check it out."

We ambled over to the dense throng, about forty strong. Several of the diminutive men invited us to have a look-see. Our physical size allowed us to peer over the raucous group. Clutching money between their fingers, screaming and hooting, the excited crowd was watching a cockfight. The men retreated in unison when the contestants in the middle came too close to them. Not surprisingly—the roosters doing battle wore razor-sharp metal spurs taped near the bottom of their bony legs. The fighters eyed each other. One was already seriously bloodied and hobbling on one leg, but unbowed. Then with a vicious thrust of the spur the healthier of the two attacked and finished off the cripple, wringing the other's neck with its beak to be sure. Even near death the vanquished refused to show fear in its eyes. A cock to the end.

The winner got to fight again and again. Lifting wire cages, owners picked the next adversaries, revving them up like racecars before the starting flag. They held the fowls' legs and wings tightly—lest humans were cut by the spurs—and smacked their beaks against each other. Onlookers settled bets after each fight and the winning owner, in addition to monetary earnings, got to keep the carcasses of the loser.

"I rather dislike this sport," Ken concluded, after we'd had enough.

"I have mixed feelings," I said. "Roosters are nasty. They pick on females and chicks unmercifully without any apparent emotion. And they wake everyone up. I can understand why they pick roosters to fight."

"Maybe we need roosters to wake us up."

Bali was a vibrant island of palm trees, greenery, flowers bursting with color, and the most spectacular sunsets I'd ever seen. As a red glow swept across the firmament, we were stopped at a pagoda temple by a two-block procession. Men in white coats and bandanas strutted down the only street, in front of women with straight black hair dressed in flowered *kambens* (the formal Balinese sarong) tucked at the shoulder. Sunset festival! Townspeople carried a statue of Durga, a semi-clad goddess carrying a spear. Meanwhile, other Balinese divine figures entertained the crowd by engaging in mock fighting. At the head of the procession, a mythical dragon threatened a kneeling repentant. The dragon had a flat nose, thick lips, large jutting teeth that clattered when it talked, a big face, bulging frog-like eyes with red and yellow circles around charcoal pupils. It was dressed in a body-length coat of feathers and boasted claws as long as a bear's. Occasionally, the dragon made threatening motions toward the crowd, and adults and children alike ran like scared rabbits. This was pure white magic.

In pursuit of some cooler air, Ken and I left Kuta Beach the next day and hopped a van to Ubud, a quaint mountain town in the clouds. Long-term travelers and tourists with big cameras shared the narrow streets and visited the tempting restaurants, quaint shops, and monkey forest. For 7,500 rupees (about $3.50), we stayed in a luxury bungalow with a bamboo roof, red-tiled floor, and porch with bamboo chairs. The scraggly frangipani trees—with their sparse shiny leaves and sweet-smelling white flowers—surrounding the bungalow added to the feeling of deep relaxation. After a nap one evening, I woke in the fresh mountain air to the sounds of crickets chirping and geckoes gecko-ing. I reflected on the amount of sleep I needed these days. Perhaps I was still making up for long years of work? Or perhaps napping was natural and I was just living more naturally now?

The spectacular and symmetrical Gunung Batur volcano, whose lava had laid waste the blackened, barren lowlands for miles in all directions, was only an hour and a half away by motorbike. The dark blue Danau Batur lake surrounded this blackness like a moat. The rain bucketed down the day Ken and I were there, in intervals under ever-changing windswept skies whose clouds flooded down on the mountains like waterfalls. Psychedelic-green rice paddies, cordoned off by mud dikes, terraced the mountains. A man knee-deep in chocolate water and mud pushed a small square wooden plough with a laughing child standing on top. We put-putted over steel bridges spanning swollen rivers, stopping to grab fat-leafed ferns to use as umbrellas. The uniformed schoolchildren on the way to the volcano, however, were unperturbed by the rain.

At the shores of the lake, Ken and I ended up drinking *kopi susu*, mud black coffee with condensed milk, and eating Indonesian style at a simple restaurant with an unobstructed view of the crater in the distance. "Indonesian style" meant washing our hands in a bowl of water, then using them to sample a variety of dishes placed on our table: chicken, jackfruit and fish curries, beans in spicy hot sauce, fried rice, fried bananas. And for desert, pineapple and *dukuh*, a small round fruit with a leatherish cover and the taste and feel of a grapefruit inside.

Staring at the black wasteland and a group of men drinking kopi susu and talking together, Ken asked, "Do you think the physical closeness of men and women back home affects how we relate?"

"It would have to. The old way of doing things has lots of time and is patriarchal. So that men and women hang out separately. Back home in the West, we shifted the emphasis from patriarchal to focus on the individual. Our mores are geared to fast relationships, sex, work tension, possessions—things like that. This means that couples end up being tied at the navel.

"I think the interesting thing is that, like Elspeth, we're still clinging to old ideas of ownership that leave little room to breathe and make mistakes. To compensate, if we make a big mistake, we don't have to live with it. Instead, we get divorced—because individual happiness is paramount. Does that make sense?"

"Right then! Our morality is in the process of development, and I am a work in progress," Ken concluded.

After five days in Ubud, Ken decided to go back to Kuta Beach to, as he put it, "party to my heart's content and share the secrets of a beautiful lass." My destination was the secluded atoll Gili Meno, via the island of Lombok just east of Bali, to spend Christmas and welcome the New Year. The traveler I spoke to said the island had white beaches with sparkling water and the temperature set at "not too hot, not too humid." I left Ken snoozing under his mosquito net and trudged through the muddy streets of Ubud in torrential rains. It was times like these, trudging with a backpack under a plastic cape to meet an early van, that hiking boots earned one's admiration.

It would be twelve hours to Gili Meno.

34

GILI MENO: BRONTE'S DILEMMA

STROKED BY A HOT, STICKY breeze, I maneuvered through the touts on Lombok to eventually climb into a canary-yellow dugout canoe with blazing-red bamboo outriggers and two mismatched outboard motors sputtering in the stern. With two bare-chested guys manning the outboards, we sliced through rough, aqua-green water. As Lombok's tropical forest shrank in our wake, the storm-shrouded volcanic peaks of Bali came into focus, looming over the smaller island like a big brother.

Sacks of food, baggage, and fresh water (since the island had none of its own) competed for space with travelers and locals. Sitting on a vibrating plank, I played with two carved figures I'd bought while in Lombok: a bone gecko and a wooden woman with a big head, small breasts, and extended belly. I'd threaded them on to a leather thong to give me a traveling necklace to replace Chimene's I'd lost in Crete. I loved the sea air and wind in my hair—that boyhood freedom of the small boat—I just hoped the motors wouldn't quit before our destination three hours away.

The engines held out and we beached in crystal waters shadowed by palm trees. Butterflies the size of birds flittered in and out of ferns that were so fat you could use their branches as fans. The Gili Meno islanders mulled around on white, glistening sand to help unload the boat and greet the newly arrived. The weather: not too hot, not too humid.

A barefoot young man with shiny, black hair flowing halfway down his back, saggy shorts, and a Chicago Bulls cap introduced himself to me as Bronte. "*Selamat pagi!*" he said. He shook my hand, and then touched his heart. Grabbing my pack and water bottle, he led the way along the beach. We passed a couple of high-rent modern guesthouses with attached seaside restaurants and manicured grounds. Bronte was taking me to accommodations he thought befitting for a backpacker. He asked whether I was married and how many children I had.

As I replied, crabs scrambled over the fine sand in front of us, reminding me of Shannon and Chimene on the beach as young kids. Little legs running from the encroaching surf, holding on to my thighs giggling and screaming. A month now, and I'd be with them. As D-day grew closer, images and feelings of family were popping into my consciousness. Those tender nights with Kathi, snuggling so close we could feel each other's breath on our skin.

The more befitting accommodation was a group of tall thatched-roof bungalows on stilts surrounding a circular open-air restaurant. Lounging around the restaurant's bamboo tables, Western women were being entertained by friendly-looking local guys with soft smiles and infectious laughs. The girls showed a dreamy affection as they interacted with these young men, who smoked incessantly, drank velvety-smooth kopi susu, shot the shit, and took turns strumming a communal guitar and singing Indonesian love songs.

A few dollars bought a large bungalow with lacquered and interlaced bamboo squares for walls, and a king-sized bed draped in turquoise netting. Light crept through crevices. There was a persistent moldy smell and no electricity. But a kerosene lamp stood on the porch, where armchairs offered a view of the sea, thirty yards away, through a path surrounded by baby evergreens and bushes with white flowers that smelled like lilacs.

Like the other local men, Bronte also chain-smoked as we lounged in the restaurant, sharing a gigantic fruit salad of mango and pineapple slices. He was telling me that same-religion weddings were law, and the government recommended two children—meaning men should hold off on marriage until thirty and women twenty-five.

"What do you use for birth control?" I asked.

"Modern methods. Old method is salted pineapple three nights a week."

"You're kidding?" I had to laugh.

He wasn't.

"Why?"

"I do not know, but I am told it works."

He took his turn on the guitar and began singing "Hotel California," then stopped to tell me about his girlfriend. She'd left to go back home to Holland and there was nothing to do on the island now that she'd gone. He wanted to work in a factory in Jakarta like his friends.

"I read that people work long hours in Jakarta's factories, for very little pay," I said.

"I do not know about that. My friends have money and I do not. How can a man marry without money?"

"You live in the Garden of Eden with time for holiday pageants and stories about your great-grandparents. You greeted me asking questions about my family. Back home, we greet people by asking what they do for a living."

"In America, you have whatever you want. I want a television."

That was the other side of the coin. Maybe balance was some point between wealth of money and a wealth of time?

"Your girlfriend is Western?"

"She *was* my girlfriend. She is beautiful. She has a large nose like yours." He pulled a wrinkled two-page letter from his shorts, and looking betrayed pointed to a section of the letter. "She says, 'Do not wait for me.'"

It wasn't hard to understand what Western women saw in the local men. They had an androgynous look about them—thin, muscular bodies with hard stomachs, lush, shiny hair, smooth cinnamon skin, and lips Hollywood starlets would drool over. As in other Islamic countries I'd visited (Gili Meno like Lombok had a Muslim majority), Western women and local men got together, but Western men rarely had romantic opportunities with local women.

"What about your friends who live here? Do they get these letters?"

"The women come, then go. They spend time with us, take us places, give us money, loving words. Then go. Then letters come, and then stop." He picked up the guitar again.

"Why do you choose to go along? And what do your women think of their guys going after tourists?"

He answered the first part with a shrug, then said, "Our women think free sex is no good. But they do not give much thought to it."

"So where are your women? I mostly see men."

"With children, in the village around the salt lake."

The day before Christmas, I met Cary at a restaurant not far from where the boat arrived. Alone at the adjoining table, he was eating with his hands, Indonesian style. In front of him were bowls of roasted chicken, jackfruit and fish curries, and beans in a spicy, hot sauce. Tall and handsome with thinning dark hair, he wore a flowery shirt open to a hairy, bronzed chest. A shadow of a beard blanketed his square face and dimples showed when he smiled and introduced himself.

"Come join me," he said. And of course I did.

We exchanged a firm handshake, and I couldn't help noticing the thick muscles of a college fullback—muscles that rippled on a flat stomach because there was so little fat. In a voice with a hint of former stutterer, Cary spoke comfortably about his life. He grew up a cowboy on his father's ranch in Texas and was a promising high school football prospect before blowing out a knee. He and his wife, Kim, came to Bali a few years before in their late twenties, "after an unsuccessful business venture and wandering, unfulfilled existence." They taught aerobics, administered massage therapy to hotel guests in Bali, and dabbled in the export of Indonesia's colorful art and clothes. Given his ease, he'd achieved simplicity of life and the ability to waste time—necessary ingredients for balance.

We left the restaurant carrying bottles of Bintang beer, to wander the beach and talk. Intimacy came naturally to Cary. He told me how he and Kim had been considering a child but were afraid to try.

"Both our parents did such a miserable job raising their kids. I don't want to foist my roots on to some poor soul. I was so fucked up when I was young! And anyway, who wants to bring kids into this chaotic dangerous world?"

"We're moving towards matriarchy, how bad can that be?"

"I loved raising kids and being a dad. You can do all sorts of things with them. Have memories.

"I remember my younger daughter, Chimene, as a two-year-old, wearing a floppy hat nearly covering her eyes, wearing my wife's galoshes up to her butt and swinging at a ball with a plastic bat as long as she was. And my older one, Shannon, at sixteen handing me a glass of wine and telling me she was *so* proud to have a father she could talk to. Then laying on me that she'd lost her virginity! But kids *are* a twenty-five-year endeavor."

"Would you do anything over with your kids?" he asked.

"I'd concentrate more on teaching them to be peacemakers. It's an art. A few years ago, my wife and I separated. We did a really good job coming back together as a family, but what remained in my craw was that neither of my girls felt it was their responsibility to get involved. To me, serious conflict was a family issue and each of us was responsible for being a peacemaker."

"That's a tough one. It takes a lot of understanding to be a peacemaker, and if you do it wrong you just make matters worse."

"That's how they felt."

We'd reached the dock and stood under a coconut tree, watching new arrivals emerge from an outrigger canoe. A local man in his thirties approached and leaned towards me whispering: "Mushroom omelet?"

"Does it have cheddar cheese and onions?" I asked, after the initial surprise.

"Mushrooms!" he said, putting his hands to either side of his head and thrusting them outwards into the sky. "Magic mushrooms!"

We told him we'd get back to him.

Cary was vacationing in one of the upscale bungalow guesthouses with marble floors, fresh sheets, a bathtub with salt water, air conditioning, and a soft chime to announce visitors. Kim joined us at dinnertime. She'd been sunning her attractively tanned and petite body—the body of a fitness expert. Her blond pageboy hair and bangs fit her round face, complemented by the gold dot earrings she wore. She had green eyes, closely spaced, which smiled easily. She came across at first as both welcoming and cautious. Nevertheless, the three of us quickly became close and they invited me over for Christmas the next day.

I'd never been away from home on Christmas or New Year's before. It was a lonely feeling being without family. Even when Kathi and I separated, it would have been unthinkable to spend holidays without our family. It wasn't the same, but I welcomed Cary and Kim's friendship and open hospitality.

Kim thoughtfully presented me gift-wrapped blackcurrant

juice and effervescent vitamin B tablets. As I fussed over the gifts, she said, "Let's see what's in store for us over the next days." She grabbed a thick New Age book on forces of energy in nature, and asked me to open it randomly. I paused to get the book's feel before opening it. The page was entitled "Living with Joy."

On New Year's Eve, we sat down to dine casually at the restaurant in front of Cary and Kim's bungalow. Wine, beer, glasses, chili sauce, and a pack of Marlboros adorned the table, but we had yet to order. Cary wore his usual flowery shirt, and Kim had her sarong tucked snugly in a way only women seemed capable of doing. Unexpectedly, a dark-haired woman climbed the wooden stairs up to our level. Her white beach dress clung elegantly to the length of her slim body. Her curly hair dropped to her shoulders, contrasting with her white skin. She was stunning. All of our mouths were open. Walking gracefully to our table with a pearly-toothed smile, she announced: "Hi, I'm Joy!"

"Pull up a chair and join us, Joy," Cary invited, while Kim and I looked at each other astonished. We ordered a round of pumpkin curry and mango shakes. One thing led to another and we decided to buy three magic mushroom omelets the next day and spend New Year's walking around the island. When the clock struck twelve, the four of us left the restaurant arm-in-arm, singing, "To Love Somebody."

35

SEEING AURAS AND FINDING JOY

"*Mau ke mana?*" two men called out. "*Jalan jalan,*" Cary and I answered in unison. We were walking behind Bakti, the magic mushroom man, to pick up our omelets. We followed him to a shack with a porch and a few tables where we sat and waited leisurely for our psychedelic snack to be prepared.

Bakti suddenly started staring at the path, pointing and laughing. There were two policemen strolling along only a coconut's throw away. My reaction was nervousness. Was it a setup? But we weren't even in possession of incriminating evidence yet.

"Police from mainland not often visit. Easy to see, look!" He pointed again. The cops wore pressed khaki uniforms and brown leather shoes that made them stand out like penguins walking down Broadway. But they weren't interested in us or our omelets, and before long Bakti handed us a hot bag weighing about three pounds. "*Tidak apa apa!*" he said. "No worries, mate."

We shared the omelets at Cary's, the girls splitting one, and began our New Year's walk around the island. The women looked stunning. Wholesomely healthy Kim wore a bikini covered by a loose rayon dress with swirling flowers and butterflies. Joy wrapped a blue sarong with white swimming fish around her hips, a delicate lace blouse meticulously covering the upper portion of her one-piece swimsuit. Cary was in fashion too, wearing psychedelic-orange sunglasses and a tight black swimsuit under a purple sarong. As for me, I had on lightweight blue and white Indonesian pants with my red bathing suit underneath, blue bandana and dolphin sarong wrapped around my waist for emergencies. And, of course, my daypack.

The magic mushrooms opened the door to dazzling dimensions, to an acute awareness of nature's smells, sounds, and tastes. Individual crystallized molecules of air and color created a sense for space—the distant peak of Bali's volcano, shrouded in a mist that turned into a mellow orange swirl around its crater, looked close enough to fondle. "WOW!" was all I could think to say. I turned in slow motion. The shimmering molecules in sand, palm trees and people's movement elicited another WOW! Now I understood why the flower children of the sixties had loved to use that word.

We walked in this lazy, bright atomic cloud down the beach—no talking, just enjoying nature. Nature had strung everything together so well, with such balance. Cary strolled into the turquoise molecular bubbles of the sea and dove below the surface. I could only imagine what he must be seeing down there amid the coral. When he re-emerged dripping sparkling hydrogen and oxygen, he began to excitedly describe the rainbow of colors, the huge eyes of the fish, and the symmetry with which they interacted. "Wow!" I said.

After walking a while we naturally split into couples: Kim and I, Cary and Joy. Collecting seashells in the warm breeze and speaking in a high voice tinged with vulnerability, Kim told me that her mom divorced early and that they moved frequently, never staying in one place long enough to have friends. As an only child with no live-in father, she had always felt alone—until she married Cary. Did married life provide what she needed, I asked.

"It's wonderful really. It's so nice to have a soulmate, someone you trust, you can confide in. With Cary, for the first time I can share my experiences, my most intimate thoughts."

Time moved slowly, its silence disturbed only by the whispering wind. I reflected on a steamy summer's night long ago, in Kathi's apartment in Greenwich Village. I was leaving for Colorado to begin graduate school. A tear fell on my back as she massaged me. That single drop had more power than all the water crashing into Victoria Falls gorge. That someone would miss me enough to cry silently opened me to Kathi's qualities as a wife. Two weeks later, in a pizza shop in Denver, I made the decision to fall in love and get married.

Back in the pliant particles of paradise, I told Kim the story. "I called my parents before proposing to Kathi. My father said I was being hasty, so I knew it was a good idea. Afterwards, love kept growing. I couldn't get enough, couldn't say I loved her enough, couldn't touch her enough."

"Falling in love is not being able to say enough good things about someone," she agreed. "My mother couldn't say many good things about me. Nothing I did was good enough for her. With Cary I feel accepted. He allows me to reveal my dark side. To face it."

"My wife wants unconditional acceptance. 'Love me for who I am, not who I should be,' she says. I used to argue that marriage was a partnership, with common goals and equal sharing of responsibilities and benefits. I couldn't figure out how you could have unconditional acceptance when the actions of one affects the other."

"Did you figure it out?"

"No, but I'm working on it."

"Cary and I have been struggling with the decision to have kids. We have such resentment against our parents."

Halfway around the atoll, we stopped at the thatched Good Heart restaurant, which was no bigger than a hut. While we waited for Cary and Joy to catch up, Kim took a picture of me below with my trusty daypack slung over my shoulder. All about coral lay in heaps. And two high-and-dry outrigger canoes sparkled by the sea like crystals in the sunlight.

We were the only people except for one waiter-cook who shuttled back and forth through a kitchen door. We lunched on noodle soup with vegetables, and basked in a willowy mushroom serenity that embraced each individual moment as if it were a special event. We watched fascinated as spiders wove their webs on the bamboo ceiling and creamy, iridescent geckoes breathed in and out while waiting in suspenseful animation for their prey.

After lunch, the pairings switched. Cary's pace took us ahead of the women. We acted silly, throwing sand at each other and diving into the water to rinse off. "Hey, Moses with a backpack!" he shouted, grabbing my hair. I felt like a little boy. Then after a while the mood changed again.

"You know what you said the other day about family being a

twenty-five year commitment?" he asked. "One of my fears—and I absolutely believe I'll be married forever—is what if I'm not?"

"Yeah, well, I'm concerned about whether my family and friends will accept me when I return. And should I go back to big business or sell hardware in a small town where people know each other? I'm concerned, but whatever happens, happens for the best if I'm positive. Does that make sense?"

"It does. I guess when you get right down to it families are about supporting each other and raising well-adjusted children. It's doing it right and keeping it together that scares the shit out of me."

"I know what you mean—finding the right formula or process. When Kathi and I got back together after we separated for a year, we wrote a partnership agreement to understand where the other was coming from and resolve inequities. We struggled about whether you keep it together with unconditional acceptance or partnership principles."

"The nice thing about accepting someone without conditions is that it's conceptually easier. A partnership seems so businesslike. Also, if people don't know who they are, they'll compromise themselves. How many of us know who we are? And if one compromises, will the other person be flexible enough to understand something has been given up?"

Wow, what a thought. I had to mull that over. Our high state gave an awesome life to everything. The smell of seaweed. The hot air pulsating like a heartbeat. Palm trees waving. Even the green in beach grass had a life of its own. A rooster's cranky crow shattered this consciousness, but was then quickly folded back into it. I felt present and removed from reality at the same time. We threw flat shells skipping against the glittering tips of waves dancing in the fading sun, and then began to talk again.

"I belonged to a fraternity in college," Cary said. "Camaraderie has been so important to me, but I've never been friends with an older man. I need that experience."

"Who'd have thought a Texas football player could be such a softy?" I said, punching him playfully on the arm. "Does that mean I'm the older man?"

"There's a fair amount of gray surrounding those golden locks."

"You and Kim would make terrific parents," I said. "First of all you want kids. And you seem to have the temperament to teach them what you want to come back to you. Like politeness, for instance."

He turned and lifted me off the sand in a bear hug. There's a nice loss of control and sense of security in a big guy's hug. The women caught up and we switched partners again. Kim and Cary keen for deep conversation immediately fell behind.

Joy had a bashful yet confident nature that hinted at something jingling loose inside her heart. Her demeanor was older than her twenty-nine years, but youth remained apparent in her profile, taught skin, and lack of wrinkles around her eyes. Her British-Australian formality, a noble stiffness, began to soften as she talked about her job in movie production. But when the conversation moved to her marriage and divorce, her young face took on a melancholy air.

"When I got married my husband wanted to have kids—like Kim and Cary do now—and shut the light off by ten. I was far too young for that kind of thinking. I wanted to go out. Boredom set in. We fought about stupid things. That's where relationships falter. When you can't get beyond the hurtful. Someone usually shuts down about a *real* issue, and the other doesn't want to bring it up again for fear of a bloody confrontation. Issues linger."

"I know what you mean. What caused the divorce?"

"I met another man to take up the slack. Funny thing is, we didn't do anything. But I never denied wrongdoing when my husband accused. We divorced three years ago.

"The last two years, I lived with the man of my dreams. Then one night he didn't come home until very late. Out with an old friend, he said. One thing led to another and the friend turned out to be his former main squeeze. I accused him of fucking her. Didn't believe his denials—I was so keen on being jealous—screamed and told him to leave.

"Then I reckoned the problem might be my own insecurities. I wanted to be everything to him. Now he's gone. And it turns out I was mistaken about the woman."

"I often misjudged my wife too, didn't have the patience to understand where she was coming from. Can you write him a letter?"

"I did. He wrote a rather sensitive letter back saying we needed faith in our own value, and trust in each other. 'What else is love?' is the way he phrased it. And if I didn't trust him, what was the sense of carrying on?" she recalled, her nose with that wrinkled prelude to tears. "It took a long time to realize that what I had done to my husband my boyfriend did to me. I don't have a plan right now."

She cried. The tears streamed down her cheek. I held her for a while, rocking gently. She was so beautiful and the intimacy made her more so. I moved my mind off her beauty.

We disengaged and, wiping her eyes, she shifted the conversation. "Tell me about your wife."

"My youngest daughter, Chimene, told me recently that she'd spent a lot of her life developing the male in her, and now wanted to explore her feminine. 'And who better a person to do that with than Mom.'

"My wife's comfortable with silence, doesn't bitch about people, and has lots of talents." I told her about Kathi's doctoral thesis, how it established that both massage therapy and creative visualization improved self-esteem.

"That's what I need," Joy said, "self-esteem. How did you meet her?"

"The summer before my senior year of college, I was at Brandy's bar in New York City with my oldest brother and his ruggedly handsome roommate Paul. Two women joined us and demanded a seat for their friend who was coming. I usually rebelled against people using gender to get what they didn't deserve, and besides I had a bum knee.

"Anyway, I felt like a schmuck for not offering my seat when Kathi limped in with an Ace bandage wrapped around her ankle and since Paul had given up his seat, he also got first crack at the wooing ritual.

"I remember her hair was short like a pixie, and she had graceful curves and penetrating gray eyes. There was also her sense of quiet elegance. She eventually noticed me. We had an easygoing quality to our discourse right from the beginning. I played the country boy with a city boy's charm, while Kathi was actually the city girl with a country girl's shyness."

The sun sprayed color through drifting clouds on to the sea. One portion of the sky held the baby blue of late afternoon, another the rose brilliance of early sunset, another the red blood of dusk, and still another the purple dark of night.

Kim and Cary caught up, their eyes glistening from tears.

"We're going to have a baby!" they cried in unison.

The four of us held each other in a circle for a long time—with just the tiny sound of splashing water and heavy cry of gulls. I felt so happy.

"They're going to have a baby!" I suddenly yelled as loud as I could and we wrestled each other to the ground in happy oblivion.

"We're going to have a baby," Kim yelled on top of the pile.

As the daylight faded, we held arms again and danced in circles. Then fell about laughing. I never laughed so hard. It felt so refreshing. The sky had become a mixture of gray-brown and white. Then, before the light completely fled, we saw each other's auras.

They were energy patterns around our bodies. The overall ambiance created by the magic mushrooms must have opened a seam into another dimension of nature—like the visual adjustment needed to view certain optical illusions. One of us would describe another's aura, its patterns and colors, which exactly fit what the rest of us saw. Mine was blue and red and the pattern was easygoing with round-edged spikes that had short distances between the highs and lows. We all saw the same patterns. Were they real? Did it matter?

When the sky darkened, we swam into one of those moonbeams that follow people wherever they go. Phosphorescence lit the water and stars twinkled.

"Look! That star's moving," Kim called out from the deep.

"They're *all* moving," Cary said.

"Look, the Southern Cross is near the saucepen," Joy shouted.

"The what?"

"Huh? Saucepen!"

"Do you mean sauce-*pan*?" Kim said laughing and enjoying Joy's accent. She began splashing the water with both hands, and we all followed her lead. We were girls and boys enjoying nirvana.

Nine hours after the trek commenced, we came back to bonfires that Bronte and his friends had built to welcome the New Year. We danced with the locals to rap music—my body doing movements it hadn't performed in years. Cary concluded that this was one of the five best days of his life. For me, the New Year had brought the ability to shake hands and touch the heart, a feeling of intimacy that evoked the hippies' sense of communal love and harmony, and three raised bumps on my palm, which someone suggested were spider's eggs laid under the skin.

Travelers were hippies in the sense they enjoyed the carefree nature of owning little. It brought with it, if you were so disposed, a mellow satisfaction with life. In this sense, hippies (and travelers) were a simple but elegant improvement towards a higher order.

The trek around the island was a good reminder that I'd spent a year exercising freedom of expression and movement. Now I had three passions: family, money, and personal freedom. Like Chimene, I needed to give each a fair opportunity—a daunting task with so much potential for friction. But I had the power—we all have that power. Elbert Hubbard wrote, "Picture in your mind the able, earnest, useful person you desire to be, and the thought that you hold is hourly transforming you into that particular individual you so admire." Maybe I could finally integrate my business self with the traveler.

Joy was also deep in thought. I joined her by the water's edge and asked her what she was thinking.

"I'm considering whether I'm going to sleep alone tonight."

I also needed someone to love and to love me this New Year's. I heard Joy's words but under the influence of mushrooms and stars I didn't stop being talkative long enough to focus on her statement. By the time focus came into mind, I judged the moment had passed. Shyness—as fucking usual. I was left walking the soft warm sand back to my bungalow alone. I fell asleep telling myself I didn't want to be just another guy hitting on her. There was little consolation in that line of reasoning.

The scenario repeated itself on our last night back in Bali. Joy and I spent it with Kim and Cary at their hotel suite. That evening, we were kids again, yelling and screaming during a wild pillow fight. When it was over Joy and I slept on two cots placed side by side in the living room listening to Kim talk in her sleep and

Cary snore. We didn't do anything, but I sure wanted to. If only I'd had the nerve. Men are like that, aren't they?

The next morning, we said goodbye to Joy at the airport. I whispered to her during a hug that at least three people in this world thought she was special.

Later that day, it was my turn to go. Cary said to me, "I feel like an angel entered my life. You keep in touch, ya hear?" I was off to Perth.

AUSTRALIA
RE-ENTRY

36

LIKE PLUGGING INTO AN ELECTRICAL SOCKET

ABOUT SIXTEEN MILLION PEOPLE LIVED on the east coast of Australia, while two thousand desolate miles away Western Australia had a total population of around two million. Stranded by geography, lay its capital, Perth—a quaint coastal city with a small-town demeanor. So why head there?

I'd met Sara on the Serengeti plains somewhere between Kenya and Tanzania. And she'd invited me to visit her in her home—Perth. Only she was due to be on a mini vacation when I arrived. Luckily, I'd met up with Ken again after I got back from Gili Meno and he'd agreed to fly to Perth with me. We envisaged a few days palling around in the Northbridge suburb of town before Sara returned and he moved on to Sydney.

Perth looked clean, with shiny grass and wide asphalt streets that were antiseptic compared with where I had come from. There were bright lights, good ice cream, people wearing suits, and lots of cops. The people walked quickly and jogged with earphones. In their world of music and news, every moment counted. Did they even see the birds?

Cars cruised the main streets and fast-food eateries were everywhere: hamburgers, pizzas, chicken, heaps of fish 'n' chips, and pies filled with combinations of minced meat, steak, mushrooms, and kidneys. Unsurprisingly, heavy people were ubiquitous. How could you stay trim with all this food?

The language also took a bit of getting used to. Folks used words with "ies" on the end: *sunnies* for sunglasses, *lollies* for lollipops, and *tennies* for sneakers (tennis shoes). On the TVs in bars and restaurants, important-looking men such as former chief justice Sir Garfield Barwick debated the clash between the monarchists and republicans over interpretations of Prince Charles's Australia Day speech. The thought that England had power this far out had never occurred to me.

Comfort and convenience abounded. No question, I felt out of place in this land of plenty.

As Ken and I stood at a crossing waiting for a red light to turn, a man's voice yelled, "Hey, beautiful! Where ya going?" I looked at Ken, then over my shoulder. No beauties there. Then looking forward I thought, *What the fuck!* A black sedan waited at the light, filled with hunched-over guys staring at me. One of them, a mean-looking yokel with an ugly mouth bellowed: "Why the fuck are you lookin' around? I'm bloody talking to you, queenie!"

He was talking to me?

Obscenities flew from the car like you'd toss feed to a pig. Then the light changed and the black demon cruised through the intersection and out of view. I scanned myself. Hmm, sandals, Balinese string-pants, katmandu stenciled shirt, my hair hanging loose. Different. I immediately felt a mixture of empathy for the abused and outrage. Who the fuck did I bother?

Then a calm inner voice said, *Change the energy, my man! You're back where you can be stereotyped. That's all!* At that point, the rage subsided like a spent flashflood. I looked at Ken.

"Right then," he said, as we burst out laughing. "You should wear shorts and tennies like me, mate. This isn't Asia. It's bloody Marlboro country."

37

SARA FROM THE SERENGETI

THE FIRST TIME I SAW Sara she was hanging out the front window of a lorry in a cloud of dust. Her raven hair blowing in the wind and dark eyes sparkling, she yelled and waved at a nonplussed rhinoceros. Later, sitting by the glow of a campfire in the Serengeti night, she revealed she was also an intellectual economist working on a Ph.D.

We discussed how in the late eighties the US Federal Reserve gouged a trillion dollars in interest from security-minded Americans. In a raspy voice that reminded me of Katharine Hepburn, she argued that the Federal Reserve, itself owned by a select group of banks, was the US's tool for shoveling money from the middle class into the coffers of banks and corporate America to bail them out of their latest Ponzi scheme.

My mother was among those fleeced investors in certificates of deposit (CDs). She watched her income drop seventy percent when the Fed lowered the interest rates it charged banks, from nine to two percent. Who got the difference? The banks that made bad loans and their customers—floundering real estate companies and leveraged buyouts (LBOs). The banks pocketed part of the interest spread while maintaining high interest rates on middle-class credit cards. Their corporate customers received lower interest rates on outrageous debt the banks encouraged them to borrow. It was the greatest short-term transfer of wealth in the history of the world. And few ever knew.

"What makes me nervous," Sara said at the time, "is that you Yanks look to be setting the stage for more of the same."

It was the theory of dissipative structures again: things grew and grew more unwieldy until there was an explosion, and a simpler but more sophisticated structure resulted.

I accepted Sara's invitation to Perth not just because of the mutual interest in socio-economics. There was that instant attraction you feel with people sometimes. Sara could have been the archetype of the Australian woman—tall, intelligent, hospitable, an incessant smoker, slightly crude but with charm. She was the kind of person who made you feel her home was yours. She wasn't what you'd call attractive—a ruddy complexion and the solid body of a softball player—but her eyes were striking. I entertained thoughts of a romance, of course.

Sarah rented a house in a tree-lined neighborhood with a grape barber on one side, a "barbie" (as the Aussies called a barbeque) in the back, and a no-eyes Scotty named Whoopee. Whoopee was a licker, or in other words an enthusiastic dispenser of love. It had been a long time since I'd seen a pet dog. About the same length of time since I'd slept in a house with a safe place to leave money, two fresh sheets smelling of spring, a hot bubble bath, and cooking facilities with a variety of spices. Not bad!

Whoopee's tongue woke me in the morning and then she'd run back and forth to the door with a leash in her mouth. A subtle hint. So while Sara worked, I took Whoopee for walks and played with her. And, to earn my keep, I cooked pasta for Sara and her roommate. Fresh tomatoes with lots of mushrooms, garlic, and olive oil—paradise! My body was hard and lean, eyes clear and white.

We ate dinner at her parents' the second night. They clearly thought highly of their daughter. Her father had been an administrator in Papua New Guinea for thirty years, where he and Sara's mother, a nurse, fell in love. Gutsy couple! I could hardly imagine Papua New Guinea thirty years before. Sara had lived there until she was twelve. We all hit it off immediately, four travelers swapping stories. Talking to them of faraway places and strange situations, I realized the adventurer I had become.

On the weekend, we joined Sara's best friends, Tina and Helen, to drive down to Margaret River south of Perth, in the heart of one of the major Australian wine districts. Both were husky, with long, blond hair and outrageous A+ extroverted personalities. Marlboro women!

In the company of such talkers, Sara became muted and I crawled inwards. I recalled comments by the Z (seemed like ages ago that we were in Vietnam) that extroverts sucked energy from other people. Tina alone drained me dry. And attention spans? Forget it!

"Denis, tell me every place you went," Helen demanded, puffing away and jamming her foot on the brake. She drove the curvy road through the sun-drenched flatlands and golden hills south of Perth like a rampaging elephant on the outskirts of Calcutta protesting its loss of habitat.

"Well, let's see. I started in England, flew to Zimbabwe and saw the magnificent Victoria Falls. Went to this island in Uganda where for two days I didn't see another Westerner. From there I traveled around Kenya. That's where I met Sara. We met at a campfire in the Serengeti game reserve. Then I flew to Egypt—"

"Sounds like you've done heaps of traveling. I went to Bali two months ago. Tina, remember our trip to Bali?" Then the two talked for fifteen minutes straight, shifting subjects all the while.

"Did I tell you that Bob got his knickers in a knot frying his burger with Francine?" said Tina.

"Whaddyareckon," Helen replied, "he's a couple of cards short of a deck? Everyone knows Alice is his main squeeze."

"Men are such dags."

"Liars!" said Helen waving her hand and ciggie in the air for emphasis.

"Why do you think men lie?" I asked.

"To get what they want, right, Sara?" Tina answered quickly.

Sara sat conspicuously quiet in front as the banter flew between Helen and Tina, who sat next to me in the back. Meanwhile, I was thinking that men also lied to get around women's inhibitions and fears.

In Margaret River, Sara and the girls took me to a huge bar constructed to look like a log cabin. Crowded and with a band, the place bubbled with twenty-somethings straining to hear conversation above the blaring music. Hundreds of voices making the smallest of talk and asking questions without listening to answers.

Scents of beer, perfume, and aftershave floated among the guys with beaded necklaces and women with painted faces and luxuriant hair. They frantically flapped their lips in 'conversation' while looking around for brighter pastures. A teen's pretty face tried to act grownup next to a boyfriend who ignored her most of the time. Pointed boobs, jeans, bartenders rushing, shouts, people playing pool—and me bored and feeling lonely among all these people trying to show they're popular.

Claustrophobia struck. I freaked! Groping through the crowd trying not to spill my drink, I felt my age. I felt lonely. So I split. Outside I gazed at the stars and thought of home. A guy puked in the parking lot to disturb my reverie. The Third World could be a wise elder to the full-of-itself West, I thought. There they understand the meaning of *slow*. Being back in the West was like sticking my finger in a socket.

After a while, Sara found me. "I'm so sorry," she said in her raspy voice. "It never occurred to me how much of a shock that bar must be after where you've been. When you walked out it struck me what a daft duck I was."

Two days later, Sara was driving me to the airport in her red Toyota Corolla. I was heading for Melbourne feeling clean—no travel dirt under my fingernails. Sara seemed so different from when we were in Africa, her penetrating personality cloaked with an inner silence that reminded me of myself. Passing the greenery of Kings Park overlooking the Swan River, I asked if her travels had changed her.

"I don't know. I'm a little lost actually. Tina says I've changed a little. Others say I'm an entirely different person. More than I think I am. Sometimes I want to talk to my friends like I do travelers, but it's not there. Life goes fast with little time for curiosity. My friends didn't ask about my trip, except one-question statements like: 'What was the most dangerous place?'

"Some things click into place, others I don't know how to deal with. Like who my friends think I am. I use time more judiciously, and don't want to hold on to people's problems anymore.

"And travel changed my view of economics. Economics is really *socio*-economics. They are married for life. You can't have one without the other. Understanding how the world operates firsthand makes me whole."

"I've been kicking around in my mind how to fit the round peg I've become into the square hole I built before I left."

"Me too! Traveling seems to draw out a character from inside that you vaguely knew, a personality waiting for its turn at the wheel."

"Like your personality by the campfire in Africa?"

"Right!" she squealed. "I'm a little lost. So many things in the air and everything going so fast there's little time to be curious. Take Tina and Sara. Can you believe the short shrift they gave your trip? I reckon I can accept who they are, but it's still fucking annoying. God, I wish I was traveling again."

"What would you say you learned about yourself?"

"That life is a hurricane," she replied slowly and softly. "And I want to live in the eye of the storm—peaceful inside while the hurricane swirls around outside."

"Well put. I was in the eye once, when I was kid in New York. During the first part of the storm, the winds raged at a hundred miles an hour. When it subsided I edged outside into a dreamy calm, quiet and peaceful. No sound, not even insects. But we all knew what was coming next."

"Living in the eye is so *bloody* hard to do! I've had a seven-year relationship, and recently a couple of short ones. Men make better friends than lovers sometimes.

"Hey, in the time remaining let's do all the talking we didn't do. What about you? What's your wife like?"

"Honest, likes to give gifts, is comfortable with silence, and doesn't bitch about people. If I didn't have issues with her, we could live happily ever after. She'd do anything to avoid conflict. When we were first married, I suggested we have monthly bitch sessions. The only rule was that if one bitched, the other had to empathize. No defensiveness. We sat up in bed one night. She had no bitches. So I thought of some for her. She said, 'Right!' Do you know that during twenty-five years of marriage she initiated only two bitch sessions? Where I'm aggressive, she's passive-aggressive."

"You married the opposite. Stephen Hawking says the universe is predicated on attractive and repulsive forces, from the tinniest spec to the largest sentient being. It's our nature to pick the opposite.

"All the males in my life—from my brother to boyfriends—are passive-aggressives. They move unalterably in one direction, pathologically lying—consciously or sub-consciously—to avoid the conflict that direction will cause. I can't fathom them. Maybe it's denial. Maybe lying and denial are the same. They say, 'Oh, are you mad?' You lay out the problem. They accept or reject your ideas, rarely suggesting anything helpful. Sometimes they don't get what you're saying."

"And when you lay out the problem you are judging them," I added.

"Right. You find solutions and make commitments. Only *you* made the commitment, so they don't have to keep it. I reckon I'm forever waiting for my brother to ask how I feel. Well, he never does. He never bloody does! Eventually they get what they want! You *cannot* outwait them!"

"I empathize with you. Five years ago, I took a year off from marriage to get romance back and change habits."

"And?"

"We got romance back, which helped immeasurably, but I learned not to expect change. If change was going to come, it had to come from me. A long trip seemed like a good idea."

We stopped at a massive shopping center with a merry-go-round blaring classical music at the entrance. I had to pick up essentials: dental floss, a new toothbrush, and Velcro to patch up my Tevas.

"How can you live a long-term relationship with your opposite?" I wondered as we shopped.

"Simple, marry a person of like mind."

"Ah, but then where's the attraction?"

We gabbed the rest of the way to the airport *and* all the way through it to the departure gate. We gabbed until everyone boarded the plane, until the very last possible second. Then, as we hugged tight, she whispered into my ear, "Don't become a wanker when you get back home. Stay with who you are now. If people like the change, they will be with you. If they don't, and you try to please them, you'll be miserable."

38

MELBOURNE, ANNE-LOUISE, AND THE AUSTRALIAN OPEN

"I NEVER" REALIZED AUSTRALIA WAS almost the size of the United States," I said to Vaughn, the paunchy guy in the aisle seat next to me.

"Most foreigners seem to think Australia is a tiny island," he replied. "Last month, I met a real wanker. He rented a car for three days in Melbourne without unlimited millage, drove to see the eighth wonder of the world, Ayers Rock, then back to Melbourne for a flight out."

"That's like driving a round trip from New York to Florida."

"It's a massive stone formation in the desert," he said, pointing it out in the middle of the Qantas map of Australia, "and so bloody rugged it can only be scaled from one route. And this bloke drove thirty straight hours to view the rock, but didn't have time to stay the night and see it at dawn, when it's this incredible red, because he had to catch his plane."

We laughed. I enjoyed this guy. Vaughn was thirty-eight or so, a divorced real estate agent. He was flying to Melbourne to visit his daughter. He thought his daughter saw more of him now than when they lived together. And he believed he was a better dad since the family had separated.

We talked about how I'd lost my fingernail—the new one was beginning to grow back, looking like a bulldozer pushing a mound of sand over a beach—and traveling in general. He said he'd gone round the world for two years in his early twenties.

"Why do so many Australians go for such extended periods," I asked, having constantly run into them on my trip.

"Most Aussies live far from their heritage. It's our custom to retrace our roots and sow wild oats before commitment to work and family."

People were eager to discuss their life, I found. A simple question and *pop*, out came their personal history. Maybe the hurricane blowing through modern relationships and families left little time for closeness. I too found it easy to give up information about myself. Why take who you are to the grave?

When Anne-Louise and I first met we were both crying. It was in the kitchen at Esalen during my transition from corporate crisis manager to a simpler human being, a few months before I'd set off on my world trip.

Located on a spectacular piece of ocean-front property in California's Big Sur, Esalen's atmosphere was slow and personal compared with the fast-paced pragmatism of figuring out how to keep organizations alive. There was an honesty that permeated life when nothing material was available.

And our tears? They came from slicing onions and garlic for pasta sauce. As we chopped away, three other women were conducting a tentative marital-status interrogation when Anne-Louise cut through the crap. "What we want to know, Denis, is whether you sleep with your wife in the same bed on a regular basis?"

She had the strong exterior of a city manager, which she was, but she was also fragile inside. I came to enjoy her no-nonsense way of thinking, her organized nature, and understanding of the intricacies of how things worked. Both in the kitchen slicing together and off duty, we shared the closeness of a friendship between a man and a woman.

The Anne-Louise who picked me up at Melbourne airport was a bit more haggard-looking and carrying a few extra pounds than when I last saw her. She still had straight, cherry-red hair cut evenly just above the shoulders. And she was happy to see me. We dumped my backpack at her place and she dropped me downtown before returning to work.

I wandered along one of Melbourne's small-town-looking streets—delis, hardware stores, and suburban housing—and picked up a local newspaper, *The Australian*. Paging through the news, I wondered where all the noteworthy Aussie females were because, in the entire paper, there were only two pictures of women. And one was Steffi Graff.

One headline told of a monster fire around Sydney, another screamed: "OUR CAMBODIAN REFUGEES ESCAPE INTO HELL." The related article told the story of a twenty-three-year-old Cambodian student who'd fired multiple gunshots at Prince Charles to protest about the treatment of Cambodians refugees in Australia. Yet despite the lurid headlines, I found people on the streets were much more laidback than in America.

As I was passing a soda shop, an old man asked: "You going to the Open, mate?"

I looked up from the paper. "What Open?"

"The Australian Open, the tennis tournament."

"Where is it?"

"Around the corner and down a bit."

Son of a bitch! THE AUSTRALIAN OPEN! Could I possibly get in? I walked around the corner and "down a bit" (three blocks), and there it was to my left. The ticket was cheap and I got to see Russian newcomer Kafelnikov take Pete Sampras to five sets. Just like that! What a way to while away the afternoon.

Either the constant traveling or the tension associated with the anticipation of going home began to take its toll. My back suddenly went into spasm. Anne-Louise nursed me with aspirin and hot compresses at her flat, filling me in on her life since we last met.

At Esalen, she'd told me she desperately wanted a child—"someone to love now, and love me in my old age." She was fed up with long-term relationships that didn't pay off in marriage, and, at thirty-six, if she couldn't find a man in two years she would consider artificial insemination. One year had passed since then. And she was seriously gene hunting.

She still had self-esteem problems and said she was becoming claustrophobic with people. Suddenly, she asked: "Am I pretty?"

I wouldn't have said Anne-Louise was pretty, but I'd never say that to any woman. Attractive was the way I put it to her. Which was true.

On the positive side, Anne-Louise felt a new sense of community in Melbourne. And she was going to study Chinese medicine because, using its approach, her aches and menstrual pains melted away.

We spent two whole nights in conversation, covering relationships, energy, family, and the female and male psyche. One of our many conclusions was that women's magazines were excessive-compulsive about sex in general and male behavior in particular. Our time together reaffirmed what I'd said to Malgosia in Poland about Anne-Louise: she really was a close friend.

I got a chance to check out Anne-Louise's genetic prospecting when she whisked me away for the weekend to meet her new boyfriend, Mat, who had arranged water-skiing with friends at a lake two hundred miles north of Melbourne. She said his gene pool was potentially first-rate. As we drove, I observed that much of habitable Australia was like California in summer: gnarled oak trees in scrub grass, rich warm weather, and rolling golden hills.

I had to decline the water-skiing, even the boat ride. I shrank at the thought of movement and even sitting up was seriously painful. Mat's friends moved me to a bed in a watercress-green, hippie-vintage Winnebago. The kind perpetually parked in a driveway. There I lay stiff, like the rusted Tin Man of Oz.

At night, it was barbie time. Honey-spiced sausage, thick bacon, and lamb chops sizzled on the grill. Beer flowed like rain on Noah's Ark. I could hear the festivities outside. A fat, black whirling-dervish fly buzzed around on this hot, lazy summer's night. Pain pills and beer enhanced the taste of the barbequed meat, corn, and potato salad that Anne-Louise brought for me. She began to ask me how I coped with being a busy businessman and family man in my prior life. I suspected her questions had to do with her envisioned family.

"I roughhoused with kids. It took the edge off work and energized me. Fortunately my family life was stable until the girls went to college. It gave me a competitive edge with people that had trouble at home because of workaholism."

To the faint sounds of people laughing outside, she confided her fears. "Mat's an ocker. Fun and charming, but a redneck underneath it all. The type that's boring as batshit one year later. I can't marry him. What am I going to do? I'm bloody obsessive about the genes in every available man I meet. I keep asking them about lineage."

"Well, if it's good jeans you want, I can send you a pair from back home."

Anne-Louise gave me a warm smile, forgiving my punning in light of the alcohol and painkillers.

39

FISHING WITH LITTLE MICK

Hiya, dude! A sign pasted on the faded pink wall of the Downunder Hostel in Sydney came into view as I opened my eyes. Rain tapped on the pavement outside like the clicks of dancing shoes. There was a slight smell of burnt wood from the deadly forest fires on the outskirts of the city.

An uneasy churning in the pit of my stomach had yanked me out of sleep. A distantly familiar feeling. It had lived in me for years before my carefree jaunt around the world. This pit-of-the-stomach anxiety meant one thing: the excitement of seeing Kathi and the girls—only a month away now—was mixed with uneasiness about renewed responsibility. Life was sweet without responsibility.

And there was the problem of loving two women. I respected more and more the hippie view of love. Why should there be a limit? But practically, I calculated a five percent chance anything would come of my relationship with Malgosia. She was beautiful and would be six thousand miles away. If I couldn't resist her love, there would be others who couldn't either.

Today was set to be a trial return to family. I was meeting Susan and her son, Mickey, to go fishing. Anne-Louise thought it would be a good idea to contact Susan for some fun. She described her friend as having "peculiar habits," and five-year-old Mickey as cute, sensitive, and precocious. My back miraculously healed once again, and I was looking forward to the outing. I envisaged a gentle day in a rowboat on a calm lake. My only restriction was I had to catch the last ferry from Sydney at 6:30 p.m. to visit a friend of Kathi's.

The early rain had ceased by the time I caught a train across Sydney to rendezvous with Susan. She picked me up at the station driving an antiquated four-door, blue Datsun. She also dressed in blue: blue sunglasses, navy blue shirt, faded blue cutoff jeans, and blue-rimmed mini-socks circling above white tennies. Mickey was in the back seat.

"This is Denis, Mickey. He's a friend of Anne-Louise."

He looked at me somewhat solemnly.

On the way, Susan stopped for Mickey's fishing rod at her recently deceased father's house. While she disappeared inside, Mickey sat peacefully strapped into his car seat, in shorts and a freshly ironed striped polo shirt. I was wearing standard shorts, colorful Indonesian button-down shirt, cap, and my trusty rejuvenated Tevas.

"How's life treating you, Mickey?" I asked.

"Oh fine," he said somberly. "Would you hand me my swords, Denis? I'd like to play with them."

"Swords" were a plastic baseball bat and a rolled-up newspaper. Soon we were fencing, Mickey giggling and wielding the bat while I aimed the paper at his tickle bones.

"If we catch a fish, we can look to see if it has teeth," he said.

"That's a good idea. It's always good to check for teeth."

"If he has sharp teeth, we can put him in the boat."

"What if he doesn't have sharp teeth?"

"We can put him back in the water."

"What?"

"We can be in the water, and the fish with sharp teeth can be in the boat."

"Makes sense!"

Mickey obviously had a lot on his mind, so I tickled him again. He tried staying serious at first, but was a sucker for the "What's that under your arm?" gag. He kept giggling and wanting my hand to check again.

Susan arrived back, and stowed her father's fishing pole in the trunk. She was a working mother, looked to be in her late thirties. She had short, curly, brown hair, a slight midriff bulge, and the quick movement of a person who has allotted only so much time for each segment of the day.

"Do you smoke ganja?" she asked, putting a heavy foot on the gas pedal.

"Sometimes, sure!"

"It's in my pocketbook. Can you roll a joint?"

"Now?" I laughed.

"Well, yes."

"If I roll one, we'll be picking ganja off the seat."

At the next light, Susan rolled the joint, bracing her hands on the steering wheel. Mickey was looking out the window at the lined-up cars. "Do you think we'll catch a little fish or a big fish?" he asked.

Susan assured him he'd catch just the right fish for him. She talked to her young son as if he was a responsible individual, and her nonchalant attitude to marijuana led me to believe that she and Mickey had discussed the subject. By the time we reached what I assumed was the lake, I was already floating.

But it wasn't a lake. It was one of the many bays that surrounded Sydney—an agitated and slightly angry one at that. And instead of little rowboats, a flotilla of moored sail and motorboats extended forever into the ocean.

Susan removed fishing gear, a picnic lunch, and warm garments from the trunk. "Show everyone your fishing pole, Mickey," she said. He looked around, as I did, at the lonely parking lot, then at the docks and masts swaying in the distant breeze. "Who is everyone, Mum?"

Ignoring the comment, she suggested I take Mickey for a walk while she attended to the boat and bait. Mickey and I moseyed hand-in-hand over to the closest dock. He pointed to a twenty-footer bobbing below and asked: "Does that boat keep the water out? Because the last boat let water in."

Something was amiss.

"Yeah, Mickey. That's a perfect boat. Look, there's no water in it!" Sensing that he needed assurance, I sat on my haunches, grabbed his right hand, and leveled my eyes into his. "Now, Mickey, how about if you and I sit right here? Let's look at the water and boats and dock for a while. Size up what we've got, okay!"

"Okay," he said uncertainly.

A late-afternoon breeze began to stir and an overcast sky threatened rain. I wondered about Susan. She didn't seem the fishing type. And we were going out on a rough bay with a kid afraid of water. I showed Mickey the ladder leading down the dock structure into bobbing swells. The ladder rails were thin and round like garden hoses. I held on to him at the edge of the dock not knowing his athletic capability or sense of safety, yet I didn't want to unnecessarily restrict him either.

Susan emerged from the office and grabbed her son's hand. "I need to take Mickey to the loo. Can you attend to the boat? They're getting one ready for us over there."

Buzzing from ganja, I carefully stepped down a steep wooden ramp. Why couldn't it have been a lake? Why did everything with me have to be an adventure? At water level, I found a young woman from Bayside Boats inside a fifteen-footer ripping at the starter-cord of a fifteen-horsepower Suzuki. The pull-cord took me back to childhood. She quickly showed me the engine basics.

"What happens if the engine doesn't start in the bay?" I asked skeptically.

"Pull the choke and repeat the procedure." She caught my "Are you fucking with me?" expression, and added, "Or wave down another boat."

Cruising out to sea, water spraying and lungs absorbing the fresh salty air, I sat by the motor. I'd assumed the role of man at the tiller, which was, I believed, exactly the way Susan had planned it. Gradually she softened as she talked. Her dad used to take her fishing on this bay. So she was a fishing type, I realized relieved. She felt guilty that her divorce several years before had deprived Mickey of a father. Now she felt a need to let him get some fatherly attention since his grandpa had passed away.

We decelerated and settled at a suitable fishing spot three kilometers from the harbor, near a deserted island. Decked out in yellow raingear, Mickey nervously asked about the silver-striped fish his mother was using as bait, and then got to the real point: how good was the boat at holding water out? He was a likable kid whose expressions already showed how he would look as a grown man. But he was anxious and Susan finally confessed why.

"We were fishing at the lake last week," she said, "I thought he was leaning too far. When I attempted to grab him, we both fell in. I scrambled back into the boat and pulled him in, but he got a bit ..." At that point, Mickey began to toss heads and lumps of fish bodies into the water, gazing anxiously at the swells.

"Good idea, Mickey," I said, patting him on the back. "We could use some chum to attract fish."

The latch on Grandpa's fishing-pole was broken and didn't reel in. It didn't much matter anyway. We weren't going to catch any fish. The sky looked mean. We had maybe an hour and a half before hauling up lines and motoring back to meet my train to the ferry. And when it came to fishing, I was a jinx. Nobody ever caught a real fish when I was around. Still, as I let out the two hundred and fifty feet of line on the little guy's rod, I remembered fishing at a reservoir near home with the girls when they were his age and Shannon's excitement at catching tiny fish.

However, as we ravenously devoured the picnic lunch, Mickey wasn't excited. He looked bored, and soon passed his grandfather's pole to me.

It was taut, straining against an unseen object.

"Denis, it looks like you have a fish," Susan said.

"Oh, I *reckon* it's just the weight of the line," I said, with my proficient use of Australian. I tested the line again, jerking it a few times. "There's no fish, Susan. No resistance at all."

"Sure looks like a fish!"

A brilliant idea entered my mind. I whispered it to Susan. "Nobody ever catches fish when I'm around, but what if we give Mickey the pole and help him pull the line in, pretending there is a fish. What the heck, he'll be excited just the same."

"Maybe there is a fish."

"Believe me, if there was a fish on that line, I'll be the most surprised person in this boat."

"Mickey, I think you've got a fish!" I said eagerly even though there wasn't so much as a twitch of resistance on the heavy line.

"I never caught a fish before," he said, holding the pole with care, his gas-flame-blue eyes lit like stars.

Susan called out, "The way you're reeling in, I reckon this fish must know its number is up and it decided on assisted suicide."

As the hook neared the surface, I turned to Mickey: "Sorry, Mickey. Looks like he got away."

I was wrong. A sense of bulk immediately forced my attention back to the line. A fish half the size of Mickey dangled there, resigned to its fate. Mouth and eyes wide open, the young angler said nothing but stared at his catch's teeth.

When we got back to shore, we discovered that Mickey's fish, which Susan had dispatched, was the largest bream caught in the last two years. All smiles, the little guy proudly carried it by the tail. He was thrilled by the stares of admiration and happily fielded questions such as: "Did you catch that big fish all by yourself?" I took a picture of Mickey and the bream for posterity.

Susan suggested we order hot chocolate after such an exciting day. "Don't worry about the train," she casually whispered, "I'll drive you to the ferry. It's half an hour. Last ferry leaves at six-thirty, yeah?" She proceeded to tell me about a party that night, dropping hints about what I might expect if I changed my mind about the ferry. Women were always partial to me, I figured, because I liked kids and was the ultimate family man—dedicated and a good earner.

"The fires will slow traffic, I reckon," Susan said, suddenly realizing the time. She grabbed Mickey and we rushed to the car.

Racing through city streets, Susan tossed a heavy book on my lap. "Can you read a city map? We're on Joseph Street heading south. Should be on page twenty-eight."

"Directions and maps confuse me," I exclaimed, helplessly searching page twenty-eight for "Joseph Street." Impatient with my fumbling, she grabbed the book and laid it against the wheel, weaving in and out of traffic, screeching around corners, and stretching yellow lights. Finally, with two minutes to spare, we pulled into a quaint ferry lot.

Still calm, Susan flashed me a coquettish look. "Bloody shame you can't make the party. Mickey and I are growing to fancy *you*, mate."

40

CONFESSING THOUGHTS OF HOME TO AN EX-PRIEST

Waving goodbye to Susan and little Mickey from the deck of the old wooden ferry, I turned my attention to my next slice of life. It was Kathi who'd met Jerry, a former Catholic priest, at a therapists' convention in North Carolina. She said he'd left the priesthood to marry a world-class diver turned doctor.

Now he and his wife counseled and treated terminally ill patients at their home—a comfortable house that rested on a grassy, two-acre knoll. A ladder's climb below was a sandy beach whose waters rolled in from the very bay I'd just fished with Mickey and his mom. Through the distant haze one could barely make out the majestic brilliance of Sydney's tall buildings.

In the far corner of the property stood a bungalow with two bedrooms and a facilitating room for intimate discussions with patients learning to accept the all-engulfing feeling of death—past or impending, of themselves or their loved ones. The main house had a bayside porch with enough cast-iron railing to accept and dry all my hand wash. Inside, a den and five bedrooms housed the five-member family.

Despite the New Age philosophy there was a hint of old school in the home, older generation mannerisms. For instance, mail on the kitchen counter was made out to *Mrs. Jerry Ryan*. Jerry was, after all, twenty years older than his wife, Helen.

I'd arrived just in time for appetizers on the porch with Jerry and a client. Jerry was a few inches taller than me, with silver hair and a beard. Everything about him projected a dignified ease. Meanwhile, Helen rushed about—delivering crackers and pâté, setting the table for dinner, and constantly answering phone calls from patients and friends. Of medium height and slender build, with preoccupied eyes, she wouldn't accept my offer of help and declined a (somewhat unrealistic) offer by Jerry to join us and relax. The sense I got was superwoman.

Six months before, the bereaved client lost his wife of thirty years to cancer and was finding it hard to adjust. His voice carried a mixture of love and anger for the departed, who he said had left him without any friends and bitter feelings for women in general. Despite his loss, I found myself impatient with his attitude. He was like so many men I knew that handed over their social lives to their spouses and became isolated as a result.

"Men don't know who they are anymore," he moaned. "What makes it more infuriating is that we are being made to look like either heroes or deviates."

Jerry expressed sympathy with his client. The media and entertainment had fostered that attitude, he said. Divorce and the preponderance of female-headed households had far too often taken the male out of the family equation. The woman and TV were left to provide the role models for both females and males.

"Do you think we need to worry about losing our maleness?" I inquired.

"Yes I do!" the bereaved spit out with an aggressive tone, as if he was talking to someone else. "We can't be sensitive, rugged, protective, and wise all in one. What kind of a man is that?"

His comment recalled for me the cocky mongrel Tramp in *Lady and the Tramp*. And while I agreed in general, I kept my mouth shut to see what would unfold.

"Women," Jerry said, "can't provide all these qualities themselves, and life would be dull without them." He spoke with a slight Australian accent devoid of "mates" and "bloodys," but was spirited nevertheless.

"You've got a point," I said. "The world is changing rapidly. Men had their shot at running things, and the new age is tearing down the role images of the past and substituting fresh ones. I think we guys better get used to a new order."

"I have the feeling that if we focus on self-esteem," Jerry summed up as he bade his client farewell before dinner, "we won't sacrifice basic masculinity."

That would describe the character of Tramp, I thought. A sense of self-worth and trust that did not forfeit basic cocky masculinity. It was Jerry, not the client, who most had the personality of Tramp.

Helen twisted her honey-blond hair into a bun and joined Jerry, their two early-twenties sons, and me at the table. Over a sumptuous candlelit dinner, we initially got into a philosophical discussion about dealing with the bereaved. Jerry spoke about denial and death, saying that once you got rid of denial, death was palatable. However, I was more interested in discussing life—specifically how my hosts met, since, which I did not say, the age difference intrigued me.

"I was a chaplain when we met back in the sixties," Jerry explained. "Helen had just graduated from medical school. Our mutual interest was 'incurable disease.' I left the ministry to marry her."

"Yes," Helen said timidly, "My father was very influential in Australia, and he hated Catholics."

"What was the initial attraction to Jerry then?" I asked.

"He was the first man to treat me like an individual," she said and looked fondly at her husband. The sons' eyes went from Mom to Dad, who catching his wife's look, smiled ever so faintly.

Helen went on to say the pressure following the marriage was unbearable. Journalists had hounded the famous wife and suddenly famous husband. A priest leaving his heavenly reward for an earthly one was a first for the Catholic Church in Australia.

After dinner, I followed Jerry upstairs to his study for further conversation. He carried with him two crystal glasses and a bottle of vintage port. I'd always associated port with the two pints of Gallo my grandfather drank every night. My grandmother only allowed him to drink *one* pint per night. The other one Papa Joe socked away before he arrived home from work to face his dominant partner. But it was clear even before I drank it that this port was not the sort he would have downed. It was primo.

Jerry's study marked him as a saver: oak desk and two leather armchairs, all piled with papers. He placed the glasses and port on the desk's single bare spot, and retrieved a pack of cigarettes and ashtray hidden in the center drawer. He cleared the armchairs and motioned for me to sit. Then, with a sheepish little boy's grin, he lit up.

From one of the relocated piles, he lifted a picture of Kathi taken at the conference. She was kneeling to pick up shells on the beach. It must have been chilly in North Carolina that day because she was wearing the gray suede leather jacket I sent her from Istanbul. She looked terrific, curls spilling on to her shoulders and a smile of inner calm. A pang of nostalgia ripped through me.

"She's a beautiful woman," he said, handing me a glass. "Warm and honest with her feelings. She misses you. Doesn't know what to expect when you return. She filled me in on your history together.

"No one can leave for a year without severely wanting change, but what did your family hope would happen when they encouraged you to travel?"

"I think they felt I needed to rejuvenate, bring zest back into my life, and maybe vicariously into theirs. Probably hoped I'd take the edge off and clear old baggage. I don't know. They were enthusiastic, though. I think Kathi looked forward to me leaving in a way, so that she could fashion the atmosphere in our house to her own personality—but she was also afraid."

"She said she wanted to establish better communication, and have you miss her," Jerry added in the manner of a man comfortable talking straight to people.

An arrow struck my heart. It hurt. I hadn't felt guilt for a while, and realized she didn't need to be present to inflict it. How could you convey the simple-yet-complex feeling of not missing someone you deeply care for? The chair squeaked as I shifted my weight. I took a slug of the port.

"Communication has always been an issue. Kathi has a Ph.D. in psychology, but our conversations since the trip began still seem formal, Jerry. It bothers me that I don't miss her like she wants, although I am thinking of her more and more. Traveling is absorbing ...."

"And then Kathi has a need to be treasured that I haven't been able to fill for a while. We've been married a long time. In my own defense, I wasn't exactly on her priority list when I left."

"Imagine how you fit with your family after this trip. What you want from them," he said as if he was on a mission, one that I appreciated because I needed this discussion.

"A couple of years ago," I finally said, "I asked my mom how she felt when her five kids moved out of the house. She said, 'One minute I had a family, and the next they were gone.'

"When I was a kid I wanted a powerful family, the Kennedy model, and I would be patriarch. Then I had two girls—"

"So much for the male model!" Jerry quipped.

"I wondered about that too. Kathi didn't fit the role model of the demanding Kennedy matriarch either, but she's perfect for raising individuals. We even developed a family charter about being integrated individuals within a family unit.

"I had a blast growing up with Kathi and the girls. People enjoyed coming to our house. Somewhere along the line, though, I became discouraged about everyone going their own way. I wanted to be a priority in their lives because they were a priority in mine. But the girls can barely tell you what I did for a living. When Mom said, 'the next minute they were all gone,' I began to wonder what I was working so hard for."

"No one paying attention to the patriarch?"

"Something like that. There were other issues."

"So, at that point you rebelled."

"I did. Everyone in the family was becoming their own person, why not me? Work, watching televised sports *alone*, and lusting over women wasn't enough. And the conversations! I couldn't discuss a subject without offending someone's self-esteem, delusion, sense of morality, or some societal taboo. Does that make any sense to you?"

"It does! It does! What you say pushes a lot of my own buttons, mate." (Aha! He was a real Australian after all.) "However, it sounds like you were an unbalanced wheel needing its spokes realigned."

"Fuckin' A! But by leaving and changing my environment, I purchased the ingredients for balance. Now I am happy every day! No guilt, no responsibility. *And*—and this is a big 'and'—my body and mind are healthy as a result."

"Wonderful!"

"You asked what I want from my family. Well, I've been concerned about how to fit in when I return. Of the four friends I traveled with this year from back home, two situations ended in disaster. I would like my family to be flexible and understanding. I am still a dad and hubby, but also a much different person than the one who left California a year ago. I would like them to think of me as a refurbished soulmate."

"I have the feeling *you'll* need to be the understanding one. Few of your family or friends will fathom where you've been and the changes you've made over the last year. Their life didn't change dramatically."

So true! I'd had time to understand and absorb how things developed and changed. Traveling gave me the time. He nailed the problem.

"That's a very astute observation, Jerry. In one sense I might be easier to live with now, but in another I'll be a shit-load of change and compromise for Kathi. While I don't want to control events the way I used to, the traveler in me wants to experience the world."

"Dangerous words, mate! Although, as Bruce Chatwin once said, 'Without change our brains and bodies rot.'"

"You said you'd like 'them' to think of you as their soulmate. Shouldn't that just be Kathi?"

"It used to be. But I've lived many lives along this journey, plus the knowledge you accumulate with twenty-five years of marriage, and I now think of a soulmate as one who helps develop the maturity to be happy with who you are. That definition doesn't require an exclusive relationship. Everyone in my family has opened themselves up to others. Now the challenge is to remain integrated."

"How will you fill Kathi's need to be treasured?"

"I don't know. It used to be that lying by her side was the greatest pleasure I'd ever known. Then unresolved *issues* and fights gradually sapped the bliss. I know how I *could* fill her need. I don't know if I want that. Do you think a non-exclusive soulmate fills that need?"

"No."

41

WHAT A TIME WE'VE HAD, ROSIE!

TWO THOUSAND KILOMETERS NORTH OF Sydney, Magnetic Island sat near the edge of the Great Barrier Reef. Outside my hostel, I lay on a hammock in the shade of two coconut trees and swayed wistfully in a hot breeze. I inhaled the now familiar scent of jasmine and listened to cockatoos squawking high in the air. In the hammock next to me, a Dutch baker was talking about nature. All species and individuals were what Indonesians called *same same, but different*. He figured traveling provided time to meet people you'd never become acquainted with in everyday life. The "great equalizer" was the way he phrased it. Koala bears slouched in nearby eucalyptus trees looking stoned—perhaps they were—while the baker and I talked about the price of freedom. I'd been happy without freedom in my previous life—I'd never have traded my family or career for it. But now I'd experienced total freedom, what would life be like again without it?

From the island, a three-decker boat looking like the starship *Voyager* took me to the Great Barrier Reef. Stretching across an area larger than Great Britain, the reef was a major feeding ground for a diverse ecosystem, with the largest concentration of corals and other life forms anywhere in the world. There were three varieties of reef: *ribbon reef*, thin strips that acted as a barrier for the continental shelf; *fringing reef* that inhabited shallow waters around islands and the mainland; and *oval platform reef* out in the crystal clear waters between the mainland and islands. I snorkeled amid the platform reefs. Here there was a low possibility of sharks—an important consideration. I looked down at the marine multitudes below me, theorizing that the lower on the food chain, the more colorful the organism.

Two days later, back on the mainland, I joined an excursion to Cape Tribulation where Captain Cook had run aground on his first voyage of discovery to Australia. The bus driver told us that during World War II the Japanese bombed the northern city of Darwin eight hundred kilometers to the northwest, and that they might have invaded Australia if it weren't for the Battle of the Coral Sea in which Allied forces inflicted severe damage on the Japanese fleet. I had no idea Australia was bombed!

On the way back, the tour bus stopped for a guided boat ride through dense mangrove trees growing in one of a countless number of saltwater estuaries that flowed inland from the ocean. The mangrove trees grew like reeds in this swampy jungle. They provided food and shelter to 1,500 species of animals and birds, including crocodiles. The whole scene reminded me of the Everglades. The guide said two months before a bloke was eaten in front of his family as he swam across this tributary. "Shortly after that," he continued, "a tipsy woman and two chaps chanced upon a murky monster. Croc took the smallest! Now the locals send their kids across first."

For the first time in ages, my mind was planted in the future, with little room for memories or current events. I only half-noticed that the "spider bites" from Indonesia were spreading on my palm. As one crusted over, another white bump appeared. As the boat slid down the narrow river and I gazed at thousands of furry-faced flying foxes (fruit bats) hanging upside down on branches like black peels of rotten bananas, I visualized how my women would greet me. Shannon, already three months in New Zealand, would be first. Her face would light up like a starburst, and she would talk with eagerness and warmth.

Chimene would arrive next, starting her own journey that would wind up in Africa. She'd probably fondle my long hair the way she did her Blankee as a baby, proclaiming: "That's my dad. How're ya doin', Dad?" Thoughts danced! Kathi would kiss me deeply. They danced! Sara saying, "Stay with who you are now. If people like the change, they will be with you." And danced! ... Humphrey Bogart stranded in a wasteland of reeds on the *African Queen*, "What a time we've had, Rosie!"

NEW ZEALAND

REUNION

42

WWOOFING WITH SHANNON: FREE SPIRIT MEETS RESPONSIBILITY

"DAD, OVER HERE!"
At the airport in Christchurch on the south island of New Zealand, these three words ended one life and began another.

Watching Shannon wave wildly, sudden and intense emotions flooded my heart—the euphoria of meeting up with my beautiful family, the thought that I had completed a life's vision. I felt like a ship passing through the locks on the Panama Canal. In one lock was the freedom to do as I pleased, in another was the elation of "Dad's back!" Even if *Dad* was something of a wobbly proposition. Then any thought was swept away as we were in each other's arms. We kissed and hugged and clung to each other's shoulders, stroking each other and grinning. Shannon let her feelings caress you.

"Three whole weeks I've been thinking, I can't wait till my papa comes!" she said, her words exploding like water from an open fire hydrant. "'I have so much to tell you. And I want to hear all about your trip.'" Then she tugged my long, curly hair: "Dad, you've become a hippie."

Yeah, a hippie who missed the glory days pursuing ambition.

Shannon and I had a week to ourselves before meeting Chimene and, two days later, Kathi in Auckland on the North Island. We were the family's talkers and we ripped into a year's worth of life like two starving hyenas.

For the previous three months, Shannon had been "wwoofing" her way around New Zealand. WWOOF stood for Willing Workers on Organic Farms—a scheme in which young travelers received room and board and occasionally pocket change for their labor. She filled me in on Kiwi-land. There were three million people, and the emerald-colored hills were covered with sheep. She'd found the people hospitable, rugby was their preferred sport, and they worried about ozone and anything nuclear. The Maori tribes were suing to reclaim land taken in colonial times. They claimed the treaty they signed, giving land in exchange for British protection, had something of a Mafia nature to it.

"Besides," she said, "the Maori didn't believe in land ownership. And this is horrible I know, but I read in the papers that there appears to be no prior claim to the land anyway, since the Maori had eaten the previous inhabitants hundreds of years before."

Shannon was sincere and funny at the same time. I remember when she was ten, driving in a car with a friend of ours.

"Bill," she said. "Do you believe in God?"

"Sometimes I do and sometimes I don't," he responded. "But mostly I do."

"That's the way I feel Bill," she said. "Sometimes I do and sometimes I don't, but mostly I don't."

We spent the night in a hostel, then boarded a bus going farther south to Akaroa, a tiny town where Shannon had been staying. On the bus, I stifled my urge to communicate with strangers since I knew Shannon wasn't interested. I was beginning a conscious adjusting to being "Dad," while my unconscious carried the unease I felt in Australia. The pure freedom to think and act was grinding to a halt, to be replaced once again by responsibility for the care and wellbeing of others. It was a kind of unease I'd felt in my startup days in Silicon Valley, when—despite the risk to my family's wellbeing—we executive staff had chosen to hold back our salaries so our computer company could go on living. *However*, while the old life was returning, the one-dimensional dad was gone forever.

Akaroa was a historic French and British settlement nestled in the heart of an ancient volcano. This picturesque town—so small it had no traffic lights—lay on the edge of the Banks Peninsular, a finger of land sweeping into the Pacific. Tree Crop Farm, a few kilometers up the hill from Akaroa, was where Shannon had ended up after wwoofing her way around the North and South Islands.

The farm was a rustic bed and breakfast and coffeehouse on sixty acres. Shannon and I talked through dinner, an evening repose, and until lights-out in the Green Room—which was holly-green to be exact. Shannon had booked this special room for our first night's stay. It came equipped with a woolskin rug, saddles on racks hanging from the wall, lacquered pine cabinets pitted with age, and a silver candelabra with teardrop handles, which sat comfortably on the bedside table. A fluffy holly-green comforter and warm bedding would keep us snug during the chilly night. We squeezed out every ounce of wakefulness, then resumed talking the next morning where we left off the night before.

"Come on, Dad! It's time to get up. I've got work to do," Shannon finally urged, while still submerged in the quilt. Birds chirped soliloquies outside a window framed with vines sprouting pink flowers. She hopped out of bed to attend early morning chores, while I attended my daily routine: ten minutes of stretching back muscles I abused as a teenager, and a game of solitaire on the floor to set the day's energy.

A solitaire without cheating meant a great day. A cheating solitaire meant a good day. While a bust hand meant a challenge during the day that needed to be treated with sensitivity. That morning produced a natural solitaire.

Walking through a cluttered living room whose defining features were an old piano and a scarred wooden bench laden with laundry, I found Shannon in the well-stocked kitchen. She introduced the proprietor, Lynne, who grudgingly said hello, reserving her pleasantries for Shannon who'd obviously won her over. Shannon had a way with people. She was comfortable and fun to be with. Lynne, on the other hand, had a tough demeanor, like a woman who'd seen the world in all its shades and was not about to add any unnecessary extra color. She'd spent most of her life in Akaroa, except for time traveling in China and Indonesia. She married a Dutchman, lived in Holland, and had a son, but came back when homesickness got too much. After a brief salutation to me, she gave Shannon her instructions for the day.

An all-white horse, Anne, poked her head through the top half of a Dutch door and with a tongue like a pink hot-water bottle scooped squares of sugar from Shannon's hand. Then Anne jerked her head back, glared at me with enormous eyes, and trotted off. I just didn't get on with horses. The size of their eyes intimidated me.

We ate breakfast in the "coffeehouse" adjacent to the kitchen. The Burgundy Room, as it was known, was decorated with throw rugs soft to the feet and an eclectic variety of charming antique furniture, including an oak dining table and loveseats loaded with pillows. Famous sayings donated by guests were chalked on support beams and ceiling pillars, or written in notebooks, such as: *Too many people tiptoe through life just to make it safely to death.*

Lynne and her pudgy, good-natured, ten-year-old son, Sebastian, and a middle-aged couple joined us for breakfast. I roughed Sebastian up. He roughed me up. Boys! That ingratiated me with Lynne. "Tell your dad the joke about the two kids and the psychologist," she said to Shannon.

"Ah, it's your joke. You tell him," Shannon said, grinning. Shannon had a volatile side, especially with me, but generally she carried positive energy that permeated any room she walked into. You noticed Shannon. She always got picked from audiences, like at Marineland's dolphin show when performers searched for a volunteer.

"Well, there's this psychologist," Lynne began, in a subdued-yet-hearty style designed to rescue dignity if the listeners didn't laugh. "He puts a pessimist child in a room loaded with toys, and an optimist child in a room loaded with horseshit." Her son was already laughing. "When they open the door to the room with the pessimist, the kid is banging his head on the wall, complaining that someone will steal his toys. When they look into the room with the optimist, they find her submerged in horseshit. Suddenly, the optimist pokes her head out, looks at the psychologist and says: 'There's got to be a pony in here somewhere.'"

After breakfast, Shannon led me on a tour along one of several rock-studded paths. As her long, strawberry-blond hair blew in the wind, she pointed out the barn, the chemical-free vegetable garden, and fenced grazing pastures for Anne and the sheep. The rocky pastures looked like Ireland, with groves of evergreens curtseying to each other in the wind. Everywhere cheerful yellow flowers opened to a clear blue sky studded with bachelor clouds still bold with youth. Birds squawked and chirped, and a persistent yellow-jacket zigzagged in front of my nose—an aggressive beast common to all parts of the world. A diminutive sun-speckled stream flickered as it rolled through the green land, drifting under wooden bridges.

"You added a little weight, Shannon. It looks good on you." As a teen, Shannon made the household conscious of what we ate. Then, during her year studying philosophy in France before college, she gained weight due to the French cooking, and she had quite a struggle with it for a while, both up and down. Her figure now was long and pleasantly slim.

"I don't worry about my weight any more. I've passed that stage," she said. "I'm firmly convinced that if people learn to love their bodies, they will feed them in a healthy way! And, in a nutshell, that is my philosophy about weight, Dad."

We hunted eggs from hidden hens' nests and gathered strawberries for dessert that night. Placido Domingo's "Flower Song" from *Carmen* drifted from the café across the sunlit fields. In the distant hills, a buzz saw outperformed the cicadas. Machinery sounds traveled long distances in quiet mountains.

The beauty of it all moved with an unhurried pace. The speed one experienced under the influence of soft drugs. In this mellow atmosphere, Shannon spoke of the herbal and mineral education she was absorbing in New Zealand. She'd decided to make a living in herbal medicine.

"Maybe I can avoid the fucking rat race I was in a few years ago," she said. "Did you know you have to work at cooking a bad meal if you cook with foods that grow together? Your vitamin level is down, you know. That's why your hair is graying!"

"Three months ago, it was blond!"

It was nice seeing Shannon secure with herself. Ever since Chimene became such a good athlete, Shannon had harbored sibling insecurity.

I'd miss being out in nature, I thought. Few material needs, the spatial satisfaction land provided, the sky. Nature had a way of appealing to your sense of calm. I couldn't imagine living indoors for long periods of time again.

Then, all of a sudden, I was back at the disastrous board meeting where I'd lost connection to my material. When I was left standing silent wondering what the fuck was happening to me. It felt like a lifetime ago. I'd envisioned quitting business by fifty, and today nature was reminding me of this commitment.

"Look over there, Dad! I think that's a piwakawaka, a fantail pigeon."

"A what? Where?"

"In that tree, by the bridge. Look, a fantail pigeon. Follow my finger. See the bird! See the soft blue-gray feathers and erect black crest."

"Oh, that one! Where'd you learn about birds?"

"At Berkeley. Environmental programs *are* about the earth and her inhabitants.

"Hey, Dad, tonight I can give you a massage and we can read Motherpeace tarot cards or play hearts or something! What do you think? You choose."

After the walk, I earned us a free picnic lunch from Lynne by fixing caffè lattes and waiting on customers for the first time since scooping ice-cream as a teenager at Howard Johnson's.

There was such a refreshing humility to serve rather than be served. On my year-long trip, part of me had always wanted to show off the affluence I'd worked so hard to achieve, but the stronger part loved the anonymity of a long-haired hippie with a blue headband. Most travelers worked to pay their way. And though I liked not having to work and occasionally telling fellow travelers that I lived in a big house on top of a hill. Mostly I liked being part of the flow, one of the guys. And here I was serving lattes New Zealand style—one large cup of steamed milk, and a separate cup of espresso. To a question from a customer as to the origin of poetry on the wall, I answered: "Beats me, mam, I only work here part-time."

43

THE VISION PULLED MY STRINGS

WHEN SHANNON COMPLETED THE TAROT card reading she brought out an ice bucket with champagne and two glasses that she'd been hiding. She popped the cork, poured the bubbly, and encircled my shoulder with her right arm. She lifted her glass and proposed a toast. "As they say in New Zealand, *Good on you,* Dad. You did it. You backpacked around the world."

Clink!

"What a nice surprise. I should leave more often."

"How do you feel?"

"How do I feel? I feel like I want to scream. Like I just finished a marathon only I'm not exhausted. Or found the missing ingredient to a fabulous pasta sauce. I have the feeling that a content dying man might have. Every minute of life will be gravy from here on out."

"Wow, Dad! That must feel good. But scream, don't die. You have a lot of stories to tell your grandchildren."

I screamed.

"Shh! Not too loud. And be careful of the glass, Lynne will kill me if we break them. About your vision that we discussed during the reading—the great family and enough money so no one could pull your strings. I hadn't realized you carried it around in your mind since before I was born. I've been thinking that if it wasn't for the money you earned, you never would have been able to travel."

"Good point. And if it wasn't for the family, I never would have gone."

"How's that?"

"Well, to begin with I was jealous of the freedom you guys had. Your mom's freedom to study subjects she loves to learn, the year you and Chimene each spent in France learning their language and philosophy, Chimene's junior year abroad in Germany, your travels after graduation. You guys gave me courage to leave."

"Really! It's nice to know you think I had an influence. Actually, that's my point! It's like this vision of yours pushed you to think about how to have a family and acquire money. Then those very desires—family and money—become the strings that pull you to a life with few options, leaving you feeling tired and used, right! Though, I have to admit, I don't know how I feel about being a 'string' that's binding you to what you don't want."

"What I *wanted*. Family and money were my passions. But passions can be all-consuming. In my case, I tried to control the future and wound up having it control me, leaving me burned out without balance or passion. I needed to let go of control and family for a while. Does that make sense?"

"Perfectly. But what was the motivation behind the part of your vision about enough money so that no one could pull your strings?"

"The fear someone would control me. In my early teens, I bought a motor for our old wooden boat and escaped the clutches of Dad's 'work to be done' by going full throttle down the creek and into the bay, wind in my face, hair flying, smells of salt and seaweed. I felt an easy sense of freedom in that boat. Money meant I wouldn't be subject to anyone."

"Hmm, so the way I see it, Dad, is that the vision was the one pulling the strings all along. It made you experience each element of itself in turn—family, money, and finally no strings to pull, which was basically your trip around the world. And by experiencing each individually, you can understand what it takes to achieve balance. What do you think of that?"

"Fuck, that's deep: The vision pulled my strings!"

I recalled how in India I'd understood that a vision is a life force energized by those that wanted that particular vision. It was my turn to pat her on the back.

"The greatness of our family," I continued, "is that you guys knew what was eating me and encouraged me to seek out the boy in the boat."

The Vision Pulled My Strings

"Thanks, Dad. We may have overlooked you, but we love you. I get the vision, especially needing money. I'm experiencing that angst now," she said with a laugh.

"Yeah, look at us. We have a week together because of money. The most time you and I ever spent alone were the one-day 'one-on-ones' during our travels through Europe when you were nine."

"Whatever happened to those one-on-ones? We were supposed to do them once a month when we got home."

"We did for a while."

I looked at my daughter thinking how you can't see the maturing process in your own children—as if they were camouflaged. She was part of the new community of confident women remaking the world. Part of nature taking things apart and putting them back together to fit the future—the theory of dissipative structures again.

"So, you must be excited to see Mom!" she said, changing the subject.

I said I was excited. How old love songs strummed in my ear. Apprehensive too, although I held back the exact weight of the misgivings. I asked her how she would summarize her parents' lives together.

"A lot of years of really good times, several years of turmoil starting when I was around sixteen. Then your first separation—counting this as your second—and then a revival for the three or four years before you traded the Mercedes for a backpack."

44

FATHER AND DAUGHTER SWIM WITH DOLPHINS

WE WERE GOING TO SWIM with dolphins. Lynne dropped us off downtown in the morning to wander about before heading over to the dock for an appointment with a friend of hers, Captain Bob, who owned a fishing boat. Honking mallards and preening geese roamed the two-lane "Main Street" that a blindfolded person could cross and never get clipped. "Downtown" was so sleepy that a woman in high heels sounded like a jackhammer. Heavy clouds gathered. The breeze smelled of pine needles and shellfish. A sign on a wooden-slat building read *Betsy's Meals, Dinner 6–8*. We sat down in a little park across from Betsy's.

"You look a little solemn, Dad. Do you miss being the traveler?"

"I do and I don't. I miss the clean slate of the traveler. At the same time, I'm excited about coming home, but not as the stereotyped family man dedicated to work," I said, though it didn't exactly come out the way I meant it.

"But you enjoyed your work, and got a lot of satisfaction out of family."

"My work was exciting, yes, but I enjoyed it about sixty percent of the time actually. And of course I got tremendous satisfaction from family. At the same time, there are other aspects to a man's life as he ages—a craving for romance, for instance."

"So you fooled around on your trip, huh? I'm not surprised, but don't tell me the details." Then she proceeded to tell me the details about a wonderful man she met during the summer, when they were both rafting guides on the American River in Northern California.

"I got a letter from him when I arrived in New Zealand. He'd been going with an older woman, you know, and they were breaking up. She's a guide too. I like her. So I wrote him back saying I was ready for a committed relationship but didn't want to get between him and the other woman. I always seem to attract guys involved with someone."

"How come you go out with men that have girlfriends? Single guys should be beating your door down. Are guys *that* afraid of an intelligent woman?"

"I don't know. I think I was afraid of commitment."

She talked on and on about this guy. I was giving and not receiving. My girls always discussed the details of their lives, while I silently protected secrets. I felt, as I realized in Egypt, like a package stamped *Denis Hickey, husband and father*. The only male in the family, I watched games on TV alone, and thought about things the women would never suspect. On the outside, family and job provided everything, but inside I had hidden personalities.

"How come you can tell me intimate details of your life and I can't tell you any?" I said, during a rare pause in her story. "For a year now I've been sharing intimate details with young people all over the world."

"Oh, it's me that has the problem then, right? I'm your daughter. I'm not *supposed* to be comfortable with your sex life."

From innocuous beginnings, our discussion dynamics were triggered: me, the know-it-all using lots of words to explain; she, defiant, interrupting me with *no's* of various complexities; me, getting increasingly frustrated.

"If you would stop interrupting me, Shannon, I could finish my thought! You and the whole of society have to defend and argue every fucking point. Whatever happened to listening?"

"I got what you said. You don't have to go on and on. And don't link me with the rest of society just because you've got a bug up your ass about them."

"How can you get my point if I didn't make it?"

"Well, make your fucking point!"

"I don't even know what my fucking point is anymore."

I remembered something Frank Zolfo said. "Most times we are really mad at something that happened in the past that is not articulated in the present." The *controller* was out.

"Shannon, I need understanding from you now," I said, taking her hand. "You're free to express, but why can't I mention intimacies that excite me? Take away a person's excitement, and you take away their soul."

"Dad, define intimate," she said with a smile.

"Sharing hidden parts of your life."

"Huh! I'm interested in your stories, Dad. And I'll work on hearing them. I'm accepting that you had experiences with women on your trip, and anticipated that would happen. But for now I'm not comfortable knowing the details."

"I'm not comfortable either, but wasn't that the purpose of our family meetings—to share what we actually think? If I tell you truth, I'm violating some unwritten law about what dads are supposed to share. And if I don't share, later on I'm a sleazebag for living a hidden life. Screw that!"

"I guess I put you on a pedestal, Dad, and don't want you to fall off. When you and Mom took off your rings during your first separation, I knew there was a change, but I wanted things to be as they were. I guess when people on a pedestal do something uncharacteristic, others don't want to accept it. Their hero image is tainted."

"It's lonely living on a pedestal. I want for us the type of intimacy that Shirley McLain had with her daughter in *Terms of Endearment*—individuals overcoming the age barrier to express private thoughts. We started out that way when you girls were seven. Remember the time your mom and I spelled out how two people in love make love? We wanted you to know about *good loving*, and at the same time prepare you to converse openly as you got older."

"I see your point, Pops. We have expectations from you, but you wind up with no one to talk to about your own expectations. Maybe that's how men detach from their emotions."

We crossed the street from the park and sauntered along the beach towards the wharf, stopping occasionally to examine washed up shells. "Good on us, Pops," Shannon said. "We recognized the family dynamic and changed energy in the heat of battle."

We high-fived and began dancing on the jetty to a sixties melody drifting from a boardwalk café: Ricky Nelson singing "Hello Mary Lou."

Captain Bob was a rugged chap with a square face, intense eyes, and black beard. His ship, the *Caroline,* looked like the vintage wooden fishing boats you saw in New England. As he cast off from the barnacle-encrusted jetty, we and a mousy couple from Auckland picked out wetsuits and snorkeling gear from a bin inside the cabin. Bob shouted over the motor that dolphins might be hard to find.

He was right. We were at sea for hours before spotting a pod of dolphins. But it was worth the wait. About fifty yards from the *Caroline*, they were jumping in tandem—as if they had telepathic communication. Before long they were surfing our bow waves. Then, without so much as a "Bob's your uncle," the captain cut the engine and threw a rope ladder over the side. "Dolphins are intelligent mammals," he instructed. "If you want to attract their attention, be interesting. Sing!"

I plunged into the enveloping dark-green deep. I trod water. Bait for sharks. But hope came to me. Hope that what people said about dolphins being protective of humans was true. Hope that the shy couple from Auckland smelled more appetizing than Shannon or me! I watched protectively for signs of fear on Shannon's face. Would I sacrifice my life to fight off Jaws?

But Shannon was singing and laughing. "C'mon, Dad," she implored, "don't be boring. Sing!" She began to scream the Big Bopper's song, "Chantilly Lace." Hyperventilating in my goggles, I sang along. Then we switched to Elvis's "Hound Dog" ... until I realized sharks might think of dogs as snacks.

Then there they were! A pair of dolphins whooshed within inches of me—as if I was a top to spin. They looked like gray shadows in a mirror. Dolphins so close I could touch them. I worked up the courage to reach out to them as they slowed their propulsion on the third pass. Solid velvet-like skin! Catching their intelligent eyes, I impressed upon their minds this cogent message: A-M-I-G-O! They played with us—although "observed" might be a better word—and then they were gone.

The next morning, we took the ferry to the capital, Wellington, at the southern tip of the north island. Our eventual destination was Auckland—New Zealand's biggest city. Under clouds like canyon walls, we navigated through a maze of fjords. Seagulls launched themselves above the turquoise water, and drifted like kites on the wind. So many species—dirty brown or snow-white with gray-black feathers, big as a goose or small as a blackbird—squawking shrill commands and gazing down at us as we conversed.

"Farmers benefit because they get cheap labor," Shannon said, explaining the mechanism of wwoofing, "and travelers get to experience the different farming techniques. People have their own story to tell, and opening up conversation is like unchaining a door. I learned so much about herbs and the farmers that grow them.

"And the sheepdogs! Dad, they are fucking smart. But sheep are dumb. Followers! That's why we say, 'leading sheep to the slaughter.'"

"What was the worst job you had to do?"

"Clipping dags before the sheep got sheared."

"What are 'dags'?"

"Pieces of shit that get stuck on the behind. Flies lay eggs in them. *Gross!* Shearers get paid by the number of sheep they clip, so they go fast and lots of times cut into the skin. The wooden floor gets covered with blood. I was invited to watch, but could hardly look. Ended up peeking out of one eye like I was watching a scary movie."

We both leaned over the railing, sniffing the salty air. Random thoughts surfaced like bubbles from the ocean floor. Another four weeks here, then Fiji, then across the international dateline to California. Jerry the ex-priest saying I'd started out traveling as an unbalanced wheel needing its spokes realigned. Devils and tidal waves in a dream the night before. Couldn't remember the last time I had nightmares.

Mr. Seagull, would my new personality fit back home?

45

REUNION WITH CHIMENE

IT WAS MOLD THAT HAD invaded my palm, the doctor in Auckland explained. It would clear up with a few weeks of dry California weather. It was reassuring news, but I was absorbed in thoughts of seeing Chimene, who was arriving from Tonga to commence a two-year odyssey of her own.

A Scorpio like my grandmother, she was lucky, focused, always the banker in Monopoly, stubborn, with a terrific smile, beautiful blue eyes, and the occasional Scorpian sting. All of her went into her mood. She could throw a defiantly dark glower or belt out a laugh somewhere between a cherry-blossom burst and a confident sunflower. She lived modestly according to her expectations, and would rebel only if the rules interfered with these expectations.

A friend of Chimene's called her "Egghead" as a kid, inspired by her long forehead. We both hated the name. Though, I'd swear she had no forehead when she was born, I've been thankful for elegant dimensions ever since. She had a slim, muscular body, light freckles, and was an inch shorter and a year younger than Shannon.

Chimene liked being in shape. Walking with her was like trying to keep up with Indiana Jones. Visiting her at Santa Barbara University one weekend during my working days, I desperately tried to keep my mountain bike on the rugged trail on the ocean's fringe she'd chosen. The reeds rapped my face, before the bike and I fell into a ditch. She waited for me on the trail, noticing something amiss. When I caught up, damaged and contemplating murder, she said with a deep grin, "I guess the little drop *off* might be a bit challenging for you, Dad."

The Dean, one of her many nicknames, had a love affair with Mother Earth. As a senior at university majoring in international politics, she represented the United Nations Association of the USA at the first Earth Summit in Brazil. There she met famous Kenyan woman's advocate Wangari Maathai, with whom she shared the belief that the health of the environment and plight of women in Africa were connected. Returning from South America, she wound up talking about the summit on TV. Unexpected fame followed, and she was asked to give speeches, often writing them with the help of her sister on the drive to the audience.

And here she was—walking off the plane at the Auckland airport and into my arms. Her short, brown hair flashing burgundy strands and face glowing from the Tonga sun, she stood back to take stock.

"How're ya doin', Papa-san?" she said with a long loving look. "You made it. That's my dad!"

Kathi wasn't expected for two days, so Shannon suggested we rent a car and drive two hundred kilometers to visit Roland, the sheep rancher who taught her to clip dags.

Roland's shaggy blond hair swept lightly over deep furrows on a forehead cracked by years of toil in the glaring sun. The hard work may have in fact enhanced his good looks. We joined the famer and his short fireball wife, Pam, for dinner. Around their wooden dining table, we ate potatoes and, of course, lamb chops, while the lively conversation toed and froed.

"Roland saves everything," Pam said with gusto. "He's never thrown out anything in his life, including his emotions. Holds everything inside. I get knackered quickly, toss them out, and catch you later, yeah!"

At the opposite end of the table, Roland was leaning towards Chimene making a political point. "America's cut us loose because we're non-nuclear. We're under an unofficial embargo ever since we refused to allow your nuclear warships to dock in the harbor."

"We like the Americans," Pam interjected, eyes afire. "Not the French, though."

"Didn't the French blow up the Greenpeace ship in Auckland harbor?" Chimene asked. "For protesting nuclear bombing in the Pacific?"

"They sure did!" Pam cried. "The French wouldn't think of setting off nuclear bombs in their own backyard, so they dropped them out here. Blowing up the ship was a government job! The bastards who did it got off in France with a slap on the wrist."

"That's the primary reason New Zealand is nuclear free," said Shannon. She'd worked at the ranch for two weeks, and you could tell by the warm familiarity between her and our hosts.

"Food's the way to a man's heart," Pam joked, motioning towards Roland and me devouring our meals.

I was curious about the economics of New Zealand's export of sheep.

"Mostly to the EEC, England, and Middle East," Roland said. "At least for the time being. Don't know how things will turn out with the EEC. For now, we're part of the Commonwealth. And we ship a million a year to Mecca. Rams with no blemishes or mutilation. Tail and balls included. They pay a hundred dollars US.

"They sacrifice rams to Allah, the meat goes to charity."

"Just the rams?" Chimene asked.

"Only rams go to Saudi. Don't need the ewes."

Shannon asked Roland to explain the cycle of raising sheep.

"Well, in April we put three or four rams in with the ewes. It's quite a sight. About forty or so females come running to meet them. Each year, we pick three hundred of the ewes for breeding. The rest, plus the males, go for meat and pelts. Wool sheep we shear twice a year for up to five years."

"Merino sheep make expensive suits and sweaters," Shannon added.

"Only the finer fleece," Roland added. "Rest for blankets and carpets. Right now wool prices are down and synthetics are eating us alive."

After dinner and songs around a grand piano, Roland went to bed. Shannon and Pam sat in wool-covered armchairs talking about how border collies were so intelligent and the farm's black horse, Valiant. It was a good opportunity for Chimene and me to step outside. We said hello to Valiant as we passed the barn, and strode off into the surrounding countryside.

"By the way, Dad," she said, as we crossed a gnarly pasture. "Thanks for paying for the BAM self-defense course. Shannon, Mom, and I got a lot out of it. I'm realizing the importance of knowing how to defend myself now that I'm about to begin wandering the world."

Chimene walked with the lax strut of her athletic uncles. The strut reminded me of her introduction into a French basketball game when we visited her and her host family in Lyon. She played in an industrial league. As she followed wiggly-hipped French athletes on to the court, her confident stride induced fans to yell, *"Américaine!"*

She'd had a natural affinity for sport since childhood. When Chimene was a summer away from the nine-year-old qualifying age in softball, she'd stand behind the wire-link fence in back of home plate when Shannon's team was up, swinging at pitches as if she were the batter. She'd found her thing. Once she reached playing age, she boiled if someone got a run off her pitching. Between innings, I'd whisper in her ear that if she didn't stop being a poor sport (phrased less delicately), she'd hang up the spikes for a few games. I'd get a Scorpio glare, but she settled down. Chimene was happy with the limelight, but also had an inclination to sit back and let others talk.

"I've always felt confident in myself," she said, "but now I feel confident dealing with dangers that women face."

"You're welcome, Dean. What did you learn?"

"A lot! We learned that if you're trapped, don't waste energy. Envision yourself as a coiled snake awaiting the opportunity to strike. When it comes, focus the explosion of all your energy into the attacker. The key is surprise. And never give up! I started to take the course more seriously after one of the attackers pinned me down, put a towel in my mouth, and whispered dirties in my ear."

"I heard you went from cocky to terrified."

"I was scared!"

Chimene then filled me in on her connection with Wangari Maathai, whom she'd interviewed in New York. The activist had been jailed several times in Kenya for disrupting the status quo on behalf of female and environmental justice.

"Wangari wants to involve me in village life to ease my assimilation. She originally thought maybe I could intern in Kenya for six months, then go back to the US to raise funds. Going to Africa has been a dream, but Wangari sent me a letter saying things were too dangerous right now to come to Africa, so I figured I'd travel in the East for a year or two, then go to Kenya."

"I'll miss you, sweetie. Who's gonna take me for rides on narrow trails?"

"Come visit me! You've got time now. We can have a blast."

"Be neat to travel around together, huh? But Chimene, it's a dangerous mission to change the male-female situation in the Third World. You can't help people if you get hurt."

"I'll be careful. I'm not aiming to get hurt."

"Just be crystal clear to men what you're looking at. Be careful how you use your eyes."

"What do you mean, exactly?"

"Well, you know the kind of guy that takes a glance as a come-on?"

"Yeah."

"Multiply that by five in the Third World. Men don't get the opportunity to be with women, and they think Western women are easy. In most cases, a good sense of humor and clear feedback will do the trick."

"What about you, Dad. What's next?"

"I think I'm going to sail the breezes when I get home, let events determine my fate, and whatever happens, happens."

"How will you incorporate your experiences?"

"Good question. Now that you guys are grown and I've learned to live on less, I think relationships are going to be the challenge."

"Speaking about relationships, you must be excited about Mom coming tomorrow!"

"I am. A year is a long time, sweetie."

"The house was different when you were gone, Dad. Quieter."

Sounds of geese overhead mixed with the calm summer's night.

"So why are you traveling, Chimene?"

"To go to places where I can live off the land, with time to figure out what to do with my life. Everyone's working so hard back home, moving fast to earn money to buy more things. Success is defined by what you have, as opposed to who you are."

"Cat's in the Cradle," I said, referring to the Harry Chapin song that had a big impact on me. "Chimene, do you mind if I give you some traveling advice?"

"You don't have to ask, Dad. I like your advice."

"A habit I picked up. Here it is in a nutshell. Your smile can buy almost anything, and the trick to meeting someone substantial is 'Hi!' Drink water, the body is mostly water and it needs recycling. Eat the local food but make sure it's cooked. After a while, you'll have a sense about food.

"Let me think, oh yeah, mosquitoes hunt after 3 p.m., so dress in long pants and wear socks. They go after veins. Put DEET sparingly on your clothes to give them the smell. And as a friend once said, 'If you get sick, drink tons of water and don't eat for twenty-four hours. Starve the little bastards.' That should do it, except for one thing—"

"What's that?"

"Remember what happened the night before you pitched the perfect game to go to the nationals in LA?"

"Pitching in relief isn't exactly a perfect game."

"Nineteen batters is perfect to me."

"That's what dads are for—to be proud. That *was* a good game, wasn't it? Our team really pulled together. I could see every inch of the plate that day, where the bats were reaching. Now I remember what happened the night before the game. Mom brought out that six-page Binghamton newspaper article about the Chanecka basketball dynasty. It had pictures of Grandpa Steve and Uncle Bill playing pro ball, right down to the current generation. I went to sleep so psyched."

"Well, attitude counts! If you think you'll have a great time, you will."

"Cool, Dad! Thanks, I'm a little nervous to tell you the truth. That definitely helps. Say, how about lending me your water purifier?"

"Take it! Only used it once, on a jungle island called Ssese in Uganda."

46

TWO ROADS
DIVERGED IN A WOOD

WAITING WITHOUT THE GIRLS AT the airport for Kathi's plane to arrive, I pondered beginnings. The next three weeks in New Zealand with Kathi would be another beginning.

The moment I'd stepped foot in Australia and knew my trip was nearing its end, I wondered how the traveler in me would find *mellow satisfaction* in American life. Would I worry about security? Or consider material possessions important again? Could Kathi and I understand each other enough to compromise our lifestyles? What about the family? The giant eland in Kenya standing courageous in the glen, his herd grazing peacefully because he provided security. I was coming home a more complete individual, no longer a patriarch. What would that mean? And, of course, Malgosia was always in the background. How would someone a world away fit in?

And there was always the other side of the coin. I *had* lived my dream. Whatever followed this new beginning would be gravy.

The arrivals board indicated her plane had touched down. Would Kathi wear her airport smile? The first time I saw that particular smile was right after I proposed marriage. She'd flown from New York to Denver, where I was attending graduate school. We locked eyes as she walked with a sensual gracefulness up the gangplank, her long, shiny hair swinging. Her smile of anticipation penetrated me so deeply. Our minds dissolved in a vast lovers' familiarity. We laughed as we ran into the other's arms. Nothing mattered but that exquisite moment.

I used to put myself to sleep thinking about her. In my mind's eye, I kissed her neck in the kitchen as she prepared meals, watched her grin, and put flowers behind my back, asking, "Which hand?"

Standing at the arrivals gate gripping yellow roses, I watched with some nervousness as people filtered out looking for family and friends or strode alone purposefully for the exit. How would she look after a year? How would we greet? She wouldn't scream. Me neither.

Just then, Robert Frost's poem came to mind.

Two roads diverged in a wood, and I
Took the one less traveled by,
And that has made all the difference.

www.ingramcontent.com/pod-product-compliance
Lightning Source LLC
Chambersburg PA
CBHW022033290426
44109CB00014B/846